Challenges and Issues of Gender-Based Violence

Challenges and Issues of Gender-Based Violence

A Christian Education Perspective

I. Asongla Pongen

Christian World Imprints

Edition: 2023, 2025

Christian World Imprints
Christian Publishing & Books from India
A-71 Group, Wazirpur Industrial Area
Delhi-110052
cwidelhi2017@gmail.com
www.ChristianWorldImprints.com
Phone: +91 11 41526079

ISBN: 978-93-5148-409-7 (HB)
ISBN: 978-93-5148-410-3 (PB)

Printed in India.

Contents

This book in its original form was the Dissertation submitted to the Senate of Serampore College (University), India, towards the degree of Doctor of Theology and is published with the written permission. The author is responsible for the title, contents and expressed in it.

The original title of the dissertation was 'Responding to the Challenges of Gender-Based Violence through Christian Education in Nagaland'.

Preface

This book is the result of my D.Th studies and personal experience as a woman. It was originally submitted as a doctoral thesis to the South Asia Theological Research Institute (SATHRI), Senate of Serampore College/University with the title *Responding to the Challenges of Gender-based Violence through Christian Education in Nagaland.* Other than few addition and subtraction, the original content of the thesis is presented as they are.

Gender-based violence is one of the most common and most widespread human rights abuses in the society. In many parts of the world, women are still isolated, unrecognized and constrained due to socio-cultural and legal structures that restrict their access to resources and control their movements and privileges. They find themselves under the bondage within the family, society and the church due to traditional and cultural restrictions. It is not surprising to find that even at times religions have reinforced oppression, segregation and discrimination of women. In spite of all the changes that are taking place today women and men seem to be living in different traditions.

The world Council of Churches has declared 1988-1998 as the 'Decade of women' and the United Nations also declared a 'Decade for a culture of peace and Non-violence for the children of the world' from 2001-2010, and a 'Decade to Overcome-violence,' yet, women and children's positions has not changed. During the decade many life challenging programmes were conducted with a numbers of writings, especially in support of women's condition in the society and in the church by feminist-inspired scholars, scientists, sociologists, psychologists, criminologists and theologians yet, the situation of women remain the same and becoming worse owing to the nature of facilities created by modern technology.

Despite the fact that people have moved away systematically from one age to another, from primitive to today's post modern age, and despite the progress in science and technology, economically and politically, we have no relevant means to curb away the social evil of gender-based violence. In other words, gender-based violence has not come to a stop; instead, it is intensely growing. Even though gender-based violence is a direct challenge to all, to the church in general and to the Christian educational ministry in particular, churches seem to have failed to address this issue. From the very beginning, its biblical teachings went along with all the prevalent cultural practices adopting the stereotyped roles in which men play superior and leading roles while women took the subordinate parts. Moreover, the interpretation of the Bible was also done in a biased way, teaching women subjectivity. Even the Biblical teachings were based on men superiority and women's inferiority, picking up a few Biblical references to support a negative expression on women. On the other hand, the church administration also adopted a system where men hold almost all the top positions or leading roles as decision-makers and so on. Besides, one of the great mistakes concerning the Christian educational ministry in the church is that it was understood as an activity mainly for children, and also the issue of gender-based violence was regarded as secular issue. With this perceptions, life threatening issue like gender-based was not given priority in the church educational ministry.

The goal Christian Education is to address issues of historical injustices, traditional oppressive ideology, and it is responsible for proclaiming redeeming activity and concern for all humanity. Therefore, how to overcome gender-based violence? How best to make aware of this problem in church and society? Can a new interpretation of the scriptures help? Can it be done through Christian education? These are some of the questions that this study attempts to answer. Exploring the norms, values and factors that influence gender-based violence and responding to these challenges through Church educational ministries, are the sole objectives of this book. Relevant and appropriate Christian education is required in order to build a life-sustaining community by challenging all forms of gender-based violence. The intention of this research is not to describe the violent situations alone but to critically analyze them, considering the socio-cultural, religious and customary law condition of the context.

Data for this was collected through personal interviews and questionnaires. For personal interview, fifty people were selected. A set of questionnaire was also distributed to a cross-section of three hundred people in three places-Kohima, Mokokchung and Dimapur, representing different people's group. The research critically analyzes the church educational ministry's role in the whole realm-both as the perpetrator and as a healer. Theoretical framework was worked out from the resources available in the libraries. The book has been divided into five chapters.

The first chapter is concerned with the statement of the problem, highlighting gender-based violence in the society and discusses the definitions on violence and gender-based violence. The chapter also asserts the methodology used throughout this research project. The second chapter deals with the theoretical frame work examining, important key terms, terminologies and phrases related to gender-based violence and also forms of gender-based violence. Second section discusses on different perspectives of gender-based violence and learned theories in the society, its stereotype roles based on the traditional structure and social applications, as they highlights the power and authority exercised in the patriarchal society. It also highlighted how a person develops a gender from his/her childhood as it becomes the norm of gender-based violence both at home, in the church and society. The third chapter examines the gender-based violence situation in Nagaland. An analysis follows the traditional and cultural norms that derogate women's lives, critically analyzing the customary laws imposed.

Chapter four analyses and interprets the gender-based violence situation in the Naga context based on the empirical research, bringing out the findings for the further exploration, discussion and consideration. The opinion expressed by the respondents varies from each age group. The respondents who are in the category of 50 years and above, are the opinion that traditional practices based on customary laws are good enough for the whole society and have expressed that tradition should not be changed. They further suggested that we should abide and preserve our rich cultural heritage where there are certain norms for both men and women in the society. It is observed that even among this age group, a few who are more open and adaptable, expressed that the Naga society needs to be changed towards newer applications by discarding the discriminatory practices based on gender, and allow equal opportunity to everyone irrespective of their sexes.

On the other hand, respondents in the age group of 50 years and below are more flexible and open to outside world opinions. A majority of the respondents in this age group expressed that, the present traditional practices based on the customary laws hinder women's lives and their mobility in many ways. For instance, denying leadership roles, not allowing in the decision-making both in the church and society, depriving their shares, restricting their movements, exploiting their bodies, ignoring their opinions, need to be challenged. It is indicated that women feel that the discriminations done to them is against their will, they do realized that the stereotype gender roles constructed in the human society is the root cause of gender-based violence.

The fifth chapter deals with the implications for the educational ministry of the church on gender-based violence by determining what kind of Christian educational system we need to employ to meet all those social challenges. It highlights the different concerns by bringing out few suggestions to be integrated in responding to the gender-based violence in the church educational ministry.

The church is called to witness against all these issues which demeaned women's worth and dignity by educating its faith community/congregation through its educational ministry based on the Biblical principles and show concern in taking action wherever it see the need, hurt, or wrong. Hence, Christian educational ministry needs to be very critical in exploring the reality about the faith community and the people around them. Healing broken society created by gender differences, status-quo, exercising power and authority in the human society should be the objectives of the Church Educational Ministry.

Acknowledgement

This publication is the result of four years of research and personal reflection on the issue of gender-based violence. In the course of this engagement, I have been encouraged, challenged, inspired, motivated and helped by many persons.

First of all, Professor (late) Samson Prabhakar, my supervisor (under whose supervision I have successfully completed my research work both M.Th and D.Th) and Director of Research, South Asia Theological Research Institute (SATHRI), has been of tremendous help. For his scholarly advice, sound and thorough criticism, remarkable patience and understanding, I am profoundly grateful. I have benefitted greatly from his support by granting study scholarship, and one-way traveling expenses with recommendation for my research exposure to Queen's Foundation for Ecumenical Theological Education, Birmingham, UK, from September to December, 2007. I am also grateful that he encouraged a critical approach to my research work. I wish he is around to read this humble publication with Foreword note. I am also grateful to all the SATHRI staff that has been so helpful throughout my studies in many ways.

I am greatly indebted to the Principal Professor O.V. Jadhana, his colleagues, staff and all the students' friend of the United Theological College, Bangalore for allowing me to stay and use their facilities during my research. Special thanks to Mrs. Rita Wesley, Librarian and her staff for helping in procuring needed books and kind assistance in every possible way. I also wish to acknowledge the help and support received from the librarians of Kristu Jyothi College, St Peter's Seminary and SAIACS, in Bangalore. I thank them all for every help they rendered to me. I owe my appreciation to Late Rev. Dr Fr. Paul Puthanangady, the Rector of Kristu Jyothi College, who's humbled but critical scholarship motivated my thoughts in the initial period.

I wish to acknowledge my appreciation to Rev. Dr Hewlett, the principal, Professor Rev. Adam Hood, Dean of Research, my official appointed co-tutors during my academic exposure Rev. Dr Nicola Slee and Rev. Dr Anthony Reddie, staff and students in the Queen's Foundation for Ecumenical Theological College, Birmingham, for being kind, helpful and understanding throughout my stay there. I am deeply grateful to Adam Hood, Dean of Research, for his initiative in securing the sponsorship for my exposure programme for four months. I wish to thank to all the Librarians of Queen's Foundations, Birmingham, Orchards Learning Centre and Birmingham University, for their co-operation and help.

I would like to express my sincere appreciation to Rev. Arun Wesley, Presbyter, Church of South India and Editorial consultant, CISRS, Bangalore for his timely help in editing and correcting the research, without which I would not have been able to submit the research work on time. Special thanks to my friend Rev. Dr David Joy, Professor, United Theological College, Bangalore, who came forward in introducing and recommending my name to Queen's Foundation Ecuminical Theological College, Birmingham.

Particular thanks are reserved for all the participants in the empirical research who kindly agree to act as respondents, providing their thoughts and expressing their opinions and suggestions. Without their help I would not have been able to continue my research work.

I would like to acknowledge the kind gesture shown by Late Rev. Dr Najekhu Yeptho, acting principal and all the Board members, Trinity Theological College, Dimapur, Nagaland, for granting my study leave for the development of faculty in the College.

I record my sincere thanks and appreciations to my respected teachers some of them have gone ahead of us; through their simplicity in lifestyle yet brilliant scholarship helped, inspired, motivated and shaped my understanding throughout my theological pilgrimage. Late Dr Renthy Keitzar,former principal, Eastern Theological College; Rev. Dr A. G. Behera, former Professor, ETC; Late Rev. Dr Gnana Robinson, former Principal, United Theological College, Bangalore; Late Rev. Dr K.C. Abraham, former SATHRI director, Professor in UTC; Late Rev. Dr Michael Traber, visiting professor to UTC; Rev. Dr (Mrs) R.L. Hnuni, former teacher in ETC; Late. Rev. Dr. John Hull, former professor in Queen's Foundation and Ecuminical Theological College and Birmingham University, UK. Also, special thanks is due to Rev. Dr S.K. Patro, Registrar, Senate of Serampore college, for his recommending me to publish my research work.

Finally, I am deeply indebted to my family members, relatives and friends for their prayers, encouragement, moral support and financial help. Most of all, I thank my mother, whose unceasing prayers inspired to do my work with dedication and my sisters and brothers along with their spouses, who generously and lovingly shared all the burdens. They are my strength and source of inspiration even in times of stress and strain throughout my theological journey. I wish to dedicate this book to my mother (90) who wishes to see my work in her life time. Above all, I am grateful to God Almighty who is the source of my life and wisdom.

Chapter 1

Introduction

The problem of gender-based violence is not a new phenomenon. It has been in existence since a long time. Of late it has become a global issue as men and women have become conscious of their rights and identity. Women for example, have been and are being killed, tortured and maimed from the time of their conception till death physically, psychologically, sexually, socially and also economically from time immemorial. Although, a great many advances have been made in terms of laws and rights, and in protecting the weaker sections of people, the condition of women still remains the same or becoming worse today. This is so, as many women have attained position of excellence in teaching, entrepreneurship, administration etc. However, women are the only ones who bear the brunt of violence. On the other hand, the age old traditional stereotyped roles about men and women and the cultural practice of inheritance too deprive women of their human Rights, making men superior and powerful.

Generally, gender-based violence has been visible widely because of physical violence and abuse dowry death, rape, murder, assaults etc. However, apart from mere physical and bodily abuse, gender-based violence most of the times is invisible, in terms of physical stress and pressure which traumatize, discriminate and oppress them. It could also occur in terms of subordination, derecognition, insult, and segregation etc, based on gender. It is no surprise that these forms of violence have been sustained and reinforced by tradition and culture-religion, rituals and customs. Of the many traditional and cultural influences that reinforced and perpetuated gender based violence in terms of discrimination and exploitation, religion stands prominent. In spite of its intension to bring about reforms in society in terms of equality, dignity, charity etc, religion in general has been discriminative-sacred and secular, man against woman, pure-impure etc. This attitude eventually strengthened a patriarchal mindset leading to expedite attempts at violence based on gender.

Christianity too as a religion emerging out of a patriarchal ethos, evolved measures-rituals, priestly class, vestments etc, and perpetuate discrimination. This was even provided with biblical information, basis and colour. In most cases, this kind of Christianity spread far and wide.

Christianity came to Nagaland in the context of a traditional patriarchal society. The gospel spread among those whose mindset was already built on the traditional cultural practices where each one maintained his/her distinctive role. Thus, from the very beginning, biblical teachings went along with these prevalent cultural practices adopting the stereotyped roles in which men played a superior and leading role while women took the subordinate parts. Moreover, the interpretation of the Bible was also done in biased way teaching women subjectivity. At the same time, the church administration too adopted the system where men held almost all the top positions or leading roles, making decisions for the whole community.

Thus, biblical teachings were based on men's superiority and women's inferiority, picking up suitable biblical references to support a negative expression on women. On the other hand, it was understood that Christian religious education was mainly for children, and also the issues on violence and more specifically gender-based violence was regarded as something related to secular world issues. With these perceptions/assumptions, gender-based violence issues were not given priority in the church educational ministry. Thus, gender-justice issues remained among a few educated personnel only.

Background of the Research

Gender-based Violence is a deep-rooted problem which manifests itself in different ways in different societies. It is very subtle unlike physical or psychological violence that is generally visible. The actions or attitudes that discriminate, segregate, and that violate a woman's worth, the dignity and status based merely on her gender in spite of her being made in the image of God can be termed as Gender-based Violence. These acts could be engendered and caused by tradition, religious dogmas, and culture and so on and so forth. In all those violent actions, women are the most affected group everywhere. Since this study was based on an empirical research in the author's home state, she started analyzing the problem there and then move on to see its implications in general where the problem is prevalent. Nagaland is one of the States in India, which nourishes the practice of Gender-based Violence both from the structural and situational events.

Being a so-called 'Christian State' evolved out of a traditional tribal background; Nagaland faces this problem in its attempt at engendering a healthy society. Although, Gender-based Violence is a direct challenge to the church's ministry, the church has failed to address this issue through its educational ministry, assuming that this is a social issue which can be taken care of by other civil organizations. Therefore, exploring the norms, values and factors that influence different forms of Gender-based Violence and responding to this problem by challenging those issues through the church educational ministry is the objective in this attempt.

Definition of Violence

The term 'Violence'[1] would include all its dimensions such as physical, psychological, political, economic, interpersonal, social and domestic.[2] According to Robert McAfee Brown, violence means,

> "whatever 'violates' another, in the sense of infringing upon or disregarding or abusing or denying the other, whether physical harm is done or not, can be understood as an act of violence. The basic overall definition of violence would then become violation of personhood. While such a denial or violation can involve physical destruction of person-hood in ways that are obvious, person-hood can also be violated or denied in subtle ways that are not obvious at all except to the victim. There can be violation of person-hood quite apart from the doing of physical harm."[3]

Violence is an act of negating what legitimately belongs to 'the other.' The other could be a person or community or animal or nature as a whole. It is basically destructive, depriving one of life, and in the affirmation of death. It is not only deprivation by inflicting physical injuries but deprivation of any and every aspect of person or community or nature. Since it is basically deprivation, violence can also be spoken of as lovelessness, injustice, selfishness, untruthfulness

---

[1] Violence is an offence, a wrong, and a misdeed done to another knowingly and willingly. *International Encyclopedia of Sociology,* Volume 1, (Fitzroy Dearborn Publishers, London: 1995), p. 373; again *The New Lexicon Webster's Dictionary of the English language* interprets violence in this way-use of physical force so as to damage or injure; intense natural force or energy/an abusive use of force passion, fury, distortion of meaning/desecration, to do violence to offend, outrage, to do violence to someone's sense of justice, (New York: Lexicon Publications, INC. 1988 edition), p. 1099.

[2] Sashikala Gurpur-Murphy, "Overcoming Violence: A Feminist Perspective" in *Overcoming Violence,* ed. Samson Prabhakar, (Bangalore: South Asia Theological Research Institute, 2004), p. 47.

[3] Brown, Mc-Afee R., *Religion and Violence,* 2nd ed., Philadelphia, 1987, p. 7, also Samson Prabhakar, *Essays on Christian Education and Liturgy* (Bangalore: South Asia Theological Research Institute, 2003), p. 124.

and intolerance. In other words, violence is the force of death and it is as real as death itself.[4]

The World Health Organization defines violence in the following way: "The intentional use of physical force or power, threatened or actual, against oneself, another person, or against a group or community that either results in or has a high likelihood of resulting in injury, death, psychological harm, deprivation."[5] In a broader sense, violence lies in the power dynamics of social situations. Other politically legitimated examples of violence within the socio-political arena include racist or sexist laws and social policies that eliminate equal employment opportunities.[6] Therefore, violence is not simply aggression or injury committed by one individual against another but it is more precisely the abuse of power, in which a powerful person or the one who in the higher position takes advantage of and abuses a less powerful one.

Again some scholars have defined violence as "injuries and destructive behavior, which damages the victim physically, mentally and financially."[7] When a person is damaged physically, mentally, and financially, automatically it leads to the destruction of both his/her moral and spiritual life too. Thus, violence could be either from within the family or through social-cultural, economic, political, religious environments, and through the media[8] and in society as a whole. Every society is thus surrounded by violence in reality, and it could be also projected and made available through varieties of images, appearing anywhere and at any moment through television, video games, and computer games and also through the Internet. Violence is also projected through newscasts and pictures of daily newspapers and periodical magazines.

---

[4] Samson Prabhakar, "Overcoming Violence: Some Key Issues," in *Essays on Christian Education and Liturgy* (Bangalore: South Asia Theological Research Institute, 2003), p. 124.

[5] Mary Yoder Holsopple, Ruth E. Krall and Sharon Weaver Pittman, *Building Peace: Overcoming Violence in Communities, (*Geneva: World Council of Churches, 2004), p. 18.

[6] The late Presbyterian theologian Robert Mc Afee Brown has created a typology of violence. He noted that overt violence such as murder, war or terrorism is visible and easily recognized. Overt violence can occur between individuals-spouse-battering or murder, for example. Or it can be legitimated within political systems, as in cases of invoking the death penalty or waging war, Mary Yoder and others… (2004), p. 18.

[7] Ram Ahuja, *Violence Against Women,* Jaipur and New Delhi: Rawat Publications, (2003), 31. In the above statement, Megargee (1982) has defined violence as "overtly threatened or overtly accomplished application of force which results in the injury or destruction of persons or property or reputation."

[8] Television, movies, video and computer games show scenes of violence. Magazines and newspapers are filled with the news of violence in our community and country, Mary Yoder and others…2004, p. 16.

Gender-based Violence

Gender issues are in the focus of all human development programmes today. Many lives are affected due to loss of values, potentialities, productivity, and definitely peaceful living, caused thus by gender-based violence. Gender-based violence is inextricably linked to culturally rooted systems of kinship and marriage.[9] Thus, gender-based violence is on the rise everywhere. It means any act of violence that results in, or is likely to result in physical, sexual or psychological harm or suffering to women, including threats of such acts, coercion or arbitrary deprivation of liberty, whether occurring in public or in private life on the basis of gender (Declaration on Eliminating[10] Violence against Women, Art. 1). However, violence in general whether through terrorism or fundamentalism or ideological conflict, or on the basis of gender has affected women in a drastic fashion. One of the best examples is the estimated two-lakh Kar Sevaks at Ayodhya, of which around 55,000 were women,[11] coercing them to join the crusade and also thereby projecting them allegedly as equals along with men, to promote a fundamentalistic religious upsurge.

In the modern world, gender-based violence is increasingly manifesting itself in newer forms, ranging from eve-teasing, molestation, sexual harassment and abuse, dowry deaths, prostitution, pornography, and sex selection. Horrifying cases of rape, which are violent sexual assaults against the will and consent of women, exemplify the distorted power relationship between men and women.[12] Domestic violence in general includes all acts of intimidation and cruelty, including mental, emotional, sexual and financial abuse[13] of women. Of late

---

[9] In the United States, protecting women from violence typically meant separating the woman from her battering husband. See Marjorie Agosin, *Women, Gender, and Human Rights: A Global Perspective*. (Jaipur and New Delhi: Rawat Publications, 2003), p. 90.

[10] Suraiya Kamaruzzaman, "Women Healing Themselves and Others," *Building Communities of Peace for All: Theme and Stories,* (Hongkong: Christian Conference of Asia, 2005), p. 29. (This is a summary of what Suriya Kamaruzzaman shared with CCA Staff at a chapel service on April 14, 2004 at CCA Center, Hongkong).

[11] Sashikala Gurpur-Murphy, "Overcoming Violence: A feminist Perspective," *Overcoming violence*, ed. Samson Prabhakar (Bangalore: South Asia Theological Research Institute, 2004), p. 54.

[12] Allwyn D'Silva, *Responding to India's Social Challenges: The Promotion of Human Rights* (A NBCLC Series on Current Issues), pp. 17-18.

[13] Women are the last to be hired and the first to be fired due to structural adjustments that are imposed on our societies. Women's labour is underpaid, or even unpaid, in family farms and businesses, and their sexuality is so often placed on the market or used by the advertising and media industries. The meeting of women from Asia, Africa and Latin America described it: It is the poor women in the south who suffer inordinately because of unjust structures, institutions and policies that perpetuate class-gender-and race-based subordination. The neo-liberal model has intensified the feminization of underpaid market work and unvalued care work, the feminization of forced migration, labour export and trafficking, the feminization of poverty and even the feminization of survival. This insecurity and frustration provoked by the neo-liberal model are affecting women's lives from womb to tomb. Patriarchal disciplining, including social and institutional control of

gender-based violence in general has forced women to break this silence (imposed on them so far by patriarchal culture), to speak of their oppression in their marital relationships as a way to make people aware of their plight and also to bring about a solution to their problems.

As women are the backbone of development, when women live in violent contexts or in constant fear that damage their whole personality, societies get affected as a whole. But unfortunately, this is not taken as seriously as it should be by either the church or other institutions in society. Women, especially in the rural areas are yet to be educated and made aware of this. Sadly many women are dying every moment without realizing the causes of their sufferings. Thus, gender-based violence is endemic both in the domestic sphere, the work place, and in the church circles though it is often kept hidden in society. It is very evident that, no society or country is exempt from expressions of gender-based violence. Besides, women are the most economically marginalized, unfairly burdened by the present global economic policies which are very crucial in the present global context.

Therefore, any attitude or behavior that causes infliction or reduces women's dignity to the level of abuse or harassment needs to be taken seriously. As the sociologist Ram Ahuja points out, "There are no women who have not suffered at one time or another harassment, humiliation, exploitation and violence that shadow her sex. A woman's life lies between pleasure at one end and danger at the other end. In daily life, women are routinely defined by sex, and even if not all men are potential kidnappers, rapists, batterers, molesters and torturers of women, all women are potential victims."[14]

According to the United Nations Development Fund for Women (UNDFW), 40 percent of all female homicide victims in the United Kingdom are caused by their husbands, partners or boy-friends. In Bangladesh, Colombia, India, Nigeria and Pakistan thousands of women suffer each year from dowry-related deaths or are disfigured by acid thrown in their faces by husbands or partners or by men to whom they are betrothed.[15]

---

reproductive rights, and violence against women are escalating in many parts of the world. ("Women's Voices on Alternative Globalization Addressing People and Earth," 27-29 August 2004, "Nameless and Silenced No longer, We Will Overcome Violence!" in *God's image: Asian Women Overcoming Violence,* Journal of Asian Women's Resource Centre for Culture and Theology, Vol. 24, No.1, March 2005, p. 4.

[14] Ram Ahuja, *Violence Against Women* (2003), p. 13. Violence against women the world over attacks their dignity as human beings and leaves them vulnerable and fearful. Conditioned thus it undervalues their skills and retribution. Women are thus marginalized in society and forced out of decision-making processes which shape and determine the development of their communities, in Aruna Gnanadason, *No longer A Secret: The church and violence against women* (Geneva: World Council of Churches, 1993), p. 1.

[15] Patricia Sheerattan-Bisnauth, "Men must be part of the solution in overcoming violence against women," in *WARC UPDATE.* Magazine, (January 2005), p. 1.

It is obvious then, violence against women exists in every country of the world in every culture, religion, race, class, caste and tribe, demanding a critical analysis of the situation in order to challenge the age-old practice of violence towards women especially those based on gender. Since, the violence that women experience is physical, emotional, spiritual and intellectual it must be seen within the framework of gendered power relations and within the spheres of personal, social, political, religious and also structured realities in society.

It would seem from the above said detailed explanation of violence in general that gender bias is at the root of all aggression, anger, frustration engendering gender-based violence. It would also seem that gender-based violence is engineered by nurturing discrimination among men and women in the family, society and the church, beginning from the time they are born with son-preference, which lead to foeticide; patriarchal tendencies to prefer men for leadership, authority and power; sons for inheritance of property etc. It would also seem that gender bias is an artificial construction of the circumstances engendered by culture, societal and patriarchal need and nurtured as such by society to perpetuate patriarchal hegemony, as upheld, supported and bolstered by contrived principles drawn from religious notions. If that be so can this attitude be changed such that gender-based violence can be rooted out or minimized? Can education or bringing awareness of issues concerning gender bias help? Can this be done by religious education? It is a moot point.

Where does Christian religious education come in to deal with gender-based violence is the issue here. Has Christian Religious Education in its ministry in the church and among Christians enabled a gender-based violence-free community? Has Christian Education been geared to respond to this issue, is the focus of this study. Thus, the study has chosen a typical Christian Community-a tribal community no doubt, in a so-called Christian state, to assess and analyze the situation for evaluating the need, relevance and the effectiveness of Christian Religious Education in order to respond to gender-based violence.

Thus, gender-based violence and violence in general have been the problem of the modern world. Gender-based violence continues to affect women in particular in all kinds of societies-dictatorial, monarchical, democratic and socialistic and it is not confined to any religion either. In fact, in certain societies, religion supports gender-based violence subtly enough due to its patriarchal leanings. It continues to affect the society as a whole as women from the backbone of its development, reform and in continuity of tradition. What is the church's response to this situation? Has the church come to grips with this reality? Has the church as yet evolved a paradigm to counter this issue? Has its educational ministry been effective enough to educate, nurture and bring to awareness the need for a holistic approach to this problem? In answer, this research endeavours to study and comprehend, to offer and implement solutions on the basis of an empirical study of the situation in Nagaland, bolstered as such by library research, from the perspective of Christian education.

Gender-based Violence in Nagaland

Since the research is based on an empirical study of gender-based violence in Nagaland, the author aims to examine in brief about the situation in there. The Nagas belong to the Mongolian stock, and are divided into many tribes. As such there are sixteen major tribes in Nagaland.[16] For long, the Nagas did not have a written script of their own until the Christian missionaries gave them the English script, or did they have a common language although they have had many spoken dialects, one dialect for one tribe or even more than one dialect for one tribe.[17] Though they speak different dialects,[18] the culture of the different tribes of the Naga is almost the same. They have a distinct culture of their own, and their customs and ways of living are different from those of other parts of the country. Moreover, their system of administration is different especially in the rural set up. They follow the patriarchal and patrilineal family systems where the major shares of the property go to the sons rather than to the daughters. For instance, when a Naga woman marries, she goes out of her father's family and comes under the authority of her husband. The husband is the custodian head of the family, where the wife is the manager of domestic affairs with certain restrictions.

In Naga society, women are not allowed to inherit father's properties, including land. Only the sons are entitled to inherit. In other words, women are not even entitled to co-ownership of property with brothers. A girl can be named only after her father's family. She cannot draw the title of her mother. Accordingly, on the demise of the mother in the family, even her name, which is so precious, is returned back to her clan members (father's line) after a certain period of time.[19] Though many women are more knowledgeable than men, they are restricted to take up high positions in many areas of political, social and religious concerns particularly in relation to customary practices. And even if they are given certain leadership roles they cannot discharge their responsibility as their male counterparts discourage them. Thus, the common statement used for women in the society "women-children" differentiates the status of women from that of the men folk. Sometimes they are rated as minor or secondary citizens irrespective of their status, age and qualifications.

The usage of the very term "women of a minor child" is no doubt, a derogatory term because even the highly educated and elderly women are

---

[16] Samson Prabhakar, *Overcoming Violence: Some Key Issues*, p. 130.

[17] Seabrooke Jermey, "Internationalism verses globalization," in Mathew George Chunakara, *Globalization and Its Impact on Human Rights* (Hongkong: Christian Conference of Asia, 1998), p. 91.

[18] There are three sub-dialects among the Ao tribe-*Jungli*, Mongsen and *Changki*, among those dialects *Jungli* is used for official purposes.

[19] N. Talitemjen Jamir and A. Lanunungsang, *Naga Society and Culture: A Case study of the Ao Naga Society and Cult*ure (Mokokchung: Nagaland University Tribal Research Center, 2005), p. 217.

grouped under this category. In order to defame women, very often men folk would say, 'What do these women of children know about?' Thus, women are in fact, regarded as inferior to men in society, in the church and in family circles just because of their feminine characteristics. Further, women are not allowed to come to the forefront especially in the field of socio-cultural and religious affairs. Women are not even allowed to participate in public debates or discussions. They are deprived of the privilege to express their opinions in public meetings, like village council meetings and church general meetings.

In Nagaland, male church workers continue to dominate the church's ministry. For example, there are more than 2000 churches under 20 Baptist associations.[20] None of the churches and associations appoints women as executive secretaries or local church pastors, which are the highest positions in the church ministry. Women are appointed only as associate pastors to take care of women's fellowship. In most of the ministerial decision-making, women's suggestions are ignored, and in some cases, female ministers are dehumanized and oppressed by their counterparts.

It is however not surprising that when people talk about violence in Nagaland, they usually refer to the political issues of the underground movement and the military operations. The long struggle for independence however among the different factional groups is no way away from acts of violence. Innocent deaths at the cost of freedom struggles are unnumbered, which are one of the serious problems experienced in Nagaland since 1950s. In spite of this, the age-old practice of customary law, in which women are treated as inferior by depriving their God-given opportunities, is the worst problem in Naga society. The churches in Nagaland have so far failed to address this structured violence, which abuses the rights of humans both women and men.

Therefore, keeping those realities in mind, the purpose of this research is to challenge the traditional practice of injustice and different forms of violence in Nagaland from a Christian educational ministry perspective. Because, the ultimate purpose of Christian Religious Education is "to lead people out to the kingdom of God with its personal, spiritual, and social political values."[21] Thus, one of its immediate purposes is the promotion of human freedom, which includes "freedom within one's social and political context." Therefore, Christian Religious Education needs to be centered on those issues, which hinder one's well-being, and ready to renounce the political, cultural, economic and social forces which deny the imposition of equality and uniformity of power and privileges. The goal of Christian Religious Education is also to address issues of historical injustice, traditional oppressive ideology, and it is responsible for proclaiming redeeming

[20] *NBCC News Letter*: A quarterly publication of the Nagaland Baptist Church Council, Volume IV, Issue 4, July-September 2004, p. 10.

[21] Thomas H. Groom, "Christian Education for freedom: A Shared-Praxis Approach," *Christian Religious Education,* (New York: Paulist, 1978), p. 35.

activity and concern for all humanity. Thus, the goal of Christian Religious Education needs to be achieved by challenging the socio-cultural, religious and political practices of gender-based violence in the community.

Thus, the study of Christian Religious Education is not only for acquiring the knowledge of the Bible and the Christian faith alone, but also for the holistic transformation of the society. But, many a time when we talk about Christian Religious Education, people refer only to the children's programmes in the church. Therefore, the traditional understanding of Christian Religious Education needs to be revalued and re-constructed in the light of one's life situation. As one of the Christian educators J.C. Wynn has mentioned, "As church-in-the-world we must also keep in touch with our tradition. Yet we must also avoid traditionalism, whose litanies no longer awaken any responses."[22] Today's context demands that Christian Religious Education should aim not only for change of individual persons by following church dogmas and practices, but also for change of the structural systems of the society.

The society in which women's worth is denied and violated, their personhood affected by segregating them from men's activities and devaluing their God-given body by harassing and torturing needs to be set right. Would education help bringing awareness of the injustice done to women, among men and women resolve the issue? What kind of education-religious education would be suitable? Would the Christian educational ministry of the church offer a way out of this? How far is it adequate and effective? This research attempts to assess and analyze the situation and to propose suggestions for improvement of the situation.

Importance of the Research

Violence in society is a subject of study as well as a concern more so in terms of Gender-based Violence not only for students of criminology and law but of theology, sociology, social psychology, social work, human rights, gender studies, women's study and civil society at large. In many countries of the world, civil wars and communal wars promote violence. In addition to war, many societies experience criminal violence, which is very much hard to intervene. Much more than that, structural violence continues to devastate the lives of many individuals, families, and societies throughout the world affecting women in terms of gender-based violence.

In this situation, world religious leaders and spiritual teachers from many faith traditions have begun to consider the religious and spiritual implications of violence especially gender-based violence in the world community.[23] Therefore, as

---

[22] J. C. Wynn, *Christian Education for Liberation: and Other Upsetting Ideas*, (Nashville: Abingdon, 1977), p. 19.

[23] Mary Yoder Holsopple, Ruth E. Krall and Sharon Weaver Pittman, *Building Peace: Overcoming Violence in Communities,(* Geneva: World Council of Churches publications, 2004), p. 17.

mentioned elsewhere, many programmes had been organized to bring awareness and necessary implementations in the given context.[24]

The Decade to 'Overcome Violence' calls people "to engage in theological reflection to overcome the spirit, logic and practice of violence."[25] In order to overcome all forms of violence in the society, churches need to raise their prophetic voices through their teaching ministry, and Christian Education is a means to that end. No doubt, the goal of Christian Education cannot be attained without a critical understanding of the social situation. It is also irrelevant if the church's educational activities are unable to address the contextual realities. Therefore it is very important to respond to the challenge of violence especially gender-based violence through Christian Education activities.

The Purpose of the Research

Since, the Church is called upon to play a prophetic role against all human rights violations in the world through her educational activities based on the biblical principles, this study attempts to explore ways in which the church can make its prophetic voice heard. Therefore, the purpose of this research is to critically analyze the age-old practice of gender-based violence and also to identify different forms of gender-based violence both in church and society, and to suggest relevant ways of responding to it through Christian Education. Besides, to assess the role of women in decision-makings and to identify the obstacles in the structured administration, it is necessary to find out the bottlenecks that prevent the participation of women and hence obstruct their meaningful empowerment.

It would be beyond the scope of this research to deal with all the prevailing issues involving violence like insurgency, war, riots etc., except for gender-based violence. As every community has its own age-old norms and regulations, social set up, religious practices, and so on, this study would focus only on the forms of gender-based violence in the church and society with a special reference to Nagaland context. Since a few research works have been done on political violence considering the above mentioned areas, therefore this study would investigate the issues relating to gender-based violence in general and to respond those challenges through the Educational Ministry of the Church.

A major limitation in the writing of this research is the unavailability of documented information on women in the context of Nagaland, challenging the socio-economic, political and religious factors which obstruct women's mobility. Even though there were a few writings on empowerment of women and domestic violence no one ever has attempted gender-based violence from the church educational ministry. This limitation will be quite noticeable from the resources available from the empirical study. Therefore, this study mostly depends on the

---

[24] *Ibid.*, p. 17.

[25] Ninan Koshy, "War and Peace in the age of Empire," *in Overcoming Violence,* ed. Samson Prabhakar (Bangalore: South Asia Theological Research Institute, 2004), p. 1.

empirical research done in three major Towns in Nagaland. Hence, this study does not claim to be a standardized research one bringing out all the discriminatory actions against women but can be considered the ground work for Church Educational Ministry.

Methodology Adopted

This empirical investigates the different forms of gender-based violence in society and in church, critically analyzing them, considering the socio-cultural, religious, and customary laws on different aspects in the society, particularly in the context of Nagaland. Apart from explaining important key Words, Terms and Phrases related to the research area, issues motivated by different factors have been also examined critically, to comprehend the problem of gender-based violence holistically to endeavour to offer solutions from a Christian perspective from the view of Christian educational ministry.

Collection of data was through personal interviews and questionnaires. Data was also collected through secondary sources books, reports, journals and news papers, especially for the theoretical framework, introduction and profile of Nagaland. For personal interview, a few suitable questions were formulated, and fifty (50) people were interviewed from the selected personalities. For the general information, a set of questionnaires was distributed to three hundred (300) people and it was conducted in three places: Kohima, Mokokchung and Dimapur as these are major towns and also as they are inhabited by different tribes of Nagaland.[26]

In the Empirical study, the participants were representatives of each tribal community, representing different peoples' groups' like-Christian educators, church ministers, women leaders, political leaders, village council members, parents and children. Hence, this study attempts to analyze the gender-based violence situation critically in Naga society. Theoretical framework needed for research was worked out on the resources available in the libraries. This methodology would open possibilities for the deeper perception of our thinking, and would at the same time remain faithful in our search for gender justice.

[26] There are sixteen major tribes in Nagaland as mentioned earlier.

Chapter 2

Issues Related to Gender-Based Violence and Christian Education

Identifying certain key words, defining and interpreting important ideologies behind the terms and bringing out their relevance in a given context to support the ongoing research is imperative. Therefore, in this attempt, a few important key terms and phrases will be examined in order to analyze and understand the gender-based violent situations in our society. It is imperative because whenever there is a talk about issues of violence towards women, there is always a tendency to discuss general assumptions/views about women's status and role in society, neglecting the real causes of violence to women. Critically analyzing the traditional understanding about certain phrases would be one of the prime factors while taking up the issues on gender-based violence. A few selected key words, terms and relevant phrases are discussed below.

Gender: Gender describes the socially-constructed identities, roles and expectations assigned to men and women. In other words, it is a socially constructed status, with assigned roles and behaviour that are inter-changeable. These socially-defined differences between women and men are based on deeply-held societal values and beliefs which are alleged to be biased and unjust. Such socially defined attributes and behaviors of men and women are often referred to as masculine and feminine. Hence, masculine and feminine genders are socio-cultural products. For this reason, in a society, men are normally encouraged to show dominance and aggression. Fear and sensitivity are discredited as unmanly. On the other hand, femininity is associated with softness, humility, submissiveness, being emotional and sensitive. With that gender consciousness, people have conditioned their position, and still maintain their status as men and women. We would probably be better informed if we examine some of the scholars' views on gender and the way they have constructed their philosophical analysis.

Thus, while defining the term 'gender,' Lynne Goodstein says, "We live in a gendered world, by being born as a boy or girl, in virtually all locations on the planet our life courses will be to some extent differentially determined. These differences in the lives of females and males are shaped to some extent by biological differences between the sex-hormone levels, body types, body size, and specific roles in the process of reproduction. Yet by far the larger influences on life-course differences come from how society inscribes sex differences with broad-scale meaning through the social construction of gender."[27] Thus, gender refers to the widely shared ideas and expectations about women and men: ideas about typically feminine and masculine characteristics, abilities and expectations about what men and women should do and how to behave in various situations. These roles/gender biases are also determined by social constructions, functional roles, biological interpretations, which influence the societal roles of men and women.

Ideas and expectations thus, for each person as male and female are taught, nurtured and learned from families, friends, opinion-forming leaders, religious and cultural institutions, schools, the home, through media, the workplace and the place where a person is associated. They reflect and influence different roles, social status, economic and political power of women and men in society. It is alleged that, these social construction of roles and status relegate women to an inferior position. Therefore, in every society, the concept of 'gender' determines the range of activities deemed appropriate for individuals to perform which becomes a traditional norm in society. Male/men's roles are deemed to be superior and authoritative in performing certain tasks; to be more appropriate to function in certain social situations and organizations, than female/women, and vice versa.

More precisely, the concept of 'gender' is also typically placed in opposition to the concept of 'sex,' such that gender (feminine/masculine) is a matter of culture. In this connection, the Indian sociologist Khamla Bhasi says, "gender is socially constructed, and not biologically determined. It is a matter of culture, and it refers to the social classification of men and women into masculine and feminine."[28] Gender may therefore be taken to refer to learned patterns of behaviour and action, as opposed to that which is biologically determined. Crucially, biology need not be assumed to determine gender. This is to suggest that, while what makes a person male or female is universal and grounded in laws

---

[27] Lynne Goodstein, "Women, Crime, and Criminal Justice-An overview" in *Women, Crime and Criminal Justice,* ed. Renzetli, Claire M, and Lynne Goodstein (California: Roxburg Publishing Company, 2001) p. 1.

[28] Khamla Bhasin, *Understanding Gender* (New Delhi: Kali for Women, 2002), p. 2.

of nature, the precise ways in which women, for example express their feminity, and men express their masculinity will vary from culture to culture. In other words, they vary in different cultures and at different times. Thus, gender includes a set of cultural rules designed by the immediate context.

Thus, qualities that are stereotypically attributed to women and men in every culture matters a lot in defining gender, such as greater emotional expression in women, greater tendencies to violence and aggression in men, are seen as due to their gender, which means that they could be changed. Therefore, it is universally true, that the specific attributes, tasks, and settings linked to female or male are not necessarily reflective of biological or physiological differences, as they vary to some degree from culture to culture and throughout historic periods. In this sense, gender is the prescription of appropriate attributes, behaviours, and social roles to females and males, that are socially constructed.[29] By understanding gender as a socially constructed relationship between women and men, the possibility of changing the nature of male-female relations and their roles becomes evident. Gender roles differ significantly from one society to another and from one historical period to another and it is an indication that they are socially and culturally constructed.[30] Therefore, in order to challenge gender-based violence, gender analysis or studies is imperative by identifying injustice and imbalanced attributions for men and women in a culturally constructed society, to suggest ways for correcting it for the whole society.

In other words, in order to correct the age-old concept of patriarchal society, the understanding of differences between male and female and their stereotype roles in society, one needs to critically evaluate and analyze the very concept of gender, what is meant by gender and how gender roles affect each person and how different genders compliment each other as men and women grow together. That means, whatever social structure it may be, when injustice or discrimination is done to some one the whole society suffers. And in many cases, these socially-constructed gender roles lead to violent actions. The victims are women who represent half of the human population in this universe. Therefore, the question here for us is-how can humanity live peacefully when its fellow beings amounting to half the percentage are on the ebb of danger? Gender-based violence occurs not only in certain places or times but everywhere and in every aspect of their lives.

As elucidated, our gender identity determines how we are perceived, and how we are expected to think and act as men and women, because of the way society is organized and constructed. Thus, the public domains such as political, economic, religious, and social matters are regarded as male places, and private domains such as homes, nurturing children, serving males and households as

[29] Goodstein Lynne, "*Women, Crime and Criminal Justice-An overview*"ed. Renzetti, Claire M. and Lynne Goodstein, (California: Roxbury publishing Company, 2001), p. 1.

[30] *The Unfolding Vision: An evaluative report on the LWF/DMD, Desk for Women in Church and Society 1988-1997* (Geneva, Switzerland: Lutheran World Federation, 1997), p. 28.

females' place in the society. Therefore, gender division gives unequal power relationships and status, which regards men as powerful and strong and women as weak and fragile. The issue of gender-based violence is a long standing problem of the patriarchal society. The hope for a better tomorrow in regard to gender relations in our society, would require some drastic reorientation of cultural practices, values and self convictions. This is a great challenge to every peace-loving citizen to grapple with as gender justice issues continue with determination and commitment, as traditional values, practices, and beliefs which were held for many centuries cannot be changed easily.

Gender-inequality

The word inequality implies that the two socially-constructed masculine and feminine genders are not equal, the former claiming dominance and superiority over the latter. Patriarchy socializes men to assume a higher status than women so as to subordinate women, as is evident in most cultures. Oppressive and exploitative forms of gender inequality are witnessed in every society though many people find it difficult to accept the reality of gender-based violence in the present technological context. When we talk about these issues, many educated persons are not willing to accept them, by saying, 'women are already liberated, and they can go and work anywhere." The reasons for that could be, as a few competent women are working in certain offices, industries and leading important roles in some fields. It does not mean however, women are equal to men in every respect nor liberated from all forms of discrimination.

It seems, the word equality is uttered only for public propagation, but in reality it is hard to put it in action. Therefore, what Qureshi, a sociologist comments is rather relevant to our situation when we examine gender-inequality. He says, "The modern man in India wants equality between the sexes; in principle. But, he (the modern man) feels much difficulty and pain in accepting equality with his wife, daughter, mother or sister. The women demand protection and security from him and in return for it he demands their loyalty and respect."[31] The above quotation itself is enough to show how gender-inequality is maintained in the society. In all the political fields and church ministries, men talk about equality and justice, laying down so many regulations to be implemented on reservation for women, yet, it is all in principle when it comes to real life situations.

Women and girls are generally discriminated everywhere whether at home or in the workplace, at all stages of life from womb to tomb, as mentioned elsewhere. They are discriminated against in every sphere: in caring and rearing; opportunity for education and other development; in employment, political arenas, social activities, economic shares and religious sanctions, marriages, property shares and so on. In this connection, what Jon Sobrino has mentioned is relevant. He said, "Where unjust Social, Political, Economic and Cultural inequalities are

[31] Muniruddin Qureshi, (2003), p. 5.

found, there is a rejection of the gift of the Lord's peace, even a rejection of the Lord himself."[32] Thus, we cannot deny the reality, when we talk about gender–inequality. Women are deprived of their rights in all the above mentioned areas.

When it comes to church's ministry, women are seen as bearers of the faith. Their contribution to church activities and building up of the faith is tremendously visible through various means. They are the ones who establish and maintain the family relationship and church life. Nevertheless, when it comes to leadership, it is always women, who take the second position, as men devalue their gifts and credibility. Thus, inequality between men and women in every aspect is one of the most crucial and yet one of the most persistent disparities in most societies.[33]

Besides, differences in female and male literacy rates are one aspect of this broader phenomenon of gender-based inequality in society especially in rural areas in India.[34] In the context where there are many children in the family, sons gets better opportunities for education and outside contacts, where as daughters are assigned to help parents in their work at home and are encouraged to get married so that the parents' burdens can be lightened. Since women are not regarded equal with men, they are deprived from higher learning, by saying 'you are going to be somebody's property.' Thus, whether a child is capable enough or not, based on its gender parents decide its career and future prospects, in which many a time girls are the victims in the family, and that leads to greater gender-based violence.

Patriarchy

Every society in the world has its own specific determinants for cultural roles which determine sex-roles in society. Thus, a society may have either a patrilineal or matrilineal culture, accordingly, it decides its own laws and rules to be applied. Interestingly, almost all human societies in the universe are patriarchal. Therefore, it is worth exploring the meaning of the very word 'patriarchy,' in order to examine gender-based violence. The very word patriarchy could be defined in many ways, depending on their cultural structures. The universally accepted term for 'patriarchy' means the rule of the father. It also describes a society in which there is an unequal distribution of power and privilege between males and females. Historically, and to some extent in contemporary life, men had jurisdiction over both the public sphere-politically, economically, religiously, and on cultural affairs and also on the private sphere of home, whereas women were expected to involve themselves only with the private sphere of the home and in raising children and serving their husbands.

---

[32] Jon Sobrino, *Jesus the Liberator: A Historical-Theological View* (New York: Orbis books, Maryknoll, Seventh printing, February, 2004), p. 19.

[33] Muniruddin Qureshi, (2003), p. 7.

[34] Sushama Sahay, *Women and Empowerment: Approaches and Strategies* (New Delhi: Discovering Publishing House, 1998), p. 120.

On the other hand, patriarchy also refers to the ways in which material and symbolic resources including income, wealth, and power and authority are unequally distributed between men and women, through such social institutions as the family, sexuality, the state, the church, the economy, culture, and language. It has been adopted by a majority of feminist theorists to refer to the way in which societies are structured through male domination, over the oppression of women.[35]

The relationship of male domination to biology was an early source of contention among men and women. While patriarchal structures may be found in all known human societies, the reduction of patriarchy to biological invariants, such as the roles of women and men in child-birth and nurturing, suggests that patriarchy is an essential and unchangeable natural relationship. On the other hand, the relationship of patriarchy to other forms of oppression, such as class and status, receives diverse theorization. Questions include that of the primacy of patriarchy over other forms of domination, and the way in which different forms of domination may interact and re-inforce each other.[36] Thus, gender-based violence has its basis in patriarchy, a system that positions men over women. The general characteristics of the status of women under patriarchy are one of subjugation without legal status as their right. Other aspects of this subjugated status include the following:

1. The lineage of children is passed down through the father; (2) male children are preferred to female children; (3) as wives, women's bodies, sexuality, and reproductive capacity belong to their husbands; (4) the sovereignty of the husband over his wife includes the right to beat her, divorce her and to confine her physically, sometimes even to sell her into bondage; (5) because women have very little public roles in politics, ministry, and culture, their education is usually limited to household skills and sometimes to minimal literacy; (6) their right to inherit property as daughters or widows is restricted, and what property they do inherit is usually administered by male members of the family or relatives.[37]

Thus, the very existence of gender-system and gender-inequality depends on patriarchy. The patriarchal system thus controls women's productivity both within the household and outside. It also controls women's reproductive power, sexuality, mobility, and property and also economic resources. Patriarchy even influences individual lives, family, religion, media, political forums, and the legal

---

[35] Andrew Edgar and Peter Sedgoick, *Key Concepts in Cultural Theory* (New York: Routledge Taylor and Francis Group, 2004), p. 269.

[36] Andrew Edgar and Peter Sedgwick, (2004), p. 270.

[37] Andrew Edgar and Peter Sedgwick, (2004), p. 271.

systems.[38] It could be thus concluded that the most patriarchal institution of the society is the family where male dominance is maintained and further legitimized by religion and promoted by literature. And again, this could be enforced or informed due to the media that we use.

Power and Authority

Power and authority have many faces and shapes. At a very elementary level, it is an important and necessary dynamic force in all natural and human relationships. Power is the energy, the potential to act, to effect and to shape. In fact there is no human being without power and authority. Power in itself is morally neutral if it is exercised rationally. Indeed, what makes power and authority prone to abuse is not due to its exercise per se, but due to the motive and the manner in which it is exercised.[39]

A significant feature of the exercise of power in societies, however, is that it is often encountered in structures that exist and operate on the basis of the objectification of power. For instance, as authority, law, forces etc., its internalization (e.g. loyalty, duty, fear of sanction) and the accumulation of the means required to wield it, characterizes its power. Such structures of power appear to exist by accumulating and processing the means to legitimize and perpetuate themselves.[40] It is in this sense that power and authority is seen as problematic and dangerous in itself, which leads to the question whether power and authority are morally neutral instruments or the mere force by which something can be done. In the following we will examine how patriarchal culture uses power and authority and how they affect women.

As examined in the preceding section, a patriarchal society is one in which power and authority is held by male heads of households. Usually, power and authority are taken to mean the exercise of force or control over individuals or particular social groups by other individuals or groups. Thus, in this view, it is something extrinsic to the constitution of both individuals and society. The exercise of power and authority is *a priori* coercive force in nature, since power and authority exercised within the limits of legality is taken to be justly exercised. On the other hand, liberals would regard any exercise of power which compels individuals to be coercive.[41] No doubt then, when it comes to power and authority in a patriarchal society, its effects are no other than on women because patriarchal culture supports males to control women. In this connection, Bride asserts, "Throughout history, power has been used against women to tyrannize, to terrorize, to rape and to kill, to alienate and to silence, to obliterate their history

---

[38] *Ibid.*, p. 272.

[39] Deenabandhu Manchala, *Nurturing Peace: Theological Reflections on Overcoming Violence* (Geneva: WCC Publications, World Council of Churches, 2005), p. 40.

[40] *Ibid.*, p. 41.

[41] *Ibid.*, p. 42.

and to deny their experience, to limit women's horizons and to thwart their ambitions."[42]

It is argued that, limiting one's freedom by someone who uses power and authority, keeping them away from the main streams, demeaning their mobility and keeping them silent in agony, not allowing them to exercise their rights, controlling their moments are all against human rights, because it deprives their personhood. Corresponding to the view mentioned above, Nancy Hartsock also states that, "power is often seen as a means to establish control over others because power has been understood from the position of the socially dominant the ruling class and men."[43]

When we talk about power and authority in a patriarchal society, it would be appropriate to mention an example in order to support the statements made earlier. Like any other patriarchal society, in Naga society, men dominate in every area the socio-cultural, political, economic, and religious affairs. Women's participation in the above areas is not visible. It is regarded as taboo for women to be in the village administrative decision-making system and to claim their share of property as men, unless their society grants it as a sign of sympathy. Under no circumstances can a woman become an administrator of the village council even today.[44] Women's role is thus mostly confined to household affairs. Naga society has placed women in a position of subservience and dependence on men. In many matters, women are simply following and cooperating with men's decisions, even though they don't agree with their ideas.

When speaking about power, there is also a clear separation between public and private spheres of life. In the private sphere of the household, the patriarch enjoys arbitrary power over all junior males and females. In the public sphere, power is shared between male patriarchs according to whatever other principles of stratification operate. No female holds any formal public position of economic, ideological, military or political power. Indeed, females are not allowed into the public realm of power.[45]

Against the above view of power and authority used by patriarchal culture, Letty Russel, a feminist theologian says, "All human relationships include the dynamics of power and authority, therefore human beings cannot function without structures of authority, but they can seek out structures that contribute

---

[42] Maureen Mc Bride, "Power," in Lisa Isherwood & Dorothea McEwan, ed., *An A to Z of Feminist Theology* (Sheffield: Sheffield Academic Press, 1996), p. 82.

[43] Nancy Hartsock, *Money, Sex and Power: Towards a Feminist Historical Materialism* (Boston: Northeastern University Press, 1983), p. 12.

[44] From the statement of one of the village council members at the author's researcher's village, during an interview on 29th June 2006.

[45] Crompton, Rosemary and Michael Mann, *Gender and Stratification* (New York: Polity Press, 1986), p. 41.

to communal well-being and justice."[46] It is logical that in human society power and authority is structured in order to maintain certain disciplines to function and responsibilities for the well-being of the society. In doing so citizens should feel comfortable in expressing their opinions without subjugation and dehumanization, on the pretext of power and authority being shared equally.[47]

Gender-based violence thus, is very much a power and authority problem. It is a known fact that, those who feel themselves superior to others have a tendency to exercise their power over and against the subordinate ones. But from the biblical perspective, the Genesis text clearly says that, man and woman were created in God's image, and that they are endowed with the power from God in order to present themselves as God's representatives in the world, by becoming agents of peace, justice and liberation. So, it is against God's order if women lose their power and authority and become voiceless due to the manipulation of power by their counterparts of men both in the church and society.[48]

Powerlessness in women is a form of structural sin committed against women and against God, seen from a different perspective of sin and exploitation. That is why powerless women have the right to reclaim their power, and that is what God wants women to do. Of course, when we speak about the reclaiming of power by women we do not mean that it should be done in a violent way, but being conscious of one's own rights. That means, everyone should be conscious of the fact that the accumulation of power is against God's will. When it is against the will of God, it is also against human rights and against women's rights too. When power and authority is held by certain sections of the people, it leads into violence. Based on the Word of God, we need to be taught that, power is to be shared by all and among all, irrespective of sex, caste, class and colour.

The fact cannot be denied that, those who have experienced sexual violence are the victims of the abuse of power and authority. In many cases, not only women but children are vulnerable to adult abuse of power and authority because they lack understanding and resources for self-protection. Some children are physically overpowered and raped by adults, even by their own father and brother. The use of threats and rewards to exploit a child's vulnerability is nothing but abuse of power and authority. All sexual contacts between adults and children are destructive because of the power inequities between them.[49] Thus, on many occasions women become vulnerable to assault and manipulation because of the power and authority vested in them by their patriarchal culture. In certain professional relationships such as employer-employee, doctor-patient, teacher-

[46] Letty Russel M., *Household of Freedom: Authority in feminist theology* (Philladelphia: The Westminster Press 1987), p. 22.

[47] *Ibid.*, p. 22.

[48] *Ibid.*, p. 24.

[49] James Newton Poling, *The Abuse of Power: A Theological Problem* (Nashville: Abingdon Press, 1991), p. 23.

student, and pastor-parishioners, men have resources which they can use abusively to exploit the vulnerabilities of women in a patriarchal society.[50]

The role of power and authority is thus pivotal to the understanding of any form of violence.[51] Violence, after all, is an exercise of power and authority over the powerless, or it is retaliation as such. The exercise of violence by the powerful and to some extent by the powerless may in fact indicate lack of power and authority and an awareness that power might be exercised in quite different ways which may, in turn, reflect the shallowness of the value systems which allow and attempt to justify such callous and violent acts.[52]

Thus, power and authority sustain by dominating, possessing, manipulating and controlling people's lives and systems. One of the causes of these is the fear or awe that power and authority induce. The sheer scope of this power decimates resistance even in the face of blatant victimization. Those who thus feel powerless and remain passive tend to deny their own capacity to resist, and their own innate ability to be innovative, and so are unable to hold power and authority accountable.

Misuse of Power and Authority

Only in sharing of power and authority can we affirm God's purposes in creating humankind in His own image. Daniel Day Williams suggests that the temptation to abuse power and authority arises from human fear and arrogance. He says:

> "We are created for communion with God and our neighbour in life which offers communion on terms which require courage and trust in a future we cannot see, which postpones fulfillment and does not allow every kind of immediate gratification. When we discover the risks involved in being human in the great community we are anxious, and when we do not find the hope of communion we are desperate. We willingly deny the fullness of our humanity in order to gratify some part of it...It is not a long step in the logic of emotion to will to destroy the sensitivity of life itself, to turn against ourselves and everything which symbolizes full humanity. We kill what we love because we refuse to love on the terms which life gives."[53]

---

[50] Marie Fortune, *Sexual Violence* (New York: Pilgrim Press, 1983), pp.105ff. see also, Marie Fortune, *Is Nnothing Sacred: When Sex Invades the Pastoral Relationship* (New York: Harper and Row, 1989); Peter Rutter, *Sex in the Forbidden Zone: When Men in Power-Therapists, Doctors, Clergy, Teachers, and Others-Betray Women's Trust* (Los Angeles: Jeremy Tarcher, 1989); Diana Russell, *Sexual Exploitation: Rape, Child Sexual Abuse, and Workplace Harassment* (Beverly Hills: Sage Publication, 1984).

[51] *Nurturing Peace Documents*, p. 9.

[52] *Ibid.*, p. 42.

[53] Daniel Day Williams, *The Spirit and the Forms of Love* (New York: Harper and Row, 1968), p. 153, also see, James Newton Poling, *The Abuse of Power: A Theological Problem* (Nashville:

Thus, abuse of power is motivated by fear and by the resulting desire to control the power of life. This fear and arrogance are then used to create societies in which structures of domination appear. Those who are powerful can organize societies in such a way that those who are vulnerable are denied the full resources that life has to offer. Abuse of power highly relies on institutions and ideologies. Abuse of power may be seen in the social set up, more specifically in the family circle, where male members overshadow the female counterparts.

The family is an ideological construct and institution in society that structures domination in certain ways. In the relationships between parents and children, parents are given over-all control over children, but the father is given authority over the whole family. In this case, the father can sexually and physically abuse his wife and daughters. It seems there are common rationalizations that, 'parents must hit their children in order to teach them to be good citizens.' 'Men hit women in order to show them who the boss is.' Certain professions, such as the ministry and medicine, often function as havens to protect perpetrators at the expense of victims. The extent and consequences of such abuse are denied and treated as interpersonal difficulties rather than as the abuse of power and authority, since society is structured in that way.[54] The overwhelming power and authority of parents is socially defined and protected. Thus, the ideology of family as one of the structures of domination and control create the conditions for abuse of power and authority, especially by the male members.

In patriarchal culture, the unjust power relationships of men and women perpetuated by ideologies and institutions, is another structure of domination that creates the conditions for abuse of power.[55] Rita Brock describes how patriarchal culture is exemplified in the interpersonal relationships of men and women:

> Women in patriarchy find themselves on the downside of power hierarchies. The masculine and feminine views of power remain split into two sides of a dualism as polarized opposites. The two views of power depend on each other in a gender-stratified system of dominance and submission. Exploiter male and exploited female go hand in hand, just as powerful, controlling parent and abused child fit a system of hierarchical power...Both dominance and compliance confuse personal power with positional power. Positional power has to do with our status

---

Abingdon Press,1991), p. 14.

[54] For summaries of the ideology of families see: Mary Lystad, ed., *Violence in the home: Interdisciplinary Perspectives* (New York: Brunner/Mazel, 1986); Hester Eisenstein, *Contemporary Feminist Thought* (Boston: Hall, 1983); Marianne Walters, et al., eds., *The Invisible Web: Gender Patterns in Family Relationships* (New York: Guilford, 1988); James Newton Poling,...29.

[55] Daniel Day Williams, *The Spirit and the Forms of Love* (New York: Harper and Row, 1968), p. 29.

> in social relationships and the extent to which our interpersonal world has emphasized control.[56]

Thus, within the ideology and institutionalized power and authority of patriarchy, women are denied their fundamental resources which are needed for equality, survival, and well-being. Another type of gender-based violence occurs when the ideologies and institutions of society create "blind zones," in which interpersonal violence is tacitly permitted and is not redressed, because certain relationship systems in society are regarded as normative culturally, and are not open to scrutiny. This situation may happen mostly in the sexual abuse incidences, because society thinks that if they are disclosed they might bring shame and destruction not only to their family but to the whole society. This social approval does not however protect victims, but only the perpetrators. Since, perpetrators are protected and secure in the first incidence that encourages them to do more because with that same power and authority they will be rewarded.

Thus, social injustice and the individual abuse of power and authority are ever present in the patriarchal culture. Misuse of power not only destroys individuals, it also destroys the web of relationship on which all life depends. As Poling, one of the practical theologians from the West rightly points out, "Abuse of power is denied of communion and denial of freedom for self, others, and God."[57] As long as a certain group of people exploit and discriminate another there would not be any peace and once there is no peace it creates violence. Therefore, denying a person's rights by oppressing and segregating through various forms are against the teachings of Christ.

General Understanding of Violence

Violence can be defined in many ways. It is interpreted according to a specific situation and context. Along with the above mentioned definitions there are again ample of descriptions given by different scholars. According to Adam Curle, violence is "Unnecessary, excessive, hurtful and unlawful use of force."[58] *The New Shorter Oxford English Dictionary* defines violence as, "Exercise of physical force so as to cause injury or damage to a person, property, the action or an act of constraining or forcing unnatural change upon something."[59] These definitions of violence involve the use of force against both people and property or misuse of power and strength.

---

[56] Rita Brock, *Journeys by Heart* (New York: Crossroad, 1988), pp. 30-33.

[57] Poling...(1991), p. 31.

[58] Paul L. Ballard, *Violence, in A Dictionary of Pastoral Care*, ed. Alastair V. Campell. (London: SPCK, 1987), p. 290.

[59] Lesley Brown, ed., *The New Oxford English Dictionary* (Oxford: Clarendon Press, 1993), p. 3585

According to Paul Wilkinson, "Violence is the use of unauthorized and illegal use of coercive power, whether by the state, by factions or individuals. Violence is also the illegitimate use or threatened use of coercion resulting in or intended to result in, the death injury, restraint or intimidation of persons or the destruction or seizure of property."[60] Therefore, the use of force or an act to cause physical and psychological harm to others, and also the use of verbal abuse which remain long lasting in person's mind are all termed as violence.

On the other hand, it is also defined as an overt act of aggression directed towards an opponent causing much pain, injury and fear. For instance, in a case of rape, a person has the experience of pain and injury, and fear because of social rejection and bleak future prospects. Violence is also taken as a demonstration of force and power against the other person. Violence can also be covert; hidden, veiled, subtle, and this concealed act of repression can be equally disastrous and destructive. Looking at a person violently, using hostile words and attitudes towards the opponent can be harmful and derogatory. In fact, words and attitudes can kill.[61] It is worth mentioning that, when people hear the very word 'Violence,' they realize its effect as causing character assassination, as uttering harmful words can provoke one to make negative comments on others. But, this is the kind of violence which kills people many a time. Women everywhere are the victims of that unnoticeable verbal violence, and this gradually leads to physical violence which destroys body, soul and mind.

It is perceived however, that physical harm can affect only a certain person or animal, whereas verbal abuse may cause injury even to the wider realm of lives. Thus, Carl Miller, in the *Dictionary of Pastoral Care and Counseling,* has explicitly brought out this aspect in his definition. It says, "Physical violence ranges on a continuum from superficial injury to death, while verbal violence involves violation of character of dignity."[62] Many scholars while defining violence have often neglected the effects of verbal violence yet it is found more serious when we analyze it from a psychological perspective.

Psychologically, violence is variously perceived as instinctive aggression rooted in evolution; faulty ego-development and lack of self-control; defective socialization etc. It is a response not only in human society but even in the animal kingdom, to protect oneself and to secure as an instinct. Carl Miller points out to two types of violence: (1) Personal violence, as in the case of rape, child abuse, wife battering, and homicide; (2) Collective violence, as in the form of strikes,

---

[60] Sarojini Sharan, "Establishment and Violence," ed. Nirol Sinha in *Women and Violence* (New Delhi: Vikas Publishing House pvtltd, 1989), p. 34.

[61] Vikash Agarwal, "Violence Against Women: Any Act of aggression or psychological domination by men over women-who will decide?," *Legal News and Views,* Vol 20 No. 8 August 2006, p. 4.

[62] D. Earl Miller, "Violence", in *The Dictionary of Pastoral Care and Counselling,* ed. Rodney J. Hunter (Nashville, London: Abingdon Press, 1999), pp. 1303-4.

riots, revolutionary, rebellious and terrorists' activities and war.[63] Thus, violence is not only physical and psychological but also personal and collective. Violence thus affects a whole range of human and non-human relationships.

Again, the definition of Robert McAfee Brown is insightful. He says, 'whatever violates another, in the sense of infringing or disregarding or abusing or denying the other, whether physical harm is done or not, can be understood as an act of violence.' The basic overall definition would then become violation of personhood. While such a denial or violation can involve physical destruction of person-hood in ways that are obvious, person-hood can also be violated or denied in subtle ways that are not obvious at all except to the victim. There can be violation of person-hood quite apart from the doing of physical harm.[64] The definition of violence does not end there because the word violence has many faces and it can be interpreted according to time and space.

The preceding statement presents its definition of violence in a wide range by including all realms of life, including every living thing in the universe, which is a holistic understanding of violence. Often people in general throughout the centuries assumed that violence is nothing but physical injuries inflicted by using forceful means. That is the reason why when one tries to investigate the gender-based violence in society and church, many people think that it is not a serious issue. Because gender issues are like any other issues present as long as human beings exist. But whatever may be the kind of violence, it is an act of destruction of one's life and the whole universe. This as the human rights issue becomes women's rights issue too.

Violence could be numerous as interpreted by different persons from different social contexts. As pointed out earlier, violence as brutality, force, destruction, or the unjust use and abuse of power are pervasive at all levels of society. The diverse issues of violence, including powerlessness, violence against women and children, destruction of the environment and over-exploitation of the world's resources, militarism etc, all must be recognized as violence. It is a fact that, violence provokes violence and irresistibly engenders new forms of oppression and enslavement.

When talking about violence, Archbishop Thomas Menamparampil expresses this in a more elaborate way covering a broader spectrum of life: "Ideological conflicts, terrorism, pathological forms of nationalism, racial violence, ethnic cleansing, famine, domestic violence, workplace abuse, football hooliganism, cyberspace violence, intercultural violence...and finally, 'accepting violence as normal.' Violence is insensitive to human suffering and oppressive of

[63] D. Earl Miller (1999), 1303-4.

[64] Robert Mc Afee Brown, *Religion and Violence* (Philadelphia: The Westminster Press, 1973), p. 7.

people. Violence in every form keeps growing."[65] The above mentioned forms of violence exist in every society and many a time they are accepted as normal incidents or ways of life. But, the fact is that our aggressive behaviour is created by social, political and economic circumstances of our own making therefore, we can control it. There are more such forms of violence which are often ignored and are not realized as violence though we live with all these types of violence.

As explicitly elaborated through our examination, violence is not only about war or attack, fighting and killing by using certain weapons, but abusing people, reducing their self-esteem and their self-confidence or self-worth, leading them to an experience of powerlessness and subjugation. It can also be physical, psychological or emotional, verbal, theological, cognitive, sexual, visual, institutional, structural, economic, political, social, and ecological. Besides, as General Arbuckle points out, the following activities on the list of violence covers the whole range of human activity: maligning others, calumniating, spreading negative rumours and character-assassination, deception by using euphemisms, e.g., 'downsizing' for plain sacking; political manipulation by bribes, unrealistic promises, deceptive flattery, untrue advertisements, glamorous display; intimidation, gossip, cynical humour, taunting, sneering, scorning, patriarchal, ethnic or racial jokes, ignoring conventional courtesies, being rude and ill-mannered, inhuman competition, vandalism, political witch-hunting and oppression of minorities. He also mentions political patronage, cronyism, family-rule, new forms of colonialism, imbalance in trade and economic relationships, the unbearable burdens of international debts all are regarded as forms of violence.[66]

Apart from the above mentioned forms of violence, there is also the violence done to future generations, when the present generation makes them inherit unbearable burdens of debts left behind, exhaustion of natural resources, damaged nature, e.g., by massive deforestation. In so acting, the present generation violates an unwritten contract of justice with the coming generations. There is violence implanted also by unhelpful philosophies that educate the rising generations to collective anger, cynicism, exaggerated pragmatism, narcissism and nihilism.[67] Thus, forms of violence are numerous and their effects are the untold burden on every human being who is trying to live a life meaningful and beneficial. Above all, gender-based violence aggravates untold suffering inflicted on women.

Spiral of Violence

According to Dom Helder Camarra, the former Archbishop of Brazil, the climate of institutional violence which breeds further violent behaviour is called the "spiral

[65] Archbishop Thomas Menamparampil, SDB., " Searching for Ways of Peace.1." in *Vidyajyoti Journal of Theological Reflection* (March 2006), p. 167.

[66] Samson Prabhakar (2003), p. 168.

[67] *Ibid.*, p. 170.

of violence.'[68] What the father of the nation Mahatma Gandhi mentioned when talking about non-violence as being right, was, "Violence provoked by Violence can lead only to a 'spiral of violence,' not peace. But violence, undergone patiently and lovingly for a cause, can be creative. It provokes others to think and, eventually, to change. Thus, violence becomes a non-violence strategy."[69] Camarra explains the spiral of violence in this way: "the spiral begins with Violence 1: Institutional violence, the violence in the rules or policies of institutions or systems that derive countless human beings into a subhuman condition, where they have to submit to humiliation and injustice, without hope. Their condition is that of slaves. Then the spiral proceeds to violence 2: Counter-violence that is the violence which reacts to violence 1-riots, revolution, terrorism, and much of the crime we see in our country today. Violence 3 is repression in response to Violence 2: It takes the form of bigger and better police and military forces.[70]

In the initial stage, people may not be able to comprehend or understand in what kind of situation they are, but as time goes by one could begin to realize and react to the very situation they are in. It can lead to a better or worse situation. In many cases, people begin to respond in a violent way, which leads to violence. According to one Christian educationist, the spiral of violence occurs when people feel very frustrated in a situation in which they experience repression, whether it is in school or in some organization or society. And many have thus the first-hand experience of dictatorship. They often know what it means experientially to have someone else control one's life, to be given no room to grow or to make decisions. Then one can begin to understand the effects of institutional violence at any age level.[71] Thus, the movement of women's liberation, Dalit and tribal theology, and many other communal movements are the out-come of such institutional violence in human history.

We also need to understand the so-called "war mentality" in one's culture itself which provokes violence. It is said that, the word 'war' does not simply mean the violent and bloody actions that take place in a battlefield, but an attitude that is prevalent in our culture, an attitude of 'us' against 'them.' It is also a mentality which supports military resolutions to conflict and the assumption that the security of a community, nation and its civilization rests on arms.[72] As seen from the preceding words, this war-mentality is present in every culture which spawns negative attitudes and rebellious actions against others in every aspect of one's life. It may be between nations, sexes, classes, colours, and ethnics groups, and even

---

[68] Kathleen McGinnis and James , *Education for Peace and Justice: National Dimensions,* 1985, in Samson Prabhakar, *Essays on Christian Education and Liturgy* (SATHRI / BTESSC, 2003), p. 109.

[69] Michael Amaladoss, S.J, *The Asian Jesus* (Chennai: IDCR/ISPCK, 2005), p. 116.

[70] Kathleen Mc Ginnis and James, *Parenting for Peace and Justice* (New York: Orbis Book, 1990), p. 46.

[71] Samson Prabhakar (2003), p. 110.

[72] Samson Prabhakar (2003), p. 110.

among the one family circle, etc. For instance, treating all women as inferior and unclean is to overpower them; oppressing people by rating their status; insulting and looking down by seeing their colour or race; and so on and so forth.[73]

The manifestations of the 'war mentality' in our culture could also be seen in the kind of toys children are provided with, namely the toys with which children can play war games. The other manifestation of this mentality is the kind of films and television programmes, and also varieties of games on the computer, that are popular these days. These manifestations are also closely linked to institutional violence, because toys, television programmes, computer games and films are commercialized. Most of the manifestations of the 'war mentality' in our culture are the way mass media interpret patriotism.[74]

In recent years, people are very much accustomed to bomb blasts, terrorist attacks, which they witness in reality, and in return they too learn to attack. Therefore, children growing up among all these facilities are comparatively, more ferocious and have more interest in forming groups in order to attack, fight or to challenge others. This institutionalized violence has embedded unaccountable and intolerable violence among fellow beings that we ought to love and to let live in harmony.

It cannot be denied that, for centuries in the history of human society women have gone through untold miseries from their male counterparts in many ways. They were killed, raped, tortured, insulted, deprived their rights, demeaned their dignity and worth, denied privileges, oppressed and assaulted in all sexual, moral, economic, and psychology. The impact of those experiences made women to raise their voice and start claiming their rights. Thus, in this post modern context, women have realized their discriminatory condition and have begun to retaliate against their abusers. There are ample incidents where the powerless group and weaker section of people have revolted against their discriminators by adapting the technique which their abusers had used. Thus, gender-based violence will continue until our society has a realization about its oppressive cultural traditions and is willing to accept both men and women as equal partners.

Statement of Violence

When talking about violence in human society, there are various opinions and arguments expressed by different people about its origin and how violence or violent actions are brought into existence. Has violence come about due to gender-bias? Whether gender relationships have caused human right violations? Can all violent reactions be traced back to gender bias? What makes a human being to behave in a violent manner? How do people learn violent activities? Deliberating on these in August 1987, the Council of Representatives of the American Psychological Association voted to endorse the Seville Statement.

[73] Mc Ginnis, Kathleen and James, *Parenting for Peace and Justice*, (1990), p. 47.

[74] *Ibid.*, p. 48.

The Seville Statement's purpose is to dispel the widespread belief that human beings are inevitably disposed to war as a result of innate, biologically-determined aggressive traits. They assumed that the misuse of scientific theories and data to justify violence is not new but has been made since genocide, colonialism, and suppression of the weak have been common. They stated their position in the form of five propositions.[75] Their findings and arguments are beneficial with interesting arguments, yet they widen many doubts in the process to understand violence:

(1) It is scientifically incorrect to say that we have inherited a tendency to make war from our animal ancestors. Although fighting occurs widely throughout animal species, only a few cases of destructive intra-species fighting between organized groups have ever been reported among naturally living species, and none of these involve the use of tools designed to be weapons. There are cultures which have not engaged in war for centuries, and there are cultures which have engaged in war frequently at sometime and not at others.

(2) It is scientifically incorrect to say that war or any other violent behaviour is genetically programmed into our human nature. While genes are involved at all levels of nervous system function, they provide a developmental potential that can be actualized only in conjunction with the ecological and social environment. Genes are co-involved in establishing our behavioural capacities, they do not by themselves specify the outcome.

(3) It is scientifically incorrect to say that in the course of human evolution there has been a selection for aggressive behaviour more than for other kinds of behaviour. In all well-studied species, status within the group is achieved by the ability to co-operate and to fulfill social functions relevant to the structure of the group. 'Dominance' involves social bindings and affiliations; it is not simply a matter of the possession and use of superior physical power, although it does involve aggressive behaviour. Violence is neither in our evolutionary legacy nor in our genes.

(4) It is scientifically incorrect to say that humans have a 'violent brain,' while we do have the neural apparatus to act violently, it is not automatically activated by internal or external stimuli. Like higher

.[75] The Seville Statement on Violence was drafted by an international committee of scholars at the 6th International Colloquium on Brain and Aggression held at the University of Seville, Spain, in May 1986, with support from the Spanish Commission for UNESCO. The Board of Scientific Affairs emphasized that this is not a Scientific Statement on the issue of specific inherited behavioural traits. It is, rather, a social statement designed to eliminate unfounded stereotypic thinking on the inevitability of war. Poornima Mohan, *Encyclopedia of Women* (Delhi: Indian Publisher's Distributors, 2000), p. 133.

primates and unlike other animals, our higher neural processes filter such stimuli before they can be acted upon. How we act is shaped by how we have been conditioned and socialized. There is nothing in our neurophysiology that compels us to react violently.

(5) It is scientifically incorrect to say that violence is caused by 'instinct' or any single motivation. The emergence of modern warfare has been a journey from the primacy of emotional and motivational factors, sometimes called 'instincts,' to the primacy of cognitive factors. Modern war involves institutional use of personal characteristics such as obedience, suggestibility, and idealism; social skills such as language; and rational considerations such as cost-calculation, planning, and information processing. The technology of modern war has exaggerated traits associated with violence both in the training of actual combatants and in the preparation of support for war in the general population. As a result of this exaggeration, such traits are often mistaken to be the causes rather than the consequences of the process.[76]

Thus, after careful analysis and examination from different perspectives on the causes of violence considering both animals and human species, psychologists have concluded that biology does not condemn humanity to violence, and that humanity can be freed from the bondage of biological pessimism, and that they can be empowered with confidence to undertake the transformative tasks needed in the society. Violence is not inherited through the genes or through instinctive motivational factors and neurophysiology that compels us to react violently but it is achieved by violent acts and is shaped by how we have been conditioned and socialized. Therefore, the same species who invented violence is also capable of inventing peace and harmony. The responsibility lies with each citizen, irrespective of male or female, boy or girl.

In other words, violent acts that are present in human society do not come from the animal world or are inherited from the animal. Rather it is created among human beings who have the instinct to do things and create the things through using their faculty which other animal species do not have. Thus, in certain cases human beings are made to believe that they have learned war and violence from the animal. All the war weapons and tools used for destruction and in killings among human beings are all human-inventions. It could be concluded that, the issues of gender-based violence prevailing in society are not generated or learned from the animal or biological trait due to sexes but through the concept of superiority and inferiority complex present in human instincts and subtly implementing this gender bias in the human sphere of day to day activities and bolstering that stance by quoting scripture, the authority of tradition and culture.

[76] Poornima Mohan, *Encyclopedia of Women.* (2000), pp. 133-135.

Forms of Violence in General

Acts of violence could be seen in many ways or forms. Firstly, structural violence is carried out by a dictatorial government. In some places, it is covered up by the so-called ethnic or religious differences, where social, political, cultural structures themselves oppress, segregate, exclude or marginalize groups of people. Some of the glaring examples of these are seen in caste discrimination, dowry system and customary laws on men and women in India. Structural violence also occurs when all of a society's formal and informal structures create an organization of wealth and power in which individuals and sub-groups or entire communities are exploited by the structures themselves.[77] In this instance, Brown has observed that, "structural violence usually has the effect of denying people important rights, such as economic well-being; social political and sexual equality; a sense of personal fulfillment, and self-worth."[78] Secondly, social violence occurs where forces like racism and sexism exclude people on the basis of colour, gender, caste, class and ethnicity and so on.[79] There is a tendency to mistreat, misjudge a person by just looking at his/her appearance without considering the actual inner self or dignity or worth of that person.[80]

Thirdly, domestic violence comprises those violent acts where women, children, maid and man-servants, are abused or treated brutally within established relationships. In today's world, situations exists where men too are abused or ill treated by their wives. In the traditional Indian society, where there is a joint family system, acts of violence exist even more. Joint family set-ups are the sites of oppression and violence, and are a great distress to women.[81] Fourthly, Psychological violence occurs, where persons or groups of persons in an institution, or in a society in general are kept threatened, deprived of dignity and live in fear.[82] Also psychological abuse such as intimidation, humiliation and controlling

---

[77] For example, poverty may be seen to be one pervasive form of structural violence when the wealth of the few is created on the backs of the poor. Conversely stated, the poverty of the many is guaranteed for the existence of the rich by the wealth of the few. While a small number of the world's families control vast sums of land and capital, millions more live in poverty so severe that they have no possibility of bettering their lives or those of their children. They are born into poverty, and they die in poverty, Mary Yoder and others…(2004), p. 19.

[78] Mary Yoder and others….(2004), p. 19.

[79] Ibid.

[80] Being a tribal by race, a woman by gender, and fatherless by family background, many a time the author herself has experienced acts of violence on many occasions.

[81] Kiran Prasad, "Contemporary Mass Media and Gender Justice: A Critical analysis on Empowerment of Women in India," *Journal of Dharma*, April-June 2004 Vol. XXIX, No. 154.

[82] It was in late eighties and early nineties during the army operation in Nagaland, there were firings, and from time to time houses were checked in the midnight that kept everyone in a state of fear and psychological trauma. Even today, whenever people hear any kind of cracker sound, it strikes them with fear.

behaviours cause psychological trauma.[83] Psychological violence[84] could also be due to aggression, anger, hatred, so on and so forth.

Fifthly, moral violence occurs, where the brutal force of the state or a dominant group denies peoples' human rights or the rights of people-hood.[85] Lastly, violence of warfare has taken the lives of many, for any number of reasons.[86] One of the reasons could be due to the advent of globalization, in which the poverty of the many is guaranteed by the wealth of the few, where a small number of the world's individuals or families control vast sums of land and capital, and millions of people live in poverty, and they die in poverty. On the other hand, when the powerful refuse to include the weak as full participants in a society, the resulting repression and oppression create situations in which violence breeds.[87]

In many cases, while protecting one's dignity and identity, others' sentiments are violated. Judging, classifying, ignoring or ruling over the other according to one's convenience and ability causes violence. Violence is therefore a problem in relation to the other, and otherness too. Therefore, overcoming violence in the conflicting circumstances demands overcoming one's perception of threat in the other.[88] Most violent incidents thus can be directly linked to such factors as provocation,[89] frustration incentives,[90] stimulation and stress, and so on.

---

[83] *Ibid.*, p. 47.

[84] There have been considerable studies on the psychology of violence because aggression, anger, hatred and their external expression in different forms of violence are no doubt part of human behaviour. Thus in a court of law those who commit violence that defies reason, such as killing one's own children, are subjected to psychiatric examination to determine whether they were in full control of themselves when the acts of violence was committed. The emotional state of anger can be provoked by actions of others and by the evocation of memories that makes one to lose control of oneself., S. Wesley Ariarajah, *Axis of Peace: Christian Faith in Times of Violence and War* (Geneva: World Council of Churches Publications 2004), p. 89.

[85] It was in early eighties during the army operation in Nagaland, there were firings, and from time to time houses were checked in the midnight that kept everyone in a state of fear and psychological trauma. Even today, whenever people hear any kind of cracker sound, it strikes them with fear.

[86] S. Wesley Ariarajah, *Axis of peace: Christian Faith in times of Violence and War* (Geneva: World Council of Churches, 2004), pp. 102-103.

[87] Mary Yoder Holsopple, Ruth E. Krall and Sharon Weaver Pittman, *Building Peace: Overcoming Violence in Communities (* Geneva: World Council of Churches, 2004), p. 19.

[88] Lalsangkima Pachuau, "Towards Overcoming Violence in North East India*:* A Perspective Drawn from Minority Experience*,"* *Overcoming Violence,* ed. Samson Prabhakar (Bangalore: South Asia Theological Research Institute, 2004), p. 44.

[89] A 12-year-old student from Nellore in Andhra Pradesh who attempted suicide by immolating herself died of burns. The deceased identified as Sharanya, a sixth standard student of Nellore Government School, was provoked by her teachers for coming late to the school. Upset over the scolding and questioning, she attempted suicide, *Vijay Times*, (Bangalore, Thursday September 29, 2005), p. 3.

[90] A 30 year-old woman committed suicide frustrated over her husband's loss in business, *Vijay Times*, (Bangalore, September 29, 2005), p. 3.

Provocations are direct and obvious, such as verbal insults and physical attacks. Very often provocations involve sexual or emotional infidelity or perceived insults to one's honor. On the other hand, frustration and depression occur when something blocks the attainment or threatens the continued possession of a valued goal objective. One of the examples could be the supervisor's bad report, which may prevent a promotion, etc.

Thus, factors causing violent situation need to be identified and critically analyzed in order to suggest relevant steps to overcome violence. Thus, violence takes place within the family, within the church community as well as in the wider society. But the problem is that, a majority of the people is not adequately made aware of how to overcome violence. In many cases, people are ignorant about the acts of violence hampering in their day-to-day lives. Relevant and appropriate Christian religious education is therefore urgently needed in order to build a life-sustaining community by challenging all forms of violence that affect people.

An Overview of Gender-based Violence

Although 'sex' and 'gender' are often used interchangeably by several writers on different occasions, they are quite different and should be used distinctly. The following section aims at figuring out the differences between these two words and how the human society treats its fellow beings based on the very word gender. Sex refers to the physical differences between males and females, where as 'gender' refers to the different socially prescribed roles of males and females. Gender roles are context-based and are learned through socialization.[91] The physical differences between males and females or girls and boys are universal, where as the gender roles are quite different and may prescribe all aspects of social life ranging from access to resources, public and private responsibilities, and patterns of courtship. Gender roles may change over time, but they are reflections of long-standing assumptions that a society holds about men, women, boys and girls.[92]

Thus, building upon these differentiated roles, 'gender-based violence' is therefore 'Violence' that is directed at an individual based on her or his specific gender role in a society. It can affect females or males; however gender-based violence affects women and girls disproportionately. It is violence intended to establish or reinforce gender hierarchies and perpetuate gender inequalities. Therefore, any discrimination or oppression embedded in an individual or a section of people based on sex whether it is physical or psychological, is a violation of the fundamental human rights.

Since 2001, the Reproductive Health for Refugees Consortium has preferred 'gender-based violence' as the broadest term in order to recognize the gendered

---

[91] Ward Jeanne, *If Not Now, When? Addressing Gender-based Violence in Refugee, Internally Displaced and Post-Conflict Settings* (New York: The Reproductive Health for Refugees Consortium. See also, *Save the Children*, p. 3.

[92] Ward, *If Not Now, When*? (2000), p. 3.

elements in nearly all forms of violence against women and girls, whether it is perpetrated through sexual violence or through other means.[93] As cited above, men and women, boys and girls, may all be subjected to gender-based violence, however, women and girls are by far the most affected group and will therefore be the principal focus in this study.

While defining gender-based violence, Jeanne Ward expounds that,

> any harm that is perpetrated against a person's will; that has a negative impact on the physical or psychological health, development, and identity of the person; and that is the result of gendered power inequities that exploit distinctions between males and females, among males and among females. Although not exclusive to women and girls, gender-based violence principally affects them across all cultures. Violence may be physical, sexual, psychological, economic, or socio-cultural,[94]

Gender-based violence may manifest itself in numerous ways as stated earlier: domestic violence, female foeticide,[95] rape, torture, trafficking, and forced prostitution and marriage.[96] Although rape and other sexual abuses have been recognized as serious crimes on humanitarian grounds, in many places these forms of gender-based violence are fundamental issues. Gender-based violence occurs in both public and private spheres. Many traditional cultures have their own beliefs, norms, and social institutions that legitimize and, therefore, perpetuate gender-based violence. The same acts that would be punished if directed at an employer, a spouse, children, a neighbour, or an acquaintance often go unchallenged when men direct them at women, especially within the family.

While describing the issues of gender-based violence, the United Nations Development Fund for Women (UNDFM) also notes that "The range of gender-based acts of violence is devastating, occurring quite literally from the womb to the tomb." Among other abuses, violence against women includes: prenatal

---

[93] Ward, *If Not Now, When?* (2002), p. 4

[94] Ward, *If Not Now, When*? (2002), p. 4

[95] The well-known religious leader and social activist, Swami Agnivesh, began a campaign across five north-western states against female foeticide. He says, "There's no other form of violence that's more painful, more abhorrent, and more shameful than the female foeticide," Infact, the death of foetus is demonic and it is martyrdom to the existence of life., in Thomas Manoj Samuel, "Martyrdom at Birth" in *Gurukul Daily Devotion*-2007 (Chennai: Gurukul Lutheran Theological College and Research Institute, 2007), p. 29.

[96] Ward Jeanne, *If not now, when?* (2002), p. 4.

sex selection[97] in favour of male babies, female infanticide,[98] and sexual abuse, female genital mutilation, sexual harassment, and discrimination that occurs in educational institutions or schools, the work place, shops, hospital, place of recreation clubs, trafficking, forced prostitution, dowry-related violence, domestic violence, battering, and marital rape."[99]

Take the case of dowry. Its demands are common among Indians. On the other hand, the problem of dowry is basically a problem of demand and supply. In this regard, the sociologist Ram Ahuja points out that, "Today dowry[100] is not confined to clothes, jewellery, utensils, furniture, and items of everyday use. The demands range from financing the boy's trip abroad, to investing in a business or building a house for him. The miseries of bride's parents do not end with their giving dowry at the time of marriage. The custom demands a perennial flow of gifts from the parents of the girl to the boy's family on all festivals."[101] Thus, a bride's dowry can economically cripple a poor family. Millions of women will have their lives cut short, killed by their husbands or in-laws for not fulfilling the constant demand of dowry. Besides, many young girls end their precious talented lives by committing suicide due to the poor condition of their parents, knowing that their existence could be a big burden for their parents in future. Therefore, knowing this fact, girls can often decide to take a firm decision before they attain the marriageable age. But they cannot, as they are conditioned to be submissive to the dowry-tradition as engendered by gender-bias.

Further, gender-based violence and abuse are not something that happens only in particular kind of homes or communities but it is obvious in every place, any time and in any kind of societal set up. In other words, it happens in all kinds of homes and communities, regardless of the social categories of economic class, caste, race, tribe, ethnicity, nationality, religion or age.[102] Therefore, unless

[97] Sex-selection abortions have been banned in India for more than a decade, but according to medical research, more than 10 million female births in India have been lost to abortion and sex selection in the last 20 years. Research showed that for every 1,000 male babies born in India, there were just 933 girls. This is due to an increasing tendency to prefer boys when previous children had been girls, in Thomas Manoj Samuel, "Martyrdom At Birth," in *Gurukul Daily Devotion*-2007, p. 29.

[98] Experts in India say female foeticide is mostly linked to socio-economic factors. It is an idea that many say has been carried over from the time India was predominantly an agrarian society where boys were considered an extra pair of hands in the farm. The girl child has traditionally been considered inferior and a liability. *Ibid.*, p. 29.

[99] *Violence Against the World's Women* UNIFEM, (2002).

[100] In the daily newspapers, at least three to four or more cases would appear about suicide and almost all cases are related to dowry deaths. As a regular reader of the news paper, the author herself has collected a number of documents on dowry death.

[101] Ram Ahuja, *Violence Against Women* (Jaipur and New Delhi: Rawat Publications, 2003), p. 136.

[102] *Created in God's Image: From Hierarchy to Partnership* (A Church *Manual for Gender Awareness and Leadership Development*), Switzerland: World Alliance of Reformed Churches,

gender-based violence is recognized as violence against humanity by both men and women, and by society as a whole, it will be a very slow journey to end the cycle of violence. Therefore, Thoreya Ahmed Obaid says, "If women and girls, and communities as a whole, are threatened by gender-based violence, then there is no real chance for peace and security."[103] So, long as the human community exercises and experiences discrimination and subjugation upon one section by another, there is no chance of peace and harmony in the society.

Violence may be interpreted or defined at different levels of one's life situation too as already stated in the preceding work. At the personal level, direct physical violence is manifest in the alarming rate of suicide, and attraction to violence spawns addictions such as drug and alcohol abuse which increasingly threaten poverty-stricken communities.[104]

At the interpersonal level, physical violence against women and children occurs in various forms:[105] 'wife-battering, rape, child abuse, incest; wide practice of female genital mutilation; female foeticide and infanticide in culture where male children are favoured; the brutal use of power, authority and humiliation of women through sex and pornography industry; the forced sterilization of women in countries with high population growth; life threatening work conditions both in national and in multi-national industries.' Today, due to the flourishing global market system and multiplication of industries and so on, many job opportunity advertisements seem to be very attractive and challenging. But these directly or indirectly affect women's movement, in which their lives are at stake.

Besides, at the local, national and global level, armed conflicts and communal conflicts create a spiral of violence that destroy civil societies, devastate places and cut down many young people in their youth. Among many, one of the examples is that of the armed conflict situation which create different forms of violence among ethnic groups and between various political groups in many parts of the world as in the case of Nagaland. In all these violent incidents, the most unfortunate groups are women and children. Thus, there are ample examples around the world where women and children were raped, tortured, harassed, oppressed and dehumanized. Thus, violence could be defined and interpreted in various ways and it could be generated through different forms, and this is the reality today. Becoming conscious about one's own context and responding to the real situations that are encountered leads to the need to challenge the context, through appropriate and timely education in which Christian Religious Education can play a pivotal role.

(2003), p. 122.

[103] http://www.theirc.org/what/gender-based.html, accessed on August 15, 2007.

[104] Lisa Isherwood and Dorothea McEwan, *An A to Z of Feminist Theology* (Sheffield, England: Sheffield academic Press Ltd, 1996), p. 229.

[105] *Ibid.*, p. 229

Gender-based Violence in Home/family

The home is the first institution where a person learns tremendously for the present and future life, there-by contributing to the larger society. Once a person's mind is set on the practices through certain structural settings, it would be extremely difficult to change. Here, our concern is the situation of women in the home/family. If we analyze the condition of women in the family we see that violence is gender-based. No wonder, in every family boy are given preference and valued above girls. In this connection, Malini Devananda has mentioned in her article 'Women Opting for a New Humanity' that, "In most homes the best food or bigger amount of food is given to the men who are served first and the female, especially the mothers, eat last and what is left over. For this reason, a high percentage of pregnant women are anemic 60% and 50% of the infants born are underweight (less than 2 ½ kg)."[106] Further, even at birth, girls are considered second class citizens. This status is conferred on them by both the family and society. In the home they are denied the same diet and medical care, as boys are in the family. They are forced into menial jobs being told of their worthlessness and their liability as women. Girls are discriminated against even before they are born. Often when parents discover that the fetus is female they choose to abort it. In some places unwanted female infants are done away with. Francis Sunderaraj has mentioned in his article, "Christian Education and Social Issues", that, 'the practice of drowning baby girls is so common in China's Guangxi Province that in twenty years at least one million boys will be unable to find wives.'[107] This is also true in some parts of India.

Gender-based Violence starts thus in the family, sometimes even before they are born. This is due to the gender-selective abortions which are prevalent in every country in the present world. Almost all the issues relating to decision-making in the family, not only with regard to children but also women are taken by men. It is very obvious in many homes, where the eldest son controls women including his mother and elder sisters after their father's death.

Though women face untold violence in the family, due to retribution, lack of economic means to extract themselves from the situation, emotionally dependent and concern for the children, they suffer silently. In the patriarchal society, men think that once they marry a woman she becomes his slave and that she may be treated in any way he wants i.e., battering and even murdering her. Many women also think that the scolding and battering they go through at the hands of their husbands is their fate and they must suffer silently. Of course,

---

106 Malini Devananda, "Women Opting for a New Humanity" in *In God's Image: Women Seraching for a New Huimanity,* Journal of Asian Women's Resource Centre for Culture and Thelogy. Vol. 25, No. 4, (December 2006), p. 10.

107 Francis Sunderaraj, "Christian Education and Social Issues," *Education That Transforms: Perspectives on Christian Eduaction for Asia*, ed. Edith Woods (Bangalore: Theological Book Trust, 1995), p. 118.

this understanding and attitude are gradually changing among the educated and those who are exposed to the outside world. Moreover, owing to sensitization programmes and setting up of women cells in urban areas. Further, it is also expected that women should be faithful to their husbands, but it is not so with the husbands. Owing to this, many women get infected with the HIV virus through their unfaithful husband.[108]

Moreover, many arguments and problems in the home are due to the fact that the wife and female members are over-worked, and the husband and brothers do not extend help in the household chores or look after the young ones. This tradition is very obvious in some of the tribes in Nagaland. Another cause of trouble in the family life is when the husband spends too much of his earnings on himself and other purposes without the knowledge of their wives, thinking that women cannot fight back even though they get angry. Likewise, there are numerous ways in which women suffer and experience violence in the family and in the society at large.

Violence on the Widow

It is common to feel sad that, 'If a woman is not safe in the family, what can be the condition of women who have lost their husbands or who remain single till death, in a male dominated patriarchal society?' Though women go through different kinds of violence in every society and religion, we would examine particularly the life condition of Hindu women. In other words, the life situation of Hindu widows represents the climax of gender-based violence in the Indian society. The state of widowhood in Hindu society is considered the worst and the most dreaded period. If at least, the stigma of widowhood is removed, remarriage could be socially accepted. A widow generally, in Hindu society has to undergo various kinds of socio-religious-cultural oppression as well as economic hardship.

According to Qureshi, a prominent psychologist, "A widow in high caste Hindu society is considered to be an evil omen in the family and society, who has 'eaten' her husband. Widowhood is regarded as the punishment for horrible crimes committed by the women during her present or earlier births. Disobedience and disloyalty to the husband or murdering him in an earlier existence are some of the grave crimes, which results as punishment in the present birth by widowhood."[109] Thus, in Hindu society a woman's worth is nil without her husband and widowhood is associated with the idea of inauspiciousness.[110] If that is true, every peace loving person should challenge and be able to respond to this kind of situation from the human rights perspective.

---

[108] Malini Devananda, "Women Opting for a New Humanity", *In God's Image: Women Searching for a New Humanity*, Journal of Asian Women's Resource Centre for Culture and Theology. Vol. 25, No. 4, (December 2006), p.10.

[109] M.U. Qrueshi, *Women and crime,* (2006), p. 241 and Saraswati, (1984), p. 69.

[110] *Ibid,* p. 69.

Moreover, it is said that 'in some parts of rural areas in India, to see the face of a widow in the morning before seeing any object is thought as unlucky; a man will postpone his journey if a widow crosses his path at the time of departure. There is hardly any day when a widow is not cursed for the death of her husband.'[111] The moment a woman loses her husband, she is deprived of average living conditions and benefits of worldly desires. A widow, irrespective of age, has religious and social sanctions to discard colourful clothes, jewelry, glass bangles, weaving of flowers, make up, good and delicious food, etc. They are also allowed only such bland food, which is enough for survival.[112] A widow is expected to go to the extreme form of sacrifice of self-immolation on her husband's pyre, and this gets the sanction of the widows themselves, as they do not want to get tortured in the remaining part of their life.[113]

Even today, in the twenty first century, where advanced modern technologies exist, and where there is so much awareness of women being empowered; widows are terribly abused in numerous ways in our society. M.U. Qureshi opines that all the rura and a few urban widows do not wear bright coloured saris. They do not even use coloured glass bangles and earrings after their husband's death. Regarding food, it was found that a majority of the widows have become vegetarian as it is believed that non-vegetarian meal is *tamasi* food which is not 'Satwik'. It will initiate the sexual urge of the widow, which is immoral for them.[114] It was also a traditional norm that widows should be allowed to eat only one meal in 24 hours of a general day and compelled to abstain from food totally on sacred days on the pretext of various religious customs.[115]

It is quite surprising to mention that, a widow who lost her husband early in years was deprived of normal sex life too, as there was no provision of remarriage among Hindus except in lower castes.[116] Again, according to Manu, a widow must not mention the name of another man after her husband's death. With the dedicated efforts of some of the social reformers, Widow Remarriage Act came into existence as early as 1856, but the attitude towards widow remarriage has not changed and cannot be said to be encouraging.[117] In almost all societies, widow remarriage is not encouraging, saying that, being a mother or a woman, she should look after the children and family members without going for remarriage, where as in the case of a widower, it is regarded as normal, and the society does not object to his second marriage. Rather, the society encourages him by saying, 'man cannot live without a wife' or 'man alone cannot take care of the children.'

---

[111] *Ibid.*, p. 69.

[112] M.U. Qureshi, *Media and Crime,* 2006.

[113] *Ibid.*, p. 242.

[114] *Ibid.*, p. 242.

[115] *Ibid.*, p. 242.

[116] *Ibid.*, p. 242.

[117] *Ibid.*, p. 242.

It is universally established that, the state of widowhood, which has been imposed upon them, is not due to their own fault, but a natural phenomenon. Birth can be checked, but death can't be. Any of the life partners can die any time, but it is the woman, who has to undergo different types of harassment-mental, physical, economic etc., just because she is a woman, as a part of a patriarchal society.[118] The attitude of the society towards a widow needs to change. It cannot be denied that education is a powerful medium to remove all the above mentioned maladies, if everyone is willing to accept. Only through proper education the mindset of the people in every society will certainly change.

Gender-based Violence on Media

Theories of violence are propagated continuously through the media, such that the media entertain people with violence and also with continuous images of the strong as those who defend themselves with violent means. In this, Thomas Fitzgerald has rightly mentioned in his article-'*Blessed are the Peacemakers for they shall be Called the Children of Go:'* "We need to recognize how easily we can be accosted by the vision of violence. In order to gain a larger audience and greater profits, some television shows, movies, songs and video games seem to propagate violence and dishonour the human person. In order to attract our attentions, commercials and advertisements can also easily diminish the dignity of the human person with violent images. And we cannot ignore the images of violence which are found on the dark side of the Internet."[119]

Thus, mass media like-News papers and TV give reports of war, crime and atrocities to satisfy the growing curiosity of viewers and readers. Apart from those violent incidents featured in the media, very often, young boys and girls are exposed to movies, Internet, books and magazines which project different forms of violence. Through the media, boys learn that women, as the 'objects' of their erotic desires, have to be controlled; and that as men, they are expected to know what they are doing and stay in control of the other person.[120] As a result, male sexuality in every culture is presented and experienced as something possessive, aggressive, hostile, harsh, violent, controlling, and with little hint of tenderness, gentleness, or respect. And the manifestations of this male image dominate the media and advertisements in which the majority of victims are women and children.

---

[118] *Ibid.*, p. 247.

[119] Thomas Fitzgerald, "Blessed are the peacemakers for they shall be called the children of God" in *Violence and Christian Spirituality: An Ecumenical Conversion,* ed. Emmanuel Clapsis (Geneva 2, Switzerland: WCC Publications, World Council of Churches, 2007) p. 272.

[120] Dr Anne Ganley, a therapist who works with violent men, comments: "Men define 'being in control' as having control over another person or a situation, not as self control." In Marie, M. Fortune, p. 25.

Thus, the media in today's world is not an innocent innocuous medium; rather it influences and regulates people's identity by defining normal/deviant people or culture, beauty/ugly, success/failure, power/powerlessness. It is said that, the media practitioners and academicians are of the view that the media portrayal of women both in and outside the family, project the negative and amazingly stereotypical images of women influenced by patriarchy. Women are shown as eternal sufferers who rejoice in self-sacrifice and self-denial.[121] This depiction in media whether it is the news segment, advertisement, movies or dance sequence, the focus is to perpetuate stereotypes. Messages of male superiority and female inferiority are constantly repeated and the portrayal is sexist and distorted.

According to writer Nilima Srivastava, stereotypes used by the media about the sexes fall into two main categories. One projects the ideal-the person who arouses envy or admiration by suggesting beauty or success; the other is an over simplification i.e., making human behaviour readily recognizable and on predictable patterns.[122] The men are shown as decision-makers, authoritative figures, conquering heroes and intelligent, women as sex objects, kitchen slaves, under protection, dependents, less versed and scatter-brained. This is because, for the most part men control the media from the press, radio and television to advertising, films and publishing. In all this, directly or indirectly, men use their influence to project ideas, attitudes and values of a patriarchal order. This mindset of superiority of men tends to deny women their rightful place in various ways.

Moreover, since women's position and roles are developed in patriarchal cultures, the media maintains the status quo in gender relations by reinforcing the sexual division of labour in society, resisting and subverting any radical change on the part of women. The image of women in advertisements echoes the traditional patriarchal attitudes and prejudices, reinforcing the 'myth' that a woman is born to be a housewife, mother or sex object. We have ample examples of his. One example could be-advertisements of shampoos, soaps and pastes show women to be involved in beautifying themselves to attract the gaze of men. Moreover, very often women are shown as 'soft toys' for men, emphasizing their subservience and dependence. They wear revealing clothes and take leaning and yearning postures, as signs of incompleteness or lacking in security.[123] A woman is generally portrayed as some one whose goals in life are to either catch a man or to obtain her husband's look of approval for her appearance.

When talking about gender-based violence through the media, many people have their own conclusion yet one common opinion which every one feels are exactly pointed out by Seema Bhaskaran: "men create films, men write books,

---

[121] Nilima Srivastava, "Media vis-à-vis Women," in *Women's Link,* Vol. 12, No. 2 April-June 2006, p. 33.

[122] *Ibid*, p. 33

[123] S. Santan Nago, "Media Images of Women," in *Women's Link*, Vol. 12, No. 2. April-June 2006, p. 3.

men deliver speeches, men create philosophies about what women feel, think and experience."[124] Thus, the above mentioned statement shows the logic behind every man, how they project, perceive and adjust women in every aspect of their lives, no wonder, women too unconsciously tune in with the rhythms of men's philosophy.

Thus, one of the factors through which gender-based violence is witnessed is through the media. In many cases, people use the media to spread messages of gender-based violence. That, there is overwhelming gender-based violence evidence that media violence predisposes or inspires people to violent attitudes and behaviors is certain, although the positive educational possibilities inherent in the media are endless.[125] Though the media promotes literacy, economy and helps to form opinions on a number of issues, in reality however, one experiences the negative effect of the media more than the positive impact.[126] It is said that, constant exposure to media violence[127] desensitizes people to violence. What is more troubling is the violence that has been introduced into children's television programmes.[128] Television violence by itself does not kill people but it destroys one's violent 'immune system,' and conditions people to derive pleasure from violence. Violence is a staple of our mass media.[129] It is reported that the average American child spends thirty hours a week in front of the television set.[130] No wonder, even the Indian children spend countless hours every week.

---

[124] Seema Bhaskaran, "Sexual Exploitation of an Adolescent Girl: Male-Centered Portrayal in a Malayalam Cinema," in *Women Link,* Vol. 12, No. 2 April-June 2006, p. 41.

[125] *Op. cit.*, p. 74.

[126] Instead of promoting learning, the media can distract people and cause them to waste time. Sometimes, the media also are used as tools of indoctrination, with the aim of controlling what people know, and denying them access to information the authorities do not want them to have. Gilbert DE LIMA, "Catholic Education: Challenges and Prospects" in *Vidyajyoti: Journal of Theological Reflection,* Volume 69, No. 9 September 2005, p. 676.

[127] Media violence could be the violence depicted in the media, of fighting, cheating, robbing, smoking, news reports on war, criticizing statements, suicide columns, sexy pictures which stimulate desires and leads to sexual crime by raping illegally, and many more such things seen and read through the media. Those who are accustomed to the media have witnessed all sorts of 'Media violence,' The author herself had experienced all the above mentioned media violence several times.

[128] What is more troubling is the violence that has been introduced into children's television programmes. For example, Tom and Jerry were quite fascinating because they depicted how the weak (Jerry, the mouse) could outsmart the powerful (Tom, the cat) with wit and wisdom. But gradually more and more violence has been introduced into Tom and Jerry so that Jerry's antics today have reached levels of violence that is almost repulsive., S. Wesley Ariarajah: *Axis of Peace: Christian Faith in Times of Violence and War* (Geneva: World Council of Churches Publications, 2004), p. 88.

[129] Mary Yoder and others (2004), p. 75.

[130] Researchers George Comstock and Erica Scharrer report that children's programming is much more violent than general audience prime-time programming, and also that four out of five

The media like television,[131] video games, computer games and internet[132] play a role furthering and reinforcing violence and create an atmosphere in which violence is normalized. Nowadays people are becoming more desensitized to violence because it is so pervasive in every media. Many of the television entertainment programmes and computer games depict scenes of fighting and exploitation of one against the other. As S. Wesley Ariarajah[133] states, "When it comes to the use of violence as entertainment for children, nothing is more glaring than computer games. Most of the games are nothing more than training to kill. Many contemporary events like the Gulf war and sniper shootings are reproduced as computer games so that children 'enjoy' themselves shooting down Iraqi soldiers or innocent bystanders,"[134]

The media thus contributes to both the escalation of violence, by sensationalizing violence and spreading hate, misunderstanding or conflict among the people especially children and women. Another example would be the role of local and national papers which influence vast readership and constantly focus on the events of killing and violence, suicides and martyrdom, cheating or malpractices, and also causing sickness in the long run.[135] The violent pictures

---

federal fact-finding task forces have concluded that media violence could be problematic in regard to the behaviour of the viewer.

[131] Violence existed in the animation films like 'Snow White and the Seven Dwarfs', but within an acceptable limit. Every cartoon story today revolves around violence., *Vijay times, Bangalore* Saturday, 24 September 2005, on 'Family Matters' column. Kids do not have the maturity to understand violence in the right perspective. Parents need to be aware what children are watching on the television.

[132] For example, pornographic materials are available on line for those who seek them out. It is possible, when surfing the Web, to stumble on something we would prefer not to see. It may be pornography. It may be the pornography of violence. It may be the pornography of hate. Whatever brand of pornography one may think of, it can be found somewhere on line. In David Lochhead: *Shifting Realities: Information Technology and the Church*, (Geneva: World Council Of churches, 1997), p. 80.

[133] S. Wesley Ariarajah, a Methodist pastor and scholar of religions from Sri Lanka, is professor of Ecumenical theology at the Graduate and Theological schools of Drew University, Madison, New Jersey, USA.

[134] S. Wesley Ariarajah, *Axis of Peace: Christian Faith in Times of Violence and War.*, p. 88.

[135] Kuala Lumpur: As computer gaming gains popularity worldwide, psychologists in Thailand have cautioned that it can cause serious health problems, and in extreme cases, result in blood clots and heart attacks in youngsters. They also say that the more one plays, the more one becomes addicted to such games. Dr Sirichai Hongsanguansri of the Department of Psychiatry at Bangkok's Ramathibodi Hospital, conducted research on the behaviour of computer gamers and noted that many Thai children were obsessed with such games. In some of these cases, playing computer games have caused deaths. The Korean boy who died after playing online games for 48 hours continuously is one such example, he said. Playing games could also affect a child's sleeping cycle as most games-addicted youth spents four hours or more a day playing games, the daily said. "Games addiction resembles gambling and drug addiction-playing one game tends to lead to

projected in the papers stimulate the sense of violence, and their effects remain in one's memories.

Further, gender-based violence is vitiated by modernization too. Thus, there is a direct relationship between the prevalence of violence and the process of globalization.[136] Though globalization has brought immense development to the human society, it has also promoted inequality, unrest, destruction, injustice, conflicts, exploitation, misunderstanding, all of which are different shades of violence. So, gender-based violence is not to be understood only in terms of physical injury inflicted on women, but to be seen in a much broader sense, including every aspect of human life on this earth.[137] In terms of the acts of violence, globalization requires the humiliation of hundreds of millions of people, keeping them in constant insecurity, pitting them against one another in a competitive struggle for survival.[138]

The problem of violence of any sort, exploitation, corruption, discrimination, and dehumanization are directly or indirectly related to globalization. The effects of globalization, therefore, are not limited to people's economic activities, but they touch almost every dimension of human life.[139] Thus, today violence has taken on different forms with technological and developmental changes in society, in which women are the most affected group, because they are the ones who take care of maximum daily activities.

Gender-based Pedagogical Practices in Educational Institutions

Gender-based violence is seen in the classroom in educational institutions and in the books they use. It is universally true that the classroom reinforces the stereotypical gender patterns of speech through student-teacher communication

another one and another one," Dr Sirichai said. Computer Games can cause blood clots and heart attacks?, *Vijay times,* Bangalore Wednesday, 12 Oct, 2005.

[136] The following statement of Steven Staples makes it clear: "Globalization and militarism should be seen as two sides of the same coin. On one side, globalization promotes the conditions that lead to unrest, inequality, and conflict and ultimately war. On the other side, globalization fuels the means to wage war by protecting and promoting the military industries needed to produce sophisticated weaponry. This weaponry in turn is used-its use threatened – to protect the investments of transnational corporations and their shareholders," Samson Prabhakar, *Essays on Christian Education and Liturgy*, (Bangalore: South Asia theological Research Institute, 2003), 129, also see in Ninan Koshy, "Militarism and Peace-Making in the Context of Globalization" in *Peace Initiatives fora Just Society*, ed. Samson Prabhakar, (A Consultation held on Dec. 6-8 2001), p. 18.

[137] Samson Prabhakar, *Overcoming Violence: Some Key Issues*, p. 130.

[138] Seabrooke Jermey, "Internationalism verses globalization," in Mathew George Chunakara, *Globalization and Its Impact on Human Right* (Hongkong: Christian Conference of Asia, 1998), p. 91.

[139] Huang Po Ho, "Globalization-A Challenge to the Church: A Case study on Migrant Worker and Church's Responsibility in Taiwan," in *Voices from the Third World, The Struggle of the Marginalized: Challenges to Theology and Ecumenical Movement,* Volume XXIII No. 1 June 2000, p. 129.

and through the syllabi and textbooks. Rich (1979) observes, "Language is a weapon-and that goes with language: reflection, criticism, renaming, and creation. The fact that our language itself is tainted by quality of our society, means that in teaching we need to be acutely conscious of the kind of tool we want our students to have available to understand how it has been used against them and to do all we can to ensure that language will not some day be used by them to keep the others silent and powerless" (pp. 24-25).[140] Thus, almost all the kinder garden schools provide different tools according to sex. Hard things like cars, blocks, balls to boys and dolls, cloth to stitch, colours for painting to girls.

In schools and colleges, female passivity is rewarded, and female mind is not taken seriously as girls and boys are indoctrinated in stereotypical gender roles. Even in co-educational institutions, men and women do not receive equal education. It is true that, the content of education itself validates men and invalidates women.[141] In the past, students were advised and suggested to take up different subjects according to sex, subjects like political science, mathematics and algebra for boys so that they will be expected to become political leaders and engineers, and domestic science, economics and education subjects for girls so that they will become teachers, nurses and good house keepers. Thus, academic disciplines ignore and distort the experience of women as a group by structuring their subject matter and concepts around female-deprived norms.

The dominant pedagogical style of classrooms discriminates against women's experiences and participation in a variety of ways, all of which reinforce female passivity.[142] Taking into consideration that girls are timid and shy, teachers neglect female students in interactions. On the other hand, again when it comes to teachers-male and sometimes female-tend to call on women students less in discussions to ask them less probing questions and to interrupt them more often. They make more frequent eye contact with men, and are more attentive to male questions or comments.[143] Thus, teaching and learning methods which stress the cooperative rather than the competitive may encourage more women to question, examine and express. The role of teacher and student, structure of classes and courses thus need to be analyzed and changed, to root out sex discrimination.

When it comes to text books that the students were provided with, it shows different roles for boys and girls. Especially, the pictures that appear in the school text books; boys with cars and some hard tools or playing cricket or with balls, whereas girls are found playing with soft things, cleaning, holding brooms, or helping mother in the kitchen, which teach them gender-specific roles. The

---

[140] Sadhana Nadu, "Exploring the 'Culture of Silence' through the Lens of Gender and Mental Health" in *Psychology in India: Intersecting Crossroad*, ed. U. Vindhya, (New Delhi: Concept Publishing Company, 2003), p. 225.

[141] Sadhana Nadu., (2003), p. 225.

[142] Sadhana Nadu., (2003), p. 225.

[143] Ibid., p. 227.

vocabulary used in the text books too are mostly masculine, which automatically build in the minds of learners that all the wonderful things are invented by men. They also assume that both manufacturers and consumers are men, whereas women's shares are very scanty. Since men are the manufacturers they are also destroyers too.[144] Therefore, once a person is educated, whether boy or girl, he or she may tend to apply the same set of roles they have been doing and taught, as the source from which they have learnt are the text books.

Thus, violence can take a number of forms and gender–based violence, all the more subtle, hidden and sophisticated. It can be very obvious or very subtle. The physical abuse of another person is a tragic expression of violence, but it is but one expression of violence. A person can also be abused in an emotional manner or in a spiritual manner. A person can be wounded with guns and knives. Persons can also be wounded with harassment and words of hate. A person can be hurt by lack of love and by neglect. Violence thus affects the body, the soul and the spirit. Violence harms both the victim and the victimizer. All forms of violence diminish the dignity of the human person who is created in the "image and likeness" of God. Violent situations can flare up in one's home, in the workplace, at school, at sporting events, on the street, and in the gatherings. As cited earlier, violent situations may involve strangers who were simply brought together by circumstances. Other violent situations may involve members of the same family, neighbours, colleagues at work or leaders from within our own community.

Gender-based Violence through Sexual Acts

Sexual violence[145] is a violation of human rights and a physical violence against the human body. Sexual violence is both violent and sexual, in that the nature of the assault makes clear the totality of the violation of the person, psychologically, physically, and spiritually.[146] In many cases, sexual violence is caused by unequal power relationship among gender, age, and social positions. In other words, it is a human rights violation by the more powerful against the less powerful in society, and therefore, sexual violence is against social justice and against the will of God. Since, every human is created in God's image and is as perfect and noble as any other, all human beings, men and women, are born to enjoy the rights of respect and protection. Any infringement of individual perfection and dignity

---

[144] *Ibid.*, p. 227

[145] Sexual violence is not sexual activity but violence against the human body. Sexual violence is a violent action misusing sex as an instrument to maintain control over the other. Any one who believes that humans are the transformed image of God must oppose any violence against any human body. Women's Committee of NCC-Korea " Overcoming and Preventing Sexual Violence in the Church," *In God's Image*, Journal of Asian Women's Resource Centre for Culture and Theology, Vol. 24, No.1, March 2005., p. 25.

[146] Marie, Fortune, *Sexual violence*, (New York: Pilgrim Press 1983), p. 6.

is an infringement of God's image and at the same time, a challenge to God's creation.[147]

Sexual violence includes forced intercourse in marriage and dating relationships, rape by strangers, rape by family members or close family friends or sometimes the most trusted friend, systemic rape, organized rape during armed conflicts,[148] sexual harassment,[149] sexual abuse of children, forced prostitution and sexual trafficking, child marriage and violent acts against the sexual integrity of a person, for example genital mutilation and obligatory inspections for virginity. Sexual violence also includes rape in prisons, police custody situations and refugee camps.[150] Thus, sexual violence is considered to be the most damaging act because the whole life of the victim and the entire family atmosphere is affected. As Ram Ahuja has found out in his research that, 'sexual assault is a relatively infrequent phenomenon (0.3% of total crime in India), yet among the crime against women, it constitutes a serious problem.'[151]

Though on many occasions victims of gender-based violence are not willing to disclose due to many reasons, one could witness several acts of sexual violence in society through media and research done by sociologists and also human rights commissions. A few incidents give a clear picture: a middle aged woman accused a Jain (monk) for committing rape on her in Bhinmal town in Jalore district of western Rajasthan in September 1997; a teacher of a government secondary school was accused of criminally assaulting school girls in Chatawati village in Chittorgarh district in July 1996';[152] a teenager was allegedly gang raped by four persons in a moving car near interstate bus stand in New Delhi,[153] and many more accidents in our society and other countries all over the world.

According to a report, 250,000 cases of sexual violence are reported in South Korea annually, with one rape case happening every three minutes. Victims of

---

[147] *Ibid.*, p. 23.

[148] Organized rape during armed conflicts happens every where, when military power is imposed upon the public. This kind of organized rape during armed conflict was a regular feature in many parts of North East India, particularly Nagaland. Incidents happen especially in the rural remote areas where army camps are placed.

[149] Sexual harassment is a form of violence, a direct violation of human rights, and a form of sexual discrimination, in *Asia Sunday 2005: Building Communities of Peace for All*, Christian Conference of Asia, 23.

[150] A girl of 17 years was raped by a jailor in Jhun-jhunu sub-jail. Ram Ahuja, *Violence Against women*, (Jaipur: Prem Rawat for Rawat Publications, Reprintrd 2003), p. 58.

[151] Mary Yoder Holsopple, Ruth E. Krall and Sharon weaver Pittman, *Building Peace: Overcoming Violence in Communities*, (Geneva: World Council of Churches Puplications, 2004), p. 47. .

[152] *Ibid.*, pp. 56-57.

[153] 'Gangraped in a car' *Vijay times*, (Tuesday October 18, 2005, Bangalore), p. 6.

sexual violence are increasing year after year and victims' ages are getting lower.[154] Therefore, sexual violence is a very crucial issue in every society; it destroys human dignity, threatens human survival, and disturbs the integrity of human life. In this, churches need to focus on certain principles in their teaching ministry to respond to this reality.

Life-Cycle Phases of Gender-based Violence

As discussed elsewhere, gender-based violence does not end in a certain period of time in one's life. It starts from the mother's womb and is continuous till the last breath. In each life-cycle, a female experiences the most dangerous and humiliating situations just because of her sex. Human society has placed men higher, better, stronger, and superior and that overpowers females through out their lives. Thus, gender-based violence starts from the very conception of women. We could witness this better through different Life-Cycle phases. The life-cycle phases given below may be different from one place to another, but the nature of suffering that women undergo in different stages may be similar, depending on the understanding of sex. In general, the different Life-Cycle phases are:

Prenatal: Sex selective abortion; battering during pregnancy (emotional and physical effects on women; effects on birth outcome); Coerced pregnancies; mass rapes in war and communal violence.

Infancy: Female infanticide; rejection at birth; emotional and physical abuse; differential treatment especially regarding access to food and medical care.

Childhood: Child marriages; genital mutilation; physical abuse and child labour; sexual abuse by family members and strangers; differential access to food, medical care and education; trafficking and child prostitution.

Adolescence: Menstrual taboos; dating and courtship violence (acid-throwing, date rape) economically-coerced sex (for example, school girls having to take up with benefactors to afford school fees); sexual abuse in the workplace; rape, sexual harassment; forced prostitution; forced marriages; trafficking in women.

Reproductive: Abuse of women by intimate male partners; marital rape; dowry abuse and murders; partner homicide; psychological abuse; sexual abuse in the work place; sexual harassment; marital rape; abuse of women with disabilities.

Old-age: Widowhood rituals and discriminatory practices; sexual abuse of widows by close relatives; elder abuse mostly affects women.[155] In recent times,

---

[154] By the Women's Committee of NCC-Korea, "Overcoming and Preventing sexual Violence in the Church" in *In God's Image*, p. 23. According to a report published by the Christian Women Counseling Center of the Korean Association of Women theologians, 31 cases of domestic violence and 95 cases of sexual violence were dealt in the center in 2002.

[155] Heire, Lori et al., *Violence against Women: The Hidden Health Burden.* Discussion Papers # 255, (Washington, D.C.: The World Bank, 1994), p. 5, see also *Women Icon of Liberation: A Work-Book for exploring and Achieving Total Liberation* by Sr Philomena D' Souza, FMA, (Mumbai: Better Yourself Books, 2005), pp. 215-216.

old women are the target. Since, they are regarded as weaker sex, they do not learn how to protect themselves.

Every day these kinds of incidents are reported in the daily news papers.[156] Women thus suffer physically, sexually, psychologically, socially, economically and religiously from birth to death. Women are unable to make their own opinions or protect themselves for fear of further repercussions from their male counterparts and society. Thus, for women, human rights are denied and their right to life is stolen from them by the ever present threat of gender-based violence.

Forms of Gender-based Violence

There are indeed many forms of violence which produce physical destruction of life or loss of bodily integrity and verbal intimidation constituting violence. Thus, different forms of gender-based violence impact women and girls' physical, emotional, psychological, spiritual, and social well-being. Moreover, forms of violence could be owing to the age-old understanding of unequal power between the sexes. A few of which could be considered important to be examined here:

1. Structural Violence

Above all, one of the most insidious forms of violence is structural or institutional violence, because, in many places it is accepted as 'legal.' Women experience both structural and behavioural violence more sharply than men because social definitions of their biological equipment assigned to them as a special secondary descriptor (female) acts as a limitation to their social status at every level in a given social hierarchy.[157] According to Boulding (1975), "The concept of structural violence refers to the organized, institutionalized and structural patterning of the family and the economic cultural and political systems that determine that some individuals shall be victimized through a withholding of society's benefits and rendered more vulnerable to suffering and death than others."[158]

The structural patterning also determines the socialization practices that induce individuals to inflict or to endure according to their role, through which, social inequalities are generated in the society. Sexual harassment, the commodification of women through beauty contests and the movie industry, sex tourism and the mail-order bride-trade combined with the forces of spiritual and social control heaped on women, violate their human rights in the name of decency and moral values. Inflicted through government and church sanctions, social pressure and stigmatization, camouflaged violence strips women of their voices and deadens their sense of outrage.[159]

---

[156] *The Times of India*, Bangalore, Friday, February 22, 2008, p. 3.

[157] M.U. Qureshi, *Women and Crime*, (2006), p. 42.

[158] Ibid.

[159] Maureen McBride, "Violence (1)" in *An A to Z of Feminist Theology*, ed. Isherwood, Lisa & Dorothea (England: Sheffield Academic Press Ltd, 1996) pp. 229-230.

Human beings find meaning, purpose and a sense of identity through belonging to structures like family, community, ethnicity and religious institutions. However, these structures themselves sometimes can become instruments of violence. Their influence is so subtle that structural violence often goes unnoticed and is collectively maintained and validated for the sake of order and stability in the given society as gender-based violence is deeply rooted in power relations between women and men.[160] This is so, since power becomes abusive when a choice is made to use it to control women. In society, women are socialized to believe that women are powerless and have no right to own power. This has strong images of authority and in many cases women do not like to be seen as authoritarian persons. Thus, women are taught and often believe that violence may be deserved.

On the other hand, 'Sexism' too perpetuates the belief that persons are either superior or inferior to one another on the basis of their biology. Historically, sexism has maintained that persons of the male sex are inherently superior to persons of the female sex by nature, that is by the very order of things and it has acted in discriminatory ways to enforce this order. In a pattern analogous to racism, this prejudice classifies a group of human beings as deficient, ordains subordinate roles for them and denies them certain rights on the basis of personal physical and/ or psychological characteristics alone. Just as racism assigns an inferior dignity to people on the basis of their ethnic heritage or on the basis of biological sex and its attendant functions, sexism considers women essentially less valuable than men, and labors mightily to keep them in their 'proper' social 'place'. In both 'isms' bodily characteristics are made to count for the whole essence of the human being so that, the fundamental dignity of the person is violated.[161] Sexism is thus a multi-dimensional factor that fixes stereotyped roles for men and women. Particular role expectation denies girls or women the opportunity to study or choose their subject of work, confining them to limited jobs, specific roles or a small geographical area.[162]

This is a very important point, because for centuries women have been socialized to give up their will by catering to the will of their father or husband or even to their brothers. In many cases, women have been forced to do this against their will, through the power of socialization. Many women have been crushed and dehumanized under such a system. Others have fought back and

---

[160] Cf.: Gewalt Gegen Frauen. E in *Bericht im Aufrag des Rates der EKD*; teil I, Hannover 1997, p.14, *Churches Say "NO" To Violence Against Women*, (The Lutheran World Federation Department for Mission and Development Women in Church and Society, Geneva, 2000,) p. 14.

[161] Elizabeth A. Johnson. *She Who Is, the Mystery of God in Feminist Theological Discourse*, (New York: The Crossroad Publishing Company, 1998), p. 23. and *Churches Say 'NO' to Violence Against Women*, p. 15.

[162] Elizabeth A. Johnson. (1998), p. 23. and *Churches Say 'NO' to Violence Against Women*, p. 17.

become vicious and cruel. Still others, who are sensible, have learned to be subtly undercutting and slyly manipulative.[163]

2. Social Violence

According to a sociologist, M.U. Qureshi, social violence is defined as "the illegal use of physical, mental and social coercion or use of threats for personal or group ends reflected broadly in our traditional social structure and present day developmental processes."[164] Thus, the 'coercive' aspects like-battering, killing, insulting, isolating, molestation and rape, eve-teasing and the 'discriminating ' and 'oppressive' aspects like-subjugation in different walks of life i.e., child-rearing and child-bearing, employment, low wages, inequality in education, health, denial of opportunities for dissent etc, are included as social violence. Therefore, the use of force, or threats for use of such force by the patriarchal social order against womenfolk have devalued their rights, which we could term as social violence.

3. Psychological Violence

As already mentioned elsewhere, gender-based violence can be both physical and psychological or emotional. Threat or aggressive behaviour towards a woman not only to her physical being but towards her self-respect and self-confidence indicates psychological violence. According to the *Encyclopedia of Women*, "Psychological violence is carried out with psychological weapons like-threats, insults, humiliating treatment, denial of human existence, rather than physical attack."[165]

Thus, making threats to harm a woman, her family, insulting her in front of others, controlling everything she does, isolating her from friends and family, blaming her for things that are not her fault are regarded as gender-based violence. Violence of all kinds is associated with severe, long lasting physical, mental and emotional effects. It is quite true that some of these illnesses or effects are compounded by lack of access to any redress or justice. In many cases, psychological suffering is likely to be compounded by women's inability to make it public what they have endured.[166] Psychological violence in other words, is

---

[163] *Ibid.*, p. 17.

[164] M.U. Qureshi, *Women and Crime,* (2006), p. 120.

[165] Poornima Mohan, *Encyclopedia of Women* (Delhi: Indian Publisher's Distributors, (2000), p. 413.

[166] These things happen in order to defend family honour by remaining silent about it. One of the informants in Surtees' research in Cambodia, for example, felt she could not make public that she had been raped by her uncle, because she had nowhere else to live, because of a perceived obligation to her aunt, and because of the imperative to protect her family from disgrace and shame, Jill Astbury, "Whose honour, whose shame? Gender-based violence, rights and health" in *Violence Against Women in Asian Societies*, ed. Lenore Manderson and Linda Rae Bennett (London and New York: Routledge Curzon, 2003), pp. 164-165.

verbal attacks, emotional outburst and blackmail, withholding of money and so on.

4. Economic Violence

Maintaining control over money and property, not allowing a woman to have her own money and account, keeping her from getting a job or more education, making her account for every penny that is spent, giving fewer wages unlike their male counterpart, not allowing her to inherit/possess properties including land,[167] are some ways of exerting economic violence. Thus, when women's social, cultural, and economic rights are transgressed, and when they experience unequal rights regarding property, marriage and inheritance, gender-based violence is facilitated because many women lack an alternative means of survival apart from dependence on their husbands or partners as it is embedded in their minds. But, denial of women's economic rights and the perpetuation of poverty only promote the perpetration and perpetuation of violence against them. Poverty marginalizes a majority of women and denies them the right to a decent standard of living. It is said that, for women, who comprise about 70 percent of the world's 1.3 billion, they bear the brunt of economic and financial transition, and their life is severely threatened. Women thus become vulnerable to poverty for reasons beyond their control.

It is universally true that, poverty affects women in different ways than it affects men. While both men and women often live in impoverished conditions, their experiences of poverty are different, given that women's roles and responsibilities are not the same as those of men. Poverty can increase the already existing gender-based violence and insecurity in the lives of many women and girls. Poverty also includes the marginalization and fragmentation of lives through domestic and public violence against women including children.

Knowing the fact of economic constraints in women's' life in the society, a feminist economist, challenges in this way, "The fundamental requirement is that all able and willing persons should have the freedom to satisfy their own basic needs within existing economic systems. The opportunity to satisfy one's basic needs is also significant for right relationships. Women who can support themselves may also organize and develop their capabilities to love and do justice."[168] Another feminist economist, Folbre also uses property rights as an example of a category that is not necessarily gendered in law but which,

[167] Women wanted equality and, in order to achieve equality, the right to own land seemed basic to them. Even though it is not a sufficient right, in the philosophical sense, it is a necessary one. See in Ann-Cathrin Jarl, *In Justice: Women and Global Economics* (Minneapolis: Fortress Press, 2003), p. 38.

[168] Ann-Cathrin Jarl, *In Justice: Women and Global Economics* (Minneapolis: Fortress Press, 2003), p. 133.

in practice, may have grave consequences for women's economic situation.[169] Women are often at a disadvantage when it comes to legal entitlements. When property changes occur, they can turn out to be unfavorable to women.[170]

Thus, economic violence can take on many different shapes and forms-socially, culturally and legally, and all forms of economic injustices can result, in diminishing women's rights and disempowering women. Especially in a country like India, where the dowry system for example, is regarded as a cultural practice and legally accepted as a norm, the consequences of this practice victimizes women alone. Every day many women face the death penalty by committing suicide or killed by their husbands and their family members, when she and her parents do not fulfill their dowry demands. Many times even the law makers themselves become a part of the exploiters in which they are supposed to be protectors and safeguard women. Women who are from economically a poor background face more discrimination and death. Out of many, one example could be stated here which appeared in The Hindu with the heading 'Police's wife commits suicide' which says, "A 23 year old woman named Roopa, committed suicide in her house in Dinnur main Road near RT. Nagar. Parents of the victim have accused her father-in-law Kempegowda, who is an Assistant Sub-Inspector, and her husband Lokesh of dowry harassment. Roopa's parents then filed a complaint with RT Nagar police."[171]

It can be argued that, even though the Constitution is framed in such a way as to maintain and exercise equality without any discrimination, it appears only on paper. In reality, the same old patterns of traditional practices of inequality still continue, where men dominate and control women by using their power vested with them by the society. Every one who is concerned with this feels and propagates against these inhuman acts in the society. They often talk of peace, reconciliation, justice and the need of the church to be prophetic against all forms of violence, yet gender biased treatment seems unconquerable. To bring gender justice and wipe away the traditional practices which destroy humanhood, each

---

[169] Nancy, Folbre, *Who Pays? For the Kids: Gender and the Structure of Constraint* (New York: Routledge, 1994), p.4, also see, Ann – Cathrin Jarl. *In Justice: Women and Global Economics*, p. 32.

[170] *Ibid.*, p. 223.

[171] *The Hindu*, Thursday, February 28, 2008, p. 3. Another similar dowry death was also uncovered in the *Bangalore Mirror*, "The death of a 23 year old married woman in the city on 20th February has been blamed on dowry harassment. According to the father of B. V. Mamatha, her mother-in-law would repeatedly tell her, 'The 300 grams of gold given as a dowry is not enough. If you want to live with my son, go get your father's retirement benefits.' Mamatha, a science graduate and a native of Hassan, was married to Vishnu Verma, a software engineer working for Celtix Outsourcing in Victoria layout, 2nd August 2005. According to the police, the dowry harassment is alleged to have begun soon after the wedding. Mamatha's family filed a complaint with the MICO Layout police and said her mother–in–law was not arrested despite her name figuring in the FIR,' *Bangalore Mirror*, Friday, February 22, 2008, p. 5.

faith community need to be sensitized with timely education. Would Christian religious educational ministry take the cue?

5. Domestic Violence

Gender-based domestic violence as a means of control and subjugation has deep historical roots in our world and particularly in the lives of women and girls. For many centuries, women everywhere havé struggled against gender-based subordination and its multiple manifestations, including violence and abuse inflicted upon them by male partners in the society and on family members. Violence within families and the home is often defended on the basis of cultural traditions which emphasize women's subordination and inferiority to men. However, it continues to be a way of life for many women and girls in all communities. As Fanny Gerymonat-Pantelis has mentioned in her articles- *Domestic Violence Against Women in the Andean-Bolivian Context*, "Domestic violence against women is part of the family's daily life, something which is considered normal, and it is very well covered up by the social, cultural, and religious patriarchal ideology of the population and institutions. Thus, we may say that domestic violence in every society has become institutionalized."[172] Though all aspects of violence or injustice are part of the general political and Human Rights concerns, even the government of India has passed an Act on 'Domestic Violence,' it works only on paper. When brought to the public notice, officials try to solve the matter by saying, it is a private matter. Again, domestic violence is not considered an issue by the church institutions, because it is considered a private problem.

As cited above, domestic violence is often not seen as a social problem but as a private matter between a man and his wife and among family members. In many cases, men accept it as part of their married life and as a normal means of disciplining a woman in both sexual life and domestic affairs. It is also accepted that women are the property of the man and what he does with his property is his business. Thus, in many countries, violence in families has been considered a private or personal matter, and has not been taken seriously by society in general, including the church or the courts, even when it was brought to their attention. Already there are instances being reported in the media where women have gone to the court to register a complaint about domestic abuse. Instead of using the provisions of the law, usually the lawyer rather advises them to think again and tries to reconcile their differences with their husbands. Many a time, women's voices are left unheard which rather enhances the esteem of the men-folk.

Wherever it may be, the social message given to children influences a large part of their response to violence. A tendency to accept the stereotype that 'boys

---

[172] Fanny Gerymonat-Pantelis, "Domestic Violence Against Women in the Andean-Bolivian Context" in *Voices from the third World, The Struggle of the Marginalized: Challenges to Theology and Ecumenical Movement,* Vol. XXIII No. 1, p. 37.

will be boys' and that females are the 'weaker sex' too often means not questioning the negative aspects of every day gender relations. Many cultures promote and support the idea of young men being 'in charge of' or responsible for grown women, including their mothers. Male violence in society and family is motivated by the belief that gender relations are defined by physical power and control. This translates into acceptance of an aggressive response to certain challenges of male authority.

Many cases of domestic violence are kept hidden. This is due in part to the fear of being stigmatized by the community. Women are often ashamed and embarrassed to let people know that they are being battered by their partners. They feel that their dignity is threatened by others' knowledge of their plight if they disclosed it to others. No wonder, severely abused or deprived women are often kept silent. They experience themselves as mindless, voiceless, and subject to the whims of external authorities. Words are used on them as weapons in expressions of anger. Women learn that when they tried to use words, they incurred wrath and punishment.[173] In their eyes women are powerless and unable to think for themselves. They must depend on authorities for guidance, authorities who never explain why, but simply order and expect obedience.[174]

Therefore, even if women are abused they end up with the understanding that everything has been done with the consent of the abuser (colluding with their abuser), by retreating in to their private place to ensure that the abuse is done in private. They often explain the marks of violence inflicted by their partners on them as being caused by accidents or other excuses.[175] Even though women experience all forms of domestic violence which leads to divorce and even up to suicide, both society and churches keep silent. Besides, policy makers too keep silent or sometimes request the victims to compromise and adjust to the situation at the cost of forgiveness. That encourage repeating the same crimes.

The Protection of Women from Domestic Violence Act, 2005, which was ratified on October 25, 2006, is path-breaking in more ways than one. Most significant perhaps is its definition of 'domestic violence' as spelt out in Chapter 11of the Act. All forms of physical, sexual, verbal, emotional or economic abuse are defined as domestic violence by this law. It offers women victims of such violence civil remedies of a kind that were not available to them earlier.[176] However, laws alone cannot bring about a change in societal attitudes, every citizen needs to be

---

[173] Mary Field Belenky, Blythe McVicker Clinchy, Nancy Rule Goldberger, and Jill Mattuck Tarule, *Women's Ways of Knowing: The Development of Self, Voice, and Mind* (New York: Basic Books, Inc., 1986), p. 48, see also Catherine Stonehouse, "The Church: A Place where All God's Children Grow?," in *Christian Education Journal*, Autumn 1992, Volume XIII Number 1, p. 38.

[174] Mary Field and others., (1986), p. 28.

[175] *Ibid.*, p. 38.

[176] Kalpana Sharma, "The Other Half: Behind Closed door" in *The Hindu*, Sunday Nov 5, 2006, p. 3.

made aware of their rights which can be possible only through proper education. Would religious education help? Would Christian religious education and its ministry in church circles enable the people to overcome gender based violence at home, in church and society is the question.

6. Physical Violence

When we discuss about gender-based physical violence, normally it is the violence done by men to women in many cases, may be husband to wife, brother to sister, male servant to maidservant, boys to girls who think that they are physically stronger, assuming that they are stronger and smarter, having controlling nature, etc. Therefore, universally, it is accepted that, women are weaker than men, with that assumption men easily overpower them in both words and actions. Physical violence could be done through any form: slapping, hitting; punching, kicking, arm twisting; shoving, burning, throwing acid, withholding medication; threatening to use a weapon, using a weapon; shooting, stabbing, raping or cutting, etc. The above mentioned physical violence are the traditional way, yet in the scientific technological world, one could even include all types of technique which kills unborn foetus, for instance, abortion, sex determination tests, and female foeticide.[177]

When talking about sex determination tests and foeticide, it is worth mentioning the statement issued at the consultation on "Prenatal Sex determination and Sex Selection Techniques-Christian concern," organized by Christian Medical Association of India in association with The National Council of Churches in India, Commission for Health of Catholic Bishops Conference of India, New Delhi 1st August 2002.[178]

> We express our concern at the consistent decline of sex-ratio in the recent past discrimination against females in the age group of 0-6 years in India. We recognize that the practices and techniques of pre-natal sex selection and sex determination that lead to gender injustice and the selective abortion of female foetuses, are the reasons for the drastic changes in the sex ratio. We realize that these malpractices are widespread, and not restricted to any geographic region or socio-economic or religious

[177] New wedding vow: No female foeticide-the 45 couples who united in a mass marriage in a village, coming from the Das Gaam Leuva Patidaar Samaj of Patels in Gandhinagar at a wedding ceremony in Kudasan village appended a vow: "The oath came from the bottom of our hearts. We will never hanker after a male child after this pledge is incorporated in the sacred wedding vows," This is the first instance of couples being administered such an oath and could very well herald a social awakening in Gujarat, the state that has an alarmingly low sex-ratio of 878 girls per 1,000 boys, in *The Times of India,* Bangalore Saturday, February 4, 2006.

[178] This Statement of Affirmation was distributed at the Consultation on Gender, Power and Identity, Organized by Women's Studies Department, the United Theological College, Bangalore, 7th and 8th March, 2008, on account of 'International Women's Day.

group. We denounce the misuse of medical technology available for the pre selection and pre determination of the foetal sex, which leads to these malpractices.

We raise our concern over the emergence of new reproductive technologies such as pre-conception or in-conception sex selection methods that have a high potential for gross misuse in the form of discrimination against the female sex. ..We believe that these practices, if not contained, will lead irrevocably to the ultimate collapse of the social fabric of our nation.

We unconditionally oppose all and any action, which contribute to the neglect, sub-optimal health, sickness or premature death of the girl child.

We reject female foeticide and all forms of cultural, historical, religious, economic, social, or other forms of justification of this heinous and barbaric crime as a sin both against God and against humanity...We affirm that a healthy society is an inclusive society which recognizes the role and potential of both men and women and which commits itself to all that promotes and contributes to the improved condition, status, health, and well being of both sexes of all ages equally.

We demand that the Government both at the center and at the state enact appropriate laws to curtail the misuse of medical technology for sex selection and selective abortion, and that it takes aggressive steps to implement that law with all vigor and throughout our land...We also demand that the Governments actively campaign for and support actions towards the achievement of a more equable sex ratio in India.[179]

We urge the medical profession to dissociate itself from all such discriminatory practices that lead towards the misuse of medical technologies that are incompatible with the Hippocratic Oath.

We urge the medical profession to take a proactive role against pre-natal sex selection and sex determination, as these practices are unjust, unethical, and illegal. We feel the need to ensure that no form of health care is dehumanizing and that all members of the female sex, of whatever age, are fully regarded as persons, and not only as statistics or as target for programmes and their achievements.

[179] By conservative estimate, female foeticide accounts for at least half a million missing female births in India every year, according to research findings published in British Medical Journal Lancet in January 2006. The Lancet study estimates that more than 10 million female foetuses may have been aborted in India in the last two decades. The child sex ratio in Delhi was 868 girls per 1000 boys according to census 2001. In 2005, only 814 girls were born in the capital for every 1000 boys according to the MCDs registration of live births.

> We urge the Church to address the issues of pre-natal sex selection and sex determination by building awareness within the communities they serve, and sensitizing them to these matters and with urgency.
>
> We further urge that the churches specifically forbid such practices by their members, and that church related hospitals and health care programmes constantly evaluate the impact of their activities upon the girl child and upon women.
>
> We request all the people in the country to ensure that such crimes against women are not committed, and urge them to maintain the dignity of women of all ages.

Thus, through all the above mentioned means women experience physical violence every now and then. Thus, there are uncountable incidents happening in many places yet many a time they are left unnoticed and even if they came to light, the authorities do not intervene in the right time. While examining female foeticide, one of the recent incidents that appeared in the Times of India' which shakes many hearts, had the heading –"Quack admits he committed 260 foeticides": Four days after the discovery of half-burnt foetuses dumped in a septic tank in the premises of an unauthorized nursing home in Pataudi, police said the quack A.K. Singh who ran the clinic had admitted his involvement in at least 260 cases of female foeticide since 1994. In some cases, the accused had charged as much as Rs. 20,000 for prenatal sex determination followed by selective abortions. The police mentioned in the report that Singh had admitted digging the septic tank in 1994 and confirmed that it was primarily utilized to dump foetuses, most of which were female.[180]

Wife-battering is the most prevalent form of gender-based violence which has been largely supported by various cultures down the ages. Surprisingly, it was part of the Napoleanic code until a decade back. The code says: "Women like walnut trees must be beaten every day." In North Africa, the expression "women and camels need to be beaten," is still common. In Europe, they used to say that a man had a right to beat his wife with a stick not thicker than his thumb. In Indian culture we have the quotation of Tulsidas such as "Drums, donkeys and women need to be beaten."[181] Thus, uncountable wives have been beaten to death by their husbands who are supposed to love, care, and protect them. It becomes a big setback for a woman, being battered by a man whom she trusted most.

In many cases, the husband rationalizes his battering saying that it happened as he was not satisfied by the conduct of his wife. So, they are made to feel guilty of their performance at home. Every minute, everywhere, women and girls are going though a variety of crisis, out of which a very few examples could be adequate to uncover the battering incidents in society:

---

[180] *Sunday Times of India,* Bangalore, June 17, 2007, p. 3.

[181] M.U. Qureshi, (2006), p. 154,

1. A housewife of Rajouli was beaten to death by her husband as she was not cooking good food and the house being untidy, for which she alone, often at times, is not responsible. Implicit in this viewpoint is that the husband has a right to beat his wife if she does not behave according to what he desires.
2. A young woman of village Taaddih under Amarpur police station of Banka was battered to death by her husband and in-laws as she refused to go out in rain to bring 'ganja' for her husband.
3. A young housewife of Dalsingsarai was mercilessly beaten to death by her husband when she objected to his having illicit relations with his elder brother's wife.[182]
4. A housewife and a government official was beaten which caused the death of her husband when she was trying to interrogate her husband's illicit relation with his own colleague.[183]

Battering happens not only between husbands and wives, it happens among children, in whom the batterers are the sons and the battered are their sisters. Thus, gender-based violence is no other than a power game, where the powerful or stronger can overpower the weaker. Traditional sex roles taught people that women are weak and fragile. As Qureshi rightly pointed out, 'to tame a woman who does not accept the traditional role of submissiveness and subordination, any means including violence is justified."[184]

7. Sexual Violence

Sexual violence is first and foremost, an act of violence, hatred, and aggression. Whether it is viewed clinically or legally, objectively, violence is the common denominator. Like other acts of violence, there is a violation of and injury to victims. The injuries may be psychological or physical.[185] Whatever violent actions they may be, once an action is carried out against somebody's will, it is violence. So also, in acts of sexual violence, usually the injuries are both, physical and psychological. In the book, '*Sexual Violence: The Unmentionable Sin,*' the author summarizes sexual violence in such a way: "Violence is violence no matter what form it takes. The body is assaulted, injury occurs, and there is the experience of physical and emotional pain. And yet the sexual aspect of sexual violence is

[182] M.U. Qureshi, (2006), p. 155.

[183] A college lecturer in Nagaland kicked his wife on her stomach while she was pregnant, due to her objection towards his illicit relationship with one of his colleagues.

[184] *Ibid.,* p. 155.

[185] Albert Bandura, *Aggression: A Social Learning Analysis* (Englewood Cliffs, N.J,: Prentice-Hall, Inc., 1973), p. 5, Marie M. Fortune, *Sexual Violence: The Unmentionable Sin* (Cleveland, Ohio: The Pilgrim Press, 1983), p. 5.

relevant. The nature of the assault makes clear the totality of the violation of the person."[186]

Thus, rape and child sexual abuse are acts of violence which are injurious to the body, mind and spirit. Any victim of rape knows that she has experienced the most violent act possible short of murder. It is reported in the daily news paper that, a gynecologist from Nigeria has been sentenced to 20 years in prison for raping and fondling women who came to his clinic for treatment.[187] There are various such cases registered in many countries. Therefore, whatever type it may be, sexual violence is a broad category of behaviour describing the sexual violation of one person by another, which may include rape, child sexual abuse, molestation and sexual harassment. The conduct may be physical or verbal sexual contact or sexualized behaviour, against the will of the victim or in a context in which authentic consent is not possible. Sexual violence could be categorized into different aspects as cited above:

Rape-According to the *Dictionary of Feminist Theologies*, rape comes from the Latin word 'rapere,' which means 'to seize and carry away by 'force' or 'to force another person to engage in sexual intercourse.'[188] The contemporary legal and applied definitions are gender-neutral and clearly indicate that rapist and victim can be of either or the same gender. However, because of the social inequities imposed due to gender, race, age, and sexual orientation, most victims of rape are women and children of all races and non-dominant men.[189] Rape is an act of aggression and violence, not a sexual act. The intention is to humiliate and terrorize the victim, never to satisfy her.[190] Any pleasure that the rapist experienced came not from the sex but from other aspects of the assault.[191] It is clear that rape

---

[186] Traditionally, society's focus on the sexual nature of sexual assault has allowed society and the offender to avoid confronting the violence inherent in sexual assault. Now, however, we must be careful when focusing on the violence that we do not begin to view sexual assault strictly as a physical attack. Rather we need to realize the sexual and the violent nature of the experience. See also Marie M. Fortune, p. 6.

[187] Charles Momah was sentenced to nearly three months after a jury convicted him on two counts of rape and two counts of indecent liberties with patients. He also performed gynecological exams without wearing gloves, sexually touched patients, probed them unnecessarily with a vaginal ultrasound wand and flirted with them inappropriately, in *The Times of India,* Bangalore, Saturday, February 4, 2006.

[188] Letty M. Russel and J. Shannon Clarkson, *Dictionary of Feminist Theologies* (Louisville, Kentucky: Westminster John Knox Press, 1996), p. 309.

[189] Letty M. Russel, (1996), p. 309.

[190] Russell Diane E. H., "Pornography and Violence: What does the New Research Say?" in *Take back the Night Women on pornography* ed. Laura Lederer (New York, 1980), p. 46.

[191] Here is one of the experiences by an assaulter, "It was one of the most satisfying experiences I've ever had. I got more pleasure out of being aggressive, having power over her, her actions, her life. It gave me more pleasure knowing there was nothing she could do....My feelings were a mixture of sex and anger. I wanted pleasure, but I had to prove something, that I could dominate a woman..... The sex part wasn't very good at all."

is an act of violence and aggression and is experienced as such by both the victim and the offender.

Rape serves the function of expressing and perpetuating male domination of women by violence. Every successfully acculturated woman grows up to fear rape and, by implication, to fear men.[192] Even though all men do not rape, many men do. Feminists claim that the prevalence of rape in the culture in which we live is the result of the way that men see and relate to women normally; a comment from Brian Wren seems appropriate here: 'Few men commit rape, but all benefit from the violence of those who do, since it instills in women the need for male protection, thus helping to keep them in a sub-ordinate place.'[193] Rape also involves hostility (anger) and control (power) more than passion. Anger and a desire to dominate and control the victim are the primary motivations of the rapist.[194] These factors are consistent with the victim's experience of sexual violence. The victim feels violated, dominated, and powerless. Rape may happen in different forms in any situation:

a. Stranger Rape

Women are not safe anywhere, may it be the street or the fields or even her own home. Stranger rape, the least common, occurs when a rapist attacks someone who is a stranger. Although stranger rape happens, victims are not in a position to report the incident owing to several reasons, yet the stigma of those very incidents haunts them throughout their lives. Out of many, two incidents could be stated here, firstly, a married woman of Chandi mohalla of Barth was brutally assaulted by six youths at her residence as the other members of the family were out. Secondly, a Harijan girl of village Musapur under Sarairanjan police station of Dälsingsarai was raped and murdered by unidentified persons in her house while she was sleeping with her mother.[195] One of the heart-threatening incidents happened in Kohima, Nagaland, in which a three years and four months' old girl was raped by a grown up boy from her own locality.[196] Thus, there are uncountable incidents of stranger rape happening in every community.

Stranger rape would also include acts of rape carried out during wartime, as acts of terror against a community. Women and girls are particularly vulnerable

---

[192] *Ibid,* p. 45.

[193] Lisa Isherwood and Dorothea Mce Ewan, *An A to Z of Feminist Theology* (Sheffield SII9AS, England: Sheffield Academic Press Ltd, 1996), p. 231.

[194] Nicholas Groth with Jean Birnbaum, *Men Who Rape* (New York: Plenum Press, 1979), p. 2.

[195] M.U. Qureshi, (2006), p. 325.

[196] A general public of Kohima attended a mass rally in protest against the rape of a 3 year and 4 month old girl by one Kenengulie of Dihoma Village at Kohima, in *Eastern Mirror,* Dimapur, Wednesday, September 15, 2004. Again on 6 June 2006, a minor girl was raped by Mr. Itoho, son of Helingmong Sangtem, *Nagaland Post,* Monday June 12, 2006 p. 2. Vol XV1, No. 188, Dimapur.

during armed conflict, when rape is used by fighting forces to terrorize, destroy and humiliate communities, when women may be forced to exchange sex for their very survival. And when war forces them to flee their homes, the risk of rape follows them and the threat of domestic violence grows.[197] Thus, stranger rape is an act of aggression and violence, not a sexual act. The intention is to humiliate and terrorize the victim, never to satisfy her. Victims are chosen for their sex, not for their sex appeal.[198] Victims thus, can be of any age, young children or fragile seniors, and can occur in any location at any time.

b. Acquaintance Rape

Acquaintance rape, the most common, describes an assault on some one who is known to the assailant, usually friends, co-workers, neighbors, land lords, employees, or their own partners, etc., whom the assailant considered a trustworthy person. Out of the various incidents of such rape "A woman was allegedly raped by her brother-in-law and two other friends in Poonch district of Jammu and Kashmir. The 22 year old woman had gone to the market from where her brother-in–law Maroof Ahmed took her to a house on some false pretext and raped her."[199] Acquaintance rape happens in the work place, at home, in the institutions or hostels, in dating places and in any place. Besides, date rape specially describes an assault against one's dating partner. Acquaintances rape happens every time and everywhere, yet it is undisclosed and kept behind the curtain.

c. Marital Rape

Marital rape describes an assault against one's marriage partner or intimate friend. Marital rape is a common form of abuse of women in marriage. Women are not just raped by sexually-frustrated strangers but their own husbands, who are lurking inside their bedroom. It is a new dimension of rape which does not generally come to light but it is a torture on women and violation of human rights of women which has not been given importance.[200] Without any doubt, Rabi N. Misra has rightly pointed out that, "Many a wife, in a domestic set up faces atrocities from the husband in the form of forcible sexual intercourse or what is termed as marital rape. As one of the victims mentioned how he experienced it: 'It was an arranged marriage, and I was jittery of what lay ahead. Instead of tender love, my husband literally lifted my wedding ghagra and raped me,' she further says, "The 15 days that I was married were a nightmare."[201]

---

[197] *http://www.theirc.org/what/gender-based.html*...accessed on 14/8/2007.

[198] *Op. cit.*, p. 46.

[199] *The Times of India,* Bangalore Wednesday, June 13, p. 9.

[200] Rabi N. Misra, *Women Education and development* (Laxmi Nagar, Delhi: Discovery Publishing House, 2006), p. 24.

[201] Reported by Shvetal Patel, a 27- year old girl in Gurukul, who was sexually preyed upon by her husband till she could not take it any more., Radha Sharma, "When rapist is none but your

Though marital rape exists everywhere, statistics are not available on this, as it is a delicate domestic affair. Even though cases are not reported, marital rape exists both in the lower class families as well as in higher level of the family. It is worth recognizing that, presently the government of India is contemplating to provide legal protection to the wife and punishment for the husband for domestic sexual violence. The proposed Bill to be introduced in the parliament is the Violence Against Women (prevention) Bill which includes domestic violence.[202] Thus, marital rape is a common form of the physical and psychological violence on women. Therefore, whatever kind of rape it may be, forcing a woman to have sex against her wishes or making a woman do sexual act that she does not like, deprives her dignity and defames her worth because, a man does not have the right to force his wife, daughter or any body to have sex.

d. Incest Rape

Incest rape means sexual relations between children and older family members, brother and sister or daughter and father etc. According to *Oxford Advanced Learner's Dictionary*, incest means "Sexual activity between two people who are very closely related in a family, for example, a brother and sister, or a father and daughter."[203] Incest follows the general pattern of child sexual abuse, with the majority of victims being female and the majority of assailants being male. Moreover, incest is rape in the sense that it is a coerced sexual relationship. However, because of the relationship with the assailant and the victim's seeming compliance,[204] it is not always defined by society as rape. The sexual violence of incest is not necessarily the physical sexual behaviour itself but the exploitation of the power difference inherent in the parent-child relationship. The victim is overwhelmed and overpowered by both the physical strength and the hatred of the rapist. The fear expressed by victims of child sexual abuse is similar.

Incidents are available which can be drawn from both sociological and biblical perspectives. One of the incidents is expressed in this way, "I had been asleep and woke up to find my father being sexual with me. I recall being in a state of terror, not quite knowing what was going on as I lay there for a few minutes and allowed him to touch me...Mostly a feeling of growing up in an environment

husband," *The Times of India,* Bangalore, October 31, 2006. p. 7.

[202] Women's organizations are demanding to include "sexual intercourse against the will of the wife" as one of the domestic violence. The National Commission for Women has also a draft bill to the government of India to include marital rape under domestic violence and to provide some protection measures to the wife. In Rabi N. Misra, p. 28.

[203] *Oxford Advanced Learner's Dictionar* (New York: Oxford University Press, 2003), 655.

[204] Incest rape has been conservatively estimated that about one million American women are survivors of incestuous relationships with their fathers, by Judith Herman, *Father Daughter Incest* (Cambridge: 1980) p. 46, and Diana E. H. Russel, "Pornography and Violence: What does the New Research Say?"in *Take back the Night Women on Pornograpgy* ed. Laura Lederer (New York, 1980), p. 49.

that was unsafe…I never felt my body was safe from violation."[205] Out of many such incidents, this is one of the incidents coming to the public eyes which could not be hid. Even in the Bible we see a similar incident. One of the best examples is the story of Tamar's defilement by her brother Amnon (2 Samuel 13:1-37), which shows that a dysfunctional family could contribute to incidents of incest. King David's family was a dysfunctional one. A heinous crime thus happened inside the royal house of David and he did not do anything about it.[206]

The story goes like this, Amnon, the first born son of David by Ahinoam, the Jezreelite, was consumed by his desire for the beauty of his half-sister Tamar, his father's daughter by Maacah (1 Chronicles 3:1-9). Amnon, with cousin Jonadab's help, planned to get Tamar by pretending to be sick. He asked his father David to send Tamar to his house to prepare food for him, and carried out his evil plan. Amnon forced himself upon Tamar and sent her away. Amnon violated the body and person of Tamar, his sister and proceeded to reject her. Her life was destroyed as she was filled with shame and anguish. The main issue in incest could be the imbalance of power, because violence is about abuse of power.[207] Thus, sexual abuse can be incestuous abuse in which not only grown up ones but even a child or a small girl is sexually abused by a member of her family, either by her father or brothers. Incest is not simply a social problem but a theological problem as both society and church must address this frightening and ruinous issue openly.

Sexual Harassment

Sexual harassment generally refers to conduct that takes place in the workplace between a supervisor or manager and employer or between co-workers. It is "the use of one's power or authority, either explicitly or implicitly, to coerce another into unwanted sexual relations or to punish another for her refusal; or the creation of an intimidating situation through verbal, using very provocative and vulgar language towards women or physical conduct of a sexual nature."[208] It is also a form of discrimination, and violation of fundamental human rights. It is very obvious that sexual harassment has become serious and common in recent years as more women enter into the world of work sectors.

Due to globalization, large sections of women are forced on to the streets in search of jobs for their livelihood. In many cases, women have to bear the sole responsibility of supporting their families. They are compelled to enter the world

---

[205] Sandra Butler, *Conspiracy of Silence* (San Francisco: New Glide Publications, 1978), pp. 49-50 and Marie M Fortune…..p. 6.

[206] Muriel Orevillo-Montenegro, "Close Family Ties and Incest," in *In God's Image: Women and Peacemaking, Journal of Asian Women's Resource Centre for Culture and Theology,* Vol. 25, No. 2, (June 2006), p. 13.

[207] *Ibid.*, p. 15.

[208] Letty M. Russel and J. Shannon Clarkson, *Dictionary of Feminist Theologies*, p. 309. and (U.S Federal Equal Employment Opportunity Commission, 1990).

of street-vending, domestic employment and other forms of unskilled work. Omvedi comments, "The readiness of poor women to do any kind of work to maintain the survival level in the family, this fluidity, makes them the base of cheap labour everywhere, the ultimate reserve army of labour."[209] Many a time, women feel uncomfortable with male supervision at work where they face sexual harassment.[210]

As mentioned above, women are harassed by their bosses and male workers. For instance, the headmaster of an English medium school at Bhurkunda, 30 km from Ramgarh Cantt was taken into police custody for raping a lady teacher of his school. A nurse of Sardar Hospital, Giridih was criminally assaulted by two young employees of the hospital.[211] Many domestic servants are also molested by employers or the relatives or friends of employers. In many cases, instead of punishing the culprits domestic servants are sent back to their parents' home with complaints or accusations. These experiences of exploitation make women vulnerable and restive. Thus, there are unaccountable incidents experienced by women in the work place. Therefore, whatever kind of actions or attitudes it may be, harassing a woman is regarded as gender-based violence. Thus, it is a daily drama that women are raped at work, on the street, in the fields, in running trains or buses and on railway platforms, in school, in their homes by men who are their employers or employees, their acquaintances, their neighbours, their relatives, their in-laws and even by their own fathers and brothers.

Sexual violence is understood theologically and ethically as sin, as the physical, psychological and spiritual violation of a person by another person that as such, violates the bodily integrity of the victim as well as shatters any possibility of right relationship between the victim and the abuser. Traditionally, males have presumed to have sexual access to women, their acts of sexual violence have been minimized as normal male behaviour and often overlooked by the legal system and community in general. In many cases, victims of sexual violence have been blamed for their own victimization, by saying that it was due to their dresses, way of behaviour, the way they approach the opposite sex, going out in the dark, due to their softness or sexy in their looks, etc. Thus, sexual violence represents a profound violation of another person which is injurious and destructive.

---

[209] *Indian Journal of Gender Studies,* Vol 13 Number 1 January-April 2006, p.13.

[210] One of the women employers shares her experiences in the work places: Some of us, become domestic helpers in others people's homes. The male employers know that we had no choice but to sleep with them, since we had to keep gruel before our men and children at the end of the day. You think our husbands did not know about it? They just keep quiet and show their frustration by beating us.

[211] M.U. Qureshi, (2006), p. 325.

Christian Education

Christian education is the process by which a faith tradition is passed on from one generation to the next generation. It is also a process in which teaching and learning about the Christian faith takes place not for a certain stage in life but through-out one's life. On the other hand, it is also the educational task of the church for the church, and without religious education, the formation of persons within a given tradition, the church has no future.[212] According to Wayne R. Rood, "Christian Religious Education is the attempt, ordinarily by members of the Christian community, to participate in and to guide the changes which take place in their relationships with God, with the church, with other persons, with the physical world, and with oneself."[213] Thus, Christian education is not only an education which emphasize the relationship with God alone but education for all humanity; fellow human beings, irrespective of sex, colours and faiths, and also with nature around them. Thereby, Christian education does not concentrate only on and within the faith community but goes beyond that understanding. It is neither limited to specific areas, nor targeting certain groups of people, but includes the whole universe throughout the people's lives.

Moreover, Christian education arises from a person's action or ministry experience. These actions and experiences become the bases for people's reflection, and thus produce transformation-their own persons, cultures, the churches, and the societies. Thus, Christian education is a process of spiritual and social transformation, transformation in every aspect. It requires a socio-cultural transformation leading to religious, economic and political transformations in society.

In the line of above definitions, Christian religious educator Sherill has expressed that, "Christian education is the attempt to participate in and to guide changes which takes place in persons in their relationship with God, with the Church, with the other persons, with the physical world and with oneself."[214] Another well known Christian educator in India who has contributed much towards Catechetical education D. S. Amalorpavadass defined Christian religious education as "the dynamic procedure in which a group of believers are guided with due respect for their freedom, to meet and discover God in the midst of

---

212 *Concilium: Religion in the eighties, The sexual Revolution,* Baum, Gregory and John Coleman, (Edinburgh: T&T. Clarks LTD, 1984), p. 16.

213 Wayne R. Rood, *Understanding Christian Education* (New York: Abingdon Press, 1970), 241.

214 Anto Amarnad, "Religion and Education for life," in *Journal of Dharma: Religion and Education, Dharmaram College Golden Jubilee Commemoration* Volume, April – June 2006, Vol. 31, No. 2, p. 241.

their life situations and understand God's designs through the instructions and interpretation of sacred scripture."[215]

When the writer says "a group of believers," he does not mean children or people at a certain stage of their lives but those who have a heart to change the existing tradition which diminishes their whole being. In other words, those with a conscious mind to discern life which brings justice and peace within and wherever they may be: Freedom from social structural practices, which created the situation of the oppressed, and the oppressors who may have done so due to patriarchy or certain societal norms. On the other hand, when a certain group of people exercise their power and authority against another group or between men and women, education is the best means to provide consciousness about their situations, empowering them by giving appropriate awareness, and therefore Christian religious education needs to play its pivotal role by educating its faith community. Faith community however, does not mean only those who come under certain church circles and those attendees of community services regularly, but every one who are Christian by birth. Further this circle can reach out to the people in society across borders of caste, creed, clan or colour to bring about transformation on the strength of educating them to reflect and act in terms of bringing about justice, peace, and harmony. Christian education can be thus used as a liberative praxis education which is the sole purpose of the gospel of Christ.

Models of Christian Religious Education

Whatever subject or study could be, models serve as guiding principles. Thus, depending upon several propositions, a number of theories of Christian education have emerged. The five existing models discussed by Jack Seymour and E. Donald in the book, *Contemporary Approaches to Christian Religious Education*, are appropriate to mention in order to understand the purpose of the subject matter. The models are transmission model, socialization on faith community model, spiritual development model, liberation model and interpretation model.[216] Every model is equally applicable and important while dealing with the different issues, and the gender-based violence issue is one of those issues, which requires proper education in the society. They are:

(1) The goal of religious instruction is to transmit Christian understanding and practices, tradition and norms set by the community to the next generation. Here, the sole purpose of religious education is to modify the behaviour of the learners to fit into the norms set by the community.

---

[215] D.S. Amalorpavadass, *A Survey of One Decade of Catechatical Renewal in India,* (Bangalore: NBCLC, 1973), p. 7. in *Anto Amarnad, "Religion and Education for Life,"* in Journal of Dharma: Religion and Education, Dhamaram College Golden Jubilee Commemorative Volume, April – June 2006, Vol. 31, No. 2

[216] Donald E. Miller, *Story and Context: An Introduction to Christian Education* (Nashville: Abingdon Press, 1999), pp. 78-80.

(2) The goal of the 'socialization on faith community' approach is to build a congregation into a community where a person can encounter the faith and learn its life-style. Thus, the very nature of the community determines the nature of Christian religious education. Its task is to preserve the faith of the community that is vitally and purposefully embodied in the community itself. Here the primary issue is not so much what to teach and learn but what it means to be Christian together in a community and the world.

(3) The goal of liberation is to transform both the Church and the people for liberation and humanization. People are to become critically aware of oppressive structures, especially those that are racist, sexist, and economic with political and cultural inhibitions. Then they would learn to understand the ways in their private and corporate, secular and religious life patterns that contribute to the oppression of other people. The goal is to bring justice to all people.

(4) The goal of spiritual development is to grow in faith to spiritual maturity. The growth of the whole person includes emotional, moral, and spiritual development. The various stages of development can be more or less identified and these stages serve to guide the Church in its educational task. Differences between individuals are accounted as important, and each is encouraged to grow in his/her own way and at his/her own rate.

(5) The goal of interpretation is to connect Christian perspectives and practices to contemporary experiences. People are to be engaged in exploring and seeking meaning from the surrounding reality in terms of the ongoing Christian story. Thus, it sees the meaning-making process as an ongoing one rather than as a given once for all. Faith is not something prescribed but something that needs to be explored and appropriated anew continuously. In this process one continues to search for meaning in a free environment.

In addition to the above mentioned five models, a number of other models have also emerged. For example, Mary Elizabeth Moore offers a traditional model of education. She suggests that, "The primary goals of Christian religious education are knowledge with understanding and the transformation of person's actions, beliefs and values,"[217] It is knowledge with the understanding of the past events of the tradition, scripture and church history. Transformation comes in the present belief and value as persons anticipate the future. In order to achieve transformation from the present belief and value which does not bring much benefit to the individual and society, people need to be educated.

---

[217] Mary Elizabeth Moore, *Education for Continuity and Change: A New Model for Christian Religious Education* (Nashville: Abingdon Press, 1983), p. 132.

Chapter 3

Theoretical Framework of Gender-Based Violence

Perspectives on Gender-based Violence

There is no human society in the world which can boast of equality among its members without any discrimination or oppression. Prejudices against one group of people or race are common, while in return, another group retaliates or reacts to create tensions and generates different forms of violence. In the religious world too, many groups influence factors that are the driving force to reinforce or fight against prejudices or biases. Besides, one of the factors that generate challenges in the modern society to alleviate discriminations could be the media.

It is beyond the scope of the current study however, to deal with all the above mentioned issues in this limited research. Gender-based violence is the current concern. Therefore, to analyze the situation in a human community for gender bias, as that in Nagaland is an interesting project. Even though, living in the same home or community, humans make so much distinction between men and women/male and female, or boys and girls in their leadership roles, functionaries, work culture, power and strength and so forth. And thus, gender generates unequal treatment between men and women in every aspect of human activity. Therefore, the following is an attempt to examine the different theories in analyzing the human context.

Anthropological Perspectives

According to anthropologist Eleanor Leacock:

> Women suffer manifold forms of oppression: as virtual slave labor in households, unpaid for their work as mothers who create new

> generations of workers, and as wives or sisters who succor the present one; as workers, often in marginal jobs and more underpaid than men; and as members of racial minorities, or of semi colonial nations, subject to various economic, legal, and social disabilities. All the while, women bear the brunt, psychologically and sometimes physically, of the frustration and anger of their men folk, who, in miserable complicity with an exploitative system, take advantage of the petty power they have been given over the women close to them.[218]

It clearly shows that the social structure which was in use from time immemorial was exploitative guaranteeing men to use power over women. Thus, another anthropologist Eleanor admits their failure in defining gender, which she says, "women's roles as everywhere and always subordinate to men. To upset this relationship is to upset the natural order itself."[219] From the above statements it is clear how different gender roles themselves show the distinction about the strong and the weak, good and bad, superior and inferior, etc. Thus, not only the male writers define the gender roles in the society in a particular way, but females themselves define it along the line which their male counter parts have structured without realizing the prejudices done to them.

Again, the British anthropologist, E. E. Evans-Pritchard[220] affirms that 'it is difficult to believe that the relative positions of the sexes are likely to undergo any considerable or lasting alteration in the foreseeable future,' since 'men are always in the ascendancy. In this way, "there are deep biological and psychological factors, as well as sociological factors, involved, and (the facts seem to suggest) that the relation between the sexes can only be modified by social changes."[221] It could be understood that, there are several factors which make gender differences. For instance, biologically women are different, as females give birth but males do not; physiologically men are stronger, intellectual, and smarter whereas women are weaker, calm, soft and not smart; socially women are confined at home, caring, nurturing, doing household work, whereas the accepted notions for men are to rule in public, having leadership ability, firm in decision making, etc. These attitudes are passed down from generation to generation. In other words, these are the learned behavior from time immemorial which is not easy to change immediately, without critically analyzing the existing situation. As E. R. Leach, a colleague of Evans-Pritchard also says, "history and ethnography combine to show that male domination has always been the norm in human affairs." Scientists are

---

[218] Eleanor Leacock, "Women, Development, and Anthropological Facts and Fictions" in Huizer, Gerrit and Bruce Mannheim, *The Politics of Anthropology: From Colonialism and Sexism Towards a View from Below* (Paris: Mouton Publishers, 1979), p. 132.

[219] Eleanor Leacock, (1979), p. 133.

[220] *Ibid.*, p. 133.

[221] *Ibid.*, p. 134.

of the opinion that, the attitude towards women in the present conditions where they are considered as subordinate has been conditioned by the society where they live, in which social changes are needed to overcome gender bias.

To the French anthropologist Claude Levi-Strauss, "human society is and has been from its very inception essentially masculine.' In his view, 'human society was inaugurated through the exchange of women as commodities, valued by men for their sexual and other services."[222] Thus, human mind and attitudes have been framed in that understanding, in which, gender-based violence today is virtually a pivotal issue around the world. It could be argued that, the above mentioned assumptions are out of human imaginations, and they thus constructed the societal norms to benefit men and the same was made by men to be appropriated in society, where women's worth and dignity were ignored by categorizing them to the level of commodities. It is undeniable, when we say women are considered as a commodity in the society, because the way men treat and use their female counter parts, be at private places or in the public arenas shows their situations.

As one of the Brazilian educators, Paulo Freire has said about the dependent people/society in one of his books, *Cultural Action for Freedom:* "The dependent society is by definition a silent society. Its voice is not an authentic voice, but merely an echo of the voice of the metropolis–in every way, the metropolis speaks, the dependent society listens."[223] Although, he has written this in the context of political activities, it is appropriate when we talk about the differences between the inferior and the superior in our context. Paulo further says, "Only when the people of a dependent society break out of the culture of silence and win their rights to speak-only, that is, when radical structural changes transform the dependent society-can such a society as a whole cease to be silent towards the director society."[224]

As the above said anthropologists have commented, values and norms in relation to the sexes are deeply implanted in every society from the beginning of human existence. In order to bring changes in the society from the very traditionalized mind set to a newer forms where gender prejudices have no room but share equal responsibility and privilege irrespective of sex, one needs to take certain risks. And to achieve that goal everyone ought to be educated in a way that makes them realize and sensitize towards the existing gender roles in which half of their own species are victimized. Therefore, simply raising slogans, empowering a few women who are educated and who are in the top level, adding subjects on women's issues in the educational institutions and scientific experimentation on sex roles from different fields alone cannot wipe away the age-old practices of gender-based violence. Hence, sensitivity on gender issues by articulating and

---

[222] Eleanor Leacock, (1979), p. 133.

[223] Paulo Freire, *Cultural Action for Freedom* (Middlesex, England: Penguin Books, 1972), p. 59.

[224] *Ibid.*, p. 60.

examining women's ability may enhance the chances of overcoming the existing discriminations.

Psychological Perspective

From a psychological perspective, violence is variously perceived as instinctive; as aggression it is rooted in evolution, due to faulty ego development and lack of self control and defective socialization, etc. Some of the aspects by which human beings have been defined on the basis of sex roles are discussed below:

(1) Identity and Sex Role

Some psychologists-psychoanalysts have theorized on the concept of identity in a cross-cultural context where the male is projected as being tied to the mother especially in view of the mother's own longing for love, as she is in satiated by the husband in a typical, patriarchal, extended, arranged marriage setting, resulting in a weak oedipal conflict and weak resolution of the same.[225] The mother-son (Oedipal) relationship is exaggerated in the Indian context, as it is connected with son-preference in society. On the other hand, women and girl child are victims of every situation starting from conception to death. They also found out from their research that, the birth of the son alone is perceived as giving the female her identity and status, and the hope for being cared in old age.[226] Thus, studies on sex role development reiterate the belief in male superiority in society and the differential socialization of boys and girls. This perception has been passed down from generation to generation and is made mandatory to be preserved as a norm. No wonder, in each given tradition, women are the only victims.

The idea of the female being inferior that originated with the Greek philosophers has had a strong impact on personality theory, partially through its shaping of the social milieu in which such theories developed. It is said that, the personality theorists, usually male, tended to encounter women only in subordinate positions. Their theories evolved, therefore, in ways that tended to explain and justify the disadvantaged position of women by postulating differences in nature among women and men.[227] This effect can be seen in the theories of both the functionalists and the psychoanalytical schools of thoughts.

Thus, psychologists within this system came up with generalizations about sex differences in temperament that had implications for a wide range of behaviour and these generalizations gave rise to the notion of a 'maternal

---

[225] T. S. Saraswathi & Ranjana Dutta, "Current Trends in Developmental Psychology: A Life Span Perspective" in *Psychology in India, the State-of-the-Art, Volume 1: Personality and mental processes,* ed. Janak Pandey (New Delhi: Sage publications, 1988), p. 115.

[226] *Ibid.,* p. 115.

[227] Hilary M. Lips, "Theories about female and male nature" in *The Psychology of Sex Differences*, ed. Hilary M. Lip and Nina Lee Colwill (New Jersey: Prentice-Hall, 978), p. 28.

instinct' in women.[228] Because, the biological task of pregnancy, childbirth, and lactation were fulfilled by women, these theorists reasoned, that the presence of a 'maternal instinct' in women (but not in men) only made the notion of evolution sensible. Therefore, another psychologist, Spencer (1891, cited in Shields, 1975), for example, felt that as women devoted most of their energy in preparation for pregnancy and lactation, there was little left over for the development of other qualities.[229] Another psychologist Edward Thorndike conceived that women are naturally both more nurturing and more submissive than men.[230] We cannot however deny totally the analytical findings made by different theorists about the identical nature among men and women. For instance, in some tasks women can do better than men, and what men can do, women cannot. The differences in activity or ability should not be the gate way to do violence on one particular gender. On the other hand, there is no room for prejudice towards other groups on the basis of their race, colour or status in the modern society.

(2) Sexual Differentiation and Gender Identity

It would be worth discussing some of the opinions and theories which were based on sexual differentiation and gender identity, as these could be one of the reasons for gender-based violence in human history. Therefore, it is appropriate to analyze some of the theories propounded by psychologists to show their actual findings on sexual differentiation.

At the end of the nineteenth century, for example, a theory was put forward that explained all physical, intellectual, and emotional differences between the sexes on the basis of a primary difference between the metabolism of women and men. The male according to this theory, was 'catabolic,' while the female, 'anabolic.'[231] This meant that males had a relatively quicker, more active metabolism, where as females were slower and more passive. This assumed biological difference between men and women was thought 'natural' to lead to such things as greater agility, creativity, variability, and scientific insight for men and greater patience, open-mindedness, appreciation for subtle details, and intuition for women.[232]

Although this was the accepted theory then, it cannot explain how men and women are equally compatible in academic, intellectual and physical realms. On the other hand, in some cases men are more open-minded and have greater patience than women. Because of this, it is felt that owing to the restriction of education to women and due to lack of opportunities, they were left behind and developed a bias in themselves which made them vulnerable.

---

[228] *Ibid.*, p. 28.

[229] *Ibid.*, p. 28.

[230] *Ibid.*, p. 28.

[231] Hilary M. Lip and Nine Lee Colwill., p. 53.

[232] *Ibid.*, p. 53.

Besides these, there are a considerable number of opinions about sex differences in temperament and personality, as well as in cognitive style among men and women. According to some psychologists,[233] boys and men are often said to be more active, more aggressive, dominant, competitive and achievement-oriented; while girls and women, being more anxious, timid and compliant, have lower self-esteem, and are more social in orientation, more concerned with nurturance, co-operation and affiliation.[234] They also argued that, as far as the cognitive performance is concerned, for example, girls excel in verbal ability and boys in visual, spatial, and also in mathematical ability. That means, girls are adept in simple, repetitive, clerical tasks, while boys achieve more complex cognitive tasks and, above all, are creative in real life, both in science and in the arts.[235] Because of these assumptions, men were advised to study subjects which required mathematics and arts, and women were encouraged to do manual jobs, which do not require much physical strength. But, today it is hard to accept all these assumptions.

According to Hilary M. Lip, "Gender identity is the individual's private experience of his or her gender: the concept of the self as masculine or feminine."[236] For him, gender identity is such a powerful and important part of a person's self-concept that in most adults it is virtually impossible to change it. Yet research indicates that physiological sexual differentiation notwithstanding, we are not born with a gender identity: it only develops after birth.[237] But, this idea cannot be fully acceptable at this age because sex could be detected while a person is still in the womb. Moreover, research also shows that once formed, a person's gender identity is extremely resistant to change. Thus, as it is very obvious in every society, cultural norms and traditional practices are not easy to change, and thus, as a person grows up, unconsciously or not he/she adapts to the environment and identifies with the stereotyped cultural roles.

(3) Social Learning Theory

Social learning theory also suggests that a child develops a gender identity through a learning process that involves modeling, imitation, and reinforcement. The theory rests on the assumption that boys learn to be boys and girls to be girls because sex-role-appropriate behaviour is rewarded whereas sex-role-inappropriate behaviour is more likely to be ignored or punished. Children thus learn which behaviour is

---

[233] Ann Taylor, Wladyslaw Sluckin, D. R. Davies, J. T. Reason, R. Thomson and A.M. Colman, *Introducing Psychology* (New York: Penguin Books Ltd, 1982), p. 590.

[234] *Ibid.*, p. 590.

[235] *Ibid.*, p. 590.

[236] Hilary M. Lip and Nine Lee Colwill, (1978), p. 73.

[237] *Ibid.*, p. 73.

sex–role appropriate or inappropriate by observing and imitating adult and peer models as well as by trial and error.[238]

Thus, in every culture, society sets and observes certain norms for both the male and the female. It is also further suggested that, parents map out gender roles for the child, and then the child is differentially reinforced to follow the appropriate one. As the child is repeatedly reminded that he is a boy or she is a girl and differentially reinforced for doing boy-things or girl-things, gradually it becomes rewarding for him to think of himself as a boy or for her to think of herself as a girl.[239] Through observation, imitation, and reinforcement, an appropriate role identity thus is established in all private affairs and community lives, which in many cases lead to discrimination and victimization, engendering gender-based violence in society.

According to Cognitive Developmental theory (Kohlberg, 1966), "gender is a concept that cannot be learned until a child reaches a particular stage of intellectual development. It is suggested that between the ages of three to five, a child acquires 'gender constancy'-an understanding that a person's gender is fixed and cannot be spontaneously altered by a chance in hairstyle, dress, or name."[240] Before that age, according to Kohlberg, although a child may have learned that people can be categorized as either male or female, she or he sometimes makes errors in classifying the self or others and thinks that arbitrary changes in classification can occur.[241] Therefore, according to developmental psychologists, once the child has categorized herself/himself with some certainty as male or female, she/he will find the performance of sex-role-appropriate behaviour reinforcing. In a similar vein, behaviours that are perceived as sex-role-inappropriate acquire negative connotations and are avoided.[242] Along with developmental psychologists we could also observe that children till they attain a certain age, may not consciously observe their sex and their roles, but it is the society which teaches and conditions them to behave according to their sex. For example, if we leave a few tools and dolls where both boys and girls are, naturally boys will grab the tools or cars, ball or guns, whereas girls choose dolls since they were given such things by their parents from the very beginning. And as they enter the class room and experience sitting separately, they learn to keep a distance between boys and girls.

(4) Sex Difference in Ability

Women have long been regarded as members of the weaker sex. As a group, they are shorter, lighter, and less muscular than men and are regarded in society as generally unable to perform heavy manual work or to compete in certain stressful or

---

238 Hilary M. Lip and Nina Lee Colwill, (1978), p. 75.

239 Hilary M. Lip and Nina Lee Colwil (1978), p. 75.

240 *Ibid.*, p. 75.

241 M. Lip and Nina (1978), p. 75.

242 *Ibid.*, p. 75.

potentially violent athletic events. These differences have been used as justification for keeping women out of certain jobs. But psychologists, however, have found out that, women are also able to do strenuous work as male counterparts.

Thus, males although enjoy the status of being muscular and the stronger sex, appear to be constitutionally weaker than females.[243] It is also argued that, males are more likely to suffer injury or death prenatal or during the birth process, and to be victims of childhood diseases.[244] They also mention that, the illness rate is higher among females than males in most parts of the world, but females are more likely to recover from illnesses than are males, and women's life expectancies are almost universally higher than those of men.[245] Thus, there is some more comparison shown by the psychologists out of their analyses, where both the sexes have advantages and disadvantages in some areas. But, the concepts of male strength and female weakness are central to the stereotypes on which sex roles are based. Thus, people tend to assume that women have always been weaker than men and that this understanding of sex difference is basic to our species.[246]

Though, there are differences between male and female in a way they are created biologically and physically it does not mean that they are subordinate beings, who can be oppressed, exploited, killed or tortured and victimized. Both sexes have weaknesses and strengths in different ways, for instance, even though a person is physically strong he/she may not have the skill to use it appropriately or cannot protect themselves when they face certain situations. Human beings need to be thus valued and accepted according to his /her ability and capability not by their visual perception/observations.

Let us examine briefly how boys learn to be male and how do they get a sense of themselves as male from which later masculinity is constructed. How does this sense of masculinity enable them to think of themselves superior, and thus begin to rule and manipulate girls by accumulating power? Concerning this, sociologist M. Richards says, "Boys learn the kind of behaviour by which they can express their masculinity. There are many factors that contribute to this sense of 'maleness.'"[247] This is a dominant view of men in the press and other media. This view of men represents them as being tough, strong, aggressive, independent, brave, sexually active, rational, intelligent, and so on. The corresponding view of women is that they are vulnerable, weak, non-aggressive, kind, caring, passive, frightened, stupid, dependent and immature. He further says, "Baby boys and

---

[243] Montagu, 1968 quoted in Hillary M. Lip and others, "Sex Differences in Ability: Do Men and Women Have Difference Strengths and Weaknesses? in *The Psychology of Sex Differences*, (1978), p. 147.

[244] *Ibid.*, 147.

[245] *Ibid.*, 147.

[246] *Ibid.*, p. 149.

[247] Sue Askew and Carol Ross, *Boys Don't Cry: Boys and Sexism in Education* (Milton Keynes: Open University Press, 1988), p. 3.

girls are treated very differently from birth. They are spoken to differently, dressed differently, play with differently, and there are different expectations for them,"[248]

In response to the above mentioned conceptions about masculinity and femininity, it could be argued by putting forward some logical questions-are girls still dependable in every aspect? Are girls still lagging behind academic exercises which demand intelligence with self modification? Do girls feel comfortable with the traditional cultural dress code and life styles they were taught a few decades ago? Do girls have the sense of aggressiveness to respond to the violent actions meted out to them? As Richards expresses, from the very beginning of human existence they were taught and treated differently in actions, speeches and dressing, as they were provided with different objects both in playing and working. With these views in mind, boys assume they are superior and overshadow girls in every aspect, and this becomes a standard norm in society.

(5) Status and Power

The concept of status and power plays a very important role in every given society. When a psychologist talks about power, she/he generally means the ability of a person to influence another's behaviour. Out of many one example from Paula Johnson, a social psychologist can be cited. She has developed a theory that relates sex-role stereotypes to power use.[249] She suggests that there are three major dimensions in which power-use is affected by sex-role stereotypes: direct-indirect, concrete-personal, and competent-helpless. In order to support this theory let us examine its three dimensions briefly:

1. Indirect versus Direct Power

Direct power is demonstrated when a person exerts influence openly, by giving an order or making a request; indirect power is exercised when the influencer obtains the desired outcome while trying to keep the other person unaware of the influence. Indirect power is often called manipulation. Johnson further suggests that in society, there are many constraints against directness by women and that, consequently, women more than men tend to rely on indirect power.[250] The reason why women may rely more heavily than men do on indirect power is that in each culture as well as in virtually every other, men are the holders of authority.

No doubt, in every patriarchal society men decide and set the norms for both men and women who are vested with power and authority. This explanation would be more vivid as we analyze the different opinions expressed by scholars. According to Rosaldo, "Authority is a particular type of power in which power holder is recognized by the society as having a legitimate, abstract right to make

[248] *Ibid.*, p. 3.

[249] Johnson,1976 quoted in Hillary M. Lip and others (1978), p. 228.

[250] Hilary M. Lip and others, p. 229. Many feminist writers have noted that a woman who uses direct power is quickly labeled unfeminine, castrating, and bitchy.

decisions and to command obedience. Obviously, a position of authority lends considerable force to any attempt to exercise power directly."[251] It can be argued that, due to this concept of power and authority in all the human activities, men control women by exercising their strength which notion was built up from their childhood. Making decisions and laying rules and regulations are usually done by men for the whole community, which every community member ought to abide and adopt. Thus, in that situation, women directly come under power and authority, when male members control female members.[252]

2. Personal versus Concrete Power

An individual's attempt to exercise power is given weight by the amount and nature of resources under his/her control. Thus Johnson (1976) suggests that resources can be divided into two categories: those that depend on personal relationships, such as liking, and approval; and those that are concrete and independent of relationships, such as money, knowledge, and physical strength. She further argues that, in society, men have considerably more control over concrete resources than do women and those women therefore rely on personal resources more than men do.[253]

The ideas behind those resources which made women rely on men could be the reason why men control women. It is undeniable that women often expect men to confirm and approve what they are going to take up, either for her individual matters or family affairs. On the other hand, since for centuries men only were given the opportunity to study, followed by employment, they assumed physical strength. But, these perceptions and ideology does not hold good in the present context as everything has been mechanized and when education has been made mandatory irrespective of sex and classes.

3. Helplessness versus Competence

Johnson (1976) suggests that because women are often in situations where they are not regarded nor do they feel competent, they tend to rely on helplessness as a mode of influence more than do men. By being or acting helpless, women can get men to do the hard heavy work. The study also indicates that in a dating situation when the issue of sexual intimacy occurs, men are seen as using direct methods to influence a woman to have sexual intercourse, and women are perceived as being capable of equal directness in turning a man down.[254] Thus, psychologists cite

[251] Rosaldo, 1974, p. 229.

[252] In many places, soon after her husband's death her eldest son occupies their house and properties, and within a few days and months she is under the control of her son and daughter-in-law. We can not see how status and power makes women to gain importance, temporarily though as long as property rights remain, as it can be withdrawn anytime as circumstances change.

[253] Hilary M. Lip and others, (1978), p. 230.

[254] *Ibid.*, p. 233.

considerable evidence that the male state is more highly valued than the female state in our society. They therefore suggest that the male state carries with it a higher status, which is translated into higher expectations of competence for men, which leads in turn to the occupation by men rather than women of positions of power and prestige in society.[255]

In the analysis of power differences by sex as a social status, it is said that as status differences between the sexes diminish, so too should sex differences in power orientation. Lionel Tiger (1969), a noted anthropologist, tries to explain this by postulating an inherent biological male-male bond, evolving from prehistory, that causes men to cling together-the better to hunt, to build, to decide, to invent, and to protect their[256] women and children.[257] He claims that, women are never likely to play a significant part in politics because males are biologically predisposed to form and maintain all-male groups, particularly when they are involved with matters of consequence.[258] He also suggests that, females have a biologically-based inability to release the patterns of behaviour in subordinates that could be termed 'follower ship.' Therefore, he again suggests that, the evidence points to the conclusion that male dominance is a biologically-rooted condition of human nature.[259] Based on his arguments, Tiger asserts that "Even if the powerful bodies of a community become dominated by females, the male-centered dominant group will soon recur."[260] In other words, even if women are given a chance to form a group or assigned leadership, they may not be able to manage within the male dominated society.

It could be argued that, if men are willing to change their ideology by restructuring their attitudes, perceptions towards women, giving enough space to utilize ability, above all accept as they are, there would not be any question of recurrence of male dominance. However, very interestingly, after expressing his opinions and suggestions on sex biological differences, Tiger himself suggests, that a radical restructuring of our present society might overcome its alleged biological predisposition towards male dominance. From the suggestions given above by various psychologists including anthropologists it is seen that though biological differences give certain sex roles, it is the society which influences dramatically each of the sex roles according to its given culture.

---

[255] Hilary M. Lips and others, p. 235. Every known society assigns a higher value to people and tasks classified as male than to those classified as female (Rosaldo, 1974).

[256] The very word *their*, itself shows that men are the owners of women and children, in which case women become men's property. Feminist theologians are conscious of these kind of statements, and they began to critique, who are they, to women.

[257] *Ibid.*, p. 238.

[258] *Ibid.*, p. 238.

[259] *Ibid.*, p. 238.

[260] *Ibid.*, p. 238.

4. Sociological Perspective

The patriarchal nature of the dominant culture has a profound effect on women, men and heterosexual relationships in every society. Therefore, it is important to understand the patriarchal bias in order to understand the dynamics of male violence towards women. The patriarchal bias influencing the social and personal development of men and women is subtle, pervasive and often unrecognized. Patriarchal values are smoothly integrated into our gender role socialization process. That is, the process by which boys and girls learn about which behaviours, attitudes, and feelings are appropriate for members of their own sex, and which are appropriate for, members of the opposite sex. And this integration is often so successful that we have difficulty in distinguishing between a behaviour that is biologically innate and the behaviour that is learned in culture. Therefore, it is evident which is which that whether or not men's violence is innate versus learned.[261]

As a patriarchal culture, society teaches men and women that the male is the norm or standard to which all else is compared. The best instance is, when girls/women do something smart, viewers comment that they did it like a boy/man. That means that which is other than male is a deviant from the norms and, therefore inferior. Males and masculine qualities are thus valued, while females and feminine qualities are devalued. In the patriarchal scheme, there is no concept of equality.[262]

As already cited above, there are many things that contribute to violence against women in society. But its basis is the patriarchal culture and its worldview, all over the world. Patriarchal culture operates on a dualistic and hierarchical worldview that puts men and women in contradictory and hierarchical positions. In this worldview, a man is placed as superior while a woman is inferior. Even the language used differs a lot in defining women in a patriarchal society. In patriarchal language, the word 'women' is synonymous with subordination, discrimination, devaluation, oppression, powerless, voiceless, and so on.

Women are considered as objects, a piece of property owned by man, either by the father, husband or by the state. Therefore, Virginia Ramey asserts, "Our socialization has taught us that we must have one set of reactions for women, another set of reactions for men. What has been overlooked in our socialization is the importance of being able to react to one another simply as persons, as human beings."[263] Thus, socialization has emphasized the wide differences between men and women to such a tremendous degree that it has obscured some of the basic meanings of the creation stories in the Bible. So, the socialization process which

---

[261] Concilium: *Religion in the Eighties, The Sexual Revolution*, Baum, Gregory and John Coleman, (Edinburgh: T and T. Clark Ltd, 1984), p. 42.

[262] *Ibid.,* p. 42.

[263] Virginia Ramey Mollenkott, *Women Men and the Bible* (Nashville: Abingdon Press, 1978), p. 74.

emphasizes radical differences between male and female is therefore a denial of the oneness of the human race as taught in the Bible.[264]

It could be argued that, even though some of the biblical narratives talk about the oneness of the human being, peace, justice and equality, the Bible becomes one of the problematic authoritative texts for women. From the Genesis account to Paul's letter, one could see the extensive way in which women as subordinate characters have been obviously brought out, which became the basis and (the biblical) foundation for all its interpretation of human activity. As from the very inception, Christians affirmed that the Bible is the authoritative[265] and sacred account, inspired by the Holy Spirit. Therefore, they accepted its norms and interpreted their message on that foundation. Some of the biblical texts written in this understanding would be discussed separately later. No doubt, the whole message of the Bible is about the salvation of the whole humanity, without any distinction and prejudices, where every believer could experience oneness in the community.

Thus, because of the role of socialization to which women have been subjected, one assumes that certain characteristics are 'masculine' and certain characteristics are 'feminine.' Therefore, we assume, men are naturally stronger, wiser, smart, aggressive, rational, competitive, and intellectual than women, where as women are fragile, passive, romantic and weaker than men.[266] The best example is, when a man fails to do something or speaks more, the comments that he receives is that he is very talkative 'like a girl or like a woman' in a derogatory way. So the assumption is, 'men lead and women follow.' These assumptions are known as sex role stereotypes and this leads to stereotyped expectations about male and female performances in society.

Thus, in whatever professions it may be, men should be the bosses, women the secretaries. Men should be active in the business world, political world and sports ground while women's place is at home or as assistants in every work. In other words, men should be up front, women behind the scenes. Therefore, it is true that, gender-based violence is sanctioned by patriarchal culture through various ways and means. This does not mean that patriarchal culture does not victimize their counter-part, men. Of course, there are also the marginalized men in our societies those who are unable to perform like their same sex in some areas. Yet, in general, it is women who become the victims and suffer the worst. In the

---

264 *Ibid.,* p. 75.

265 "All scripture is inspired by God and is useful for teaching, for reproof, for correction, and for training in righteousness, so that everyone who belongs to God may be proficient, equipped for every good work," II Timothy 3:16-17 (NRSV).

266 It was understood in every society that men are assertive and strong, where as women are weak and submissive, that men are born to fight, to provide and to build, women to bear children and to act as companions and servants of men, Peter Swerdloff and the Editors of Time-Life Books, *Human Behaviour: Men and Women* (Nederland: Time-Life International, Second printing, 1977), p. 8.

following discussion we will examine how patriarchal culture has socialized the people to play their sex role in a given society.

Sex-role in Society

Each society illogically or not views a wide variety of personal characteristics, interests, and behaviour as the virtually exclusive domain of one sex or the other. The fact that societies vary in their definition of feminine and masculine roles is proof that sex roles are based on social rather than on biological factors. Wherever it may be, sex-roles are systematically inculcated in individuals, beginning at birth, by parents, educational and social system, peers, the media, and the religious teachings, symbols and images, and are supported by the social sciences and the economic, political, and legal structure of the society.

As Mack Kinnon puts it, "Women/men have a distinction not just of difference, but of power and powerlessness. If men are powerful and women are powerless as such, then male dominations are, on this view, pervasive."[267] From the very beginning thus individuals learn appropriate roles for each sex through role models and differentials of reinforcement.[268] Thus, in every society, males have power over females because of role definitions. It is true that, the rationality assigned to the male role gives men access to positions of expertise as well as credibility even when they are not experts. Thus, men have power and privilege over women by virtue of their sex. Though in many cases they are less competitive and have certain negative assumptions, it is always accepted that, men have higher status; this status is directly rewarding, and provides access to other highly valued statuses and rewards, through promotions, inheritance, authority and power, and that leads to domination.

As cited earlier, by virtue of their sex and their control of traditional sex-role definitions, men are able to manipulate women's behaviour by ignoring, misinterpreting, devaluing, and discrediting women or their accomplishments, especially when women deviate from traditional roles. Some examples are of the omission of women's contributions and achievements. It is undeniable that, from time immemorial, there were women, who ruled, led, fought, and invented, yet their names and their achievements are hardly recognized and totally neglected. Since there were no records or recognition of their efforts, slowly their names were forgotten both in church and society. It could be argued without hesitation that, the present women-empowerment programmes and gender justice or feminist theologies are all out of women's own propagations and achievements. They have written their own stories out of their experiences of struggles and have gathered enough evidences to picture their situation of neglect.

---

[267] Mack Kinnon Catharine, *Feminism Unmodified: Discourses on Life and Law* (Combridge: Harvard University Press, 1987), p. 123.

[268] Barbara Bovee Polk, "Male Power and the Women's Movement" in *Women: A Feminist Perspective*, ed. Jo Freeman (California: Mayfield Publishing Company, 1979), p. 591.

Thus, from its inception traditional laws were made, interpreted, and enforced with male self-interest in mind. The best example of this attempt could be the 'Naga Customary Law' which enforces much restriction on girls in terms of their moral conduct, observance of rituals and inheritance and sharing of parents' properties and many more. Those laws were laid down orally by men as the decision making body. In other words, males have suppressed feminine culture and have hindered their access to institutional power partly because they 'fit' the value structures of the institutions better than women. The confidence of being 'right,' of fitting, gives even incompetent men an important source of psychological power over women, who have not been so wholly socialized into the masculine value structure.[269]

Thus, traditional sex roles dictate not only that man should have more power, but also that the sexes should exert influence in different ways. Therefore, so long as the society prescribes sex-roles and social penalties for those who deviate from them, no meaningful choice exists for members of either sex. In all these, women are the only victims, because societal structures support men's ideologies and authority even if they deviate from certain norms. In the following discussions we will look into the patriarchal social structure adopted in the society.

Gender-based Violence and Social Structure

Social structure analysis is one of the most widely used tools in sociology and social theory. It indicates some regular and stable patterning of social action and social institutions, therefore its precise meaning is not easily determined. While 'structure' itself may be defined as the organizing relationship between parts in a whole, in social structure the whole is the society. In organic analogy, whereby a society is compared to an organism, the elements are institutions which perform functions, necessary to the survival and stability of the whole. Thus, in functionalism, social structure may be understood as roles, or as variously defined groups within the society. That society is structured, and that these structures can confront the individual as natural forces, constraining and determining their action, is taken to be indicative of a 'reified' state and thus a false society.[270]

Thus, in most cultures, girls learn from the earliest age that they must serve the needs of their family so that one day they will be equipped to serve the needs of a family of their own. It was the assumption that, to serve the needs of the other without having an opportunity to develop their own human potential, has cast women into a role inferior to men who have always sought to satisfy their inner

---

[269] Barbara Bovee Polk, "Male Power and the Women's Movement" in *Women: A Feminist Perspective*, ed. Jo Freeman, (California: Mayfield Publishing Company, 1979), p. 597.

[270] Andrew Edgar and Peter Sedgwick, *Key Concepts in Cultural Theory* (London and New York: Routledge, 2004), p. 367.

urgings for self-fulfillment. Men accept this as their right as human beings.[271] Thus, structures and systems of oppression are never open and easily visible, that so often they stand ignored and unnoticed in society as they operate through cultural conditioning.

Therefore, sex-role stereotyping goes on in family patterns, schools, institutions and academic text-books, church activities, mass media, work patterns, all through the society. Women grow up accepting this conditioning without realizing it, internalizing the image projected on them, an image shaped by male ideology.[272] Today those differences, roles and social relationship between male and female are all under challenge. Thus, Christian Religious Education needs to respond to those challenges through her church educational ministry not only within the faith community but to the extent of reaching others who do not belong to our own faith.

Gender-based Violence through Cultural Moldings

Violence is an acquired phenomenon. It is learnt in the society during the course of socialization through imitation and identification. As stated before our society is male-dominant. It does not provide equal treatment to both the sexes. As Qureshi, a sociologist also points out, "When a child takes birth he remains completely raw. He learns whatever he observed in the society and that constitutes his personality. A boy finds that he is getting preferential treatment by the society so he learns only the immediate gratification of his needs. He fails to get the opportunities to learn the use of such defensive-mechanisms as repression and suppression in controlling his desires more frequently so they remain weak."[273] In the family circle, a boy identifies himself with his father. He imitates his reaction, aggression and hostility shown towards his mother and daughters. A son also observes that his father is leading an independent life, deciding factors, being the head of the family. Moreover, he develops an anticipation of individual existence or separate entity which ultimately generates self-confidence, assertiveness, encouragement and initiation in him.[274]

All these characteristics are associated with dominance. Thus, a boy learns to develop authoritarian attitude towards his opposite sex, including his mother and sisters. As a result, a son or a younger brother could tell, 'you women keep quite or shut your mouth.' On the contrary, a girl learns to control and suppress her desires and wishes by advising them to have tolerance, patience and submission. Especially, in the family situation mostly, the mother instructs her daughters not

---

[271] Alison O'Grady, *Voices of Women: An Anthology of Writings by Asian women* based on the theme "Called to change-Committed to serve" (Asian Christian Women's Conference, 1978), 3.

[272] Alison O' Grady (1978), p. 30.

[273] M.U. Qureshi, *Women and Crime* (New Delhi: SBS Publishers & Distributors P. Ltd, 2006), p. 184.

[274] *Ibid.*, p.184.

to argue or reply back to boys or else they will only lose, being girls. In this way women and girls are forced to accept the dominance of males in the family and in society. The reasons may be the following:

a) Our socio-religious norms have affected women's status. Right from the post-Vedic era down to the modern times, the religious practices, rituals, scriptures, precepts, and historical forces have created for women their existing secondary status in society.
b) In many places still, menstruating women are treated as untouchables and unclean. Women are also considered as a property of men, to be disposed off as the master pleases.
c) Almost all the religious rituals are performed by men, as, no-where in the world, temple rituals are performed by women, and also in some religions women are not even allowed inside the places of worship.

Thus, for example among Muslims, men even from their childhood, are allowed to go to the mosque. Muslim women are required to cover their whole body except their face by black cloth, which project the norm that they are under certain religious and social practices giving others a negative connotation.[275] One of the famous prayers said by the Muslim men was, 'thank God that I am not made a woman or an animal.' There are many such examples in other religious teachings against women, and it is beyond this research to cite all of them.

For Christians, biblical teachings play a tremendous role in subjugating and devaluing women without analyzing the right situation in which it was written and for what purposes. For instance, verses like 'I have found more bitter than death the woman who is a trap, whose heart is snares and nets, whose hands are fetters; one who pleases God escapes her, but the sinner is taken by her… which my mind has sought repeatedly, but I have not found. One man among a thousand I found, but a Woman among all these I have not found' (Ecclesiastes 7:26, 28). Concerning this, Ann Brown, a feminist theologian says, "At every step of the way, feminists had to fight the conception that they were violating the God-given nature of women. Clergymen interrupted women's rights conventions, waving Bibles and quoting from the scriptures: 'Saint Paul said;…and the head of every woman is man …..Let your women be silent in the churches, for it is not permitted unto them to speak….And if they will learn anything, let them ask their husbands at home; for it is a shame for a woman to teach, nor usurp authority over the man, but to be in silence; for Adam was first formed, then Eve."[276]

---

[275] In many places we notice Muslim women roaming around with black cloth even in the hot climate, restricting them, where as men are free to wear according to their convenience. The black colour itself shows the unhealthy condition, and projects the bias in life style.

[276] Ann Brown, *Apology to Women: Christian Images of the Female sex* (Leicester, England: InterVarsity Press, 1991), p. 155.

Besides these, there are many more biblical quotations quoted by the preachers as they become a stumbling block for women to raise their voice and to come out from their oppressive situations. Since, from the very beginning people strongly assumed the Bible to be authoritative, they accepted as it is. In this way women were taught to be faithful to their husbands. It was also taught and believed that a woman who is beaten deserved it, since it was her fault as if her husband has a right to beat his wife. All these traditions make the rebellious silent among women which strengthens the authoritarian mentality of males. These kinds of understanding and perception need to be corrected through the religious educational ministry.

Thus, women have been since time immemorial the subject and the victim of male humour. A popular myth perpetrated through such jokes is the quarrelsome nature of women. For example, it is said, 'women can never get along well with one another,' 'Women's gatherings resemble a fish market' etc. But, what does history tell us? Who were the people who indulged in invasions, riots, arson and wars? They were and are men, of course not every one. However, all these acts of theirs are glorified as 'bravery,' and acts of courage. The same acts when committed by women are termed as aggressive, 'excesses' committed by them, because, the system has labeled aggressiveness as a male virtue. Hence, whenever young boys weep, they are ridiculed as girls. A boy defeating his opponent in a bout of boxing or in street-fights is encouraged. Even a five year old boy is sent as an 'escort' with his sixteen year old sister.[277] It stereotypes the virtues of aggressiveness, and protectiveness is inculcated in men right from childhood.

It is undeniable that the process of education begins in the family. And the family performs its role to the fullest satisfaction of the society. It teaches boys to be aggressive, studious, playful and energetic and trains them to do outside activities to share financial responsibilities and to protect the womenfolk of the family. Similarly, it cultivates in girls the 'feminine virtues' of delicateness, inertness, docility and obedience, keeping the family matters confined to the house.[278] In this way gender-based violence becomes a way of life, an accepted mode of behaviour, sanctioned by folkways and conventional morality as a subculture.[279]

Theological and Biblical Perspectives

Christianity developed amid patriarchal societies in which women were treated as objects rather than persons. To this day, women have neither been accorded equal rights within society or equal rights within religious communities. Even in Christian communities therefore, it is quite evident, how theological thought was framed and expounded in such a way that led to women's subordination, making

[277] Poornima Mohan, *Encyclopedia of Women* (Delhi: Indian Publisher's Distributors, 2000), p. 407.

[278] Ibid.

[279] S. K, *Women and Crime*, pp. 185-86.

them submissive to positions of authority throughout the Christian era. Beginning from the early Church Fathers, leading theologians were no exception and down to the present theologians and their articulations suppressed women in numerous ways. No doubt, many women too have supported their male counterparts in constructing their theological understanding towards male domination.

As Margaretha Hendricks-Ririmase[280] remarks, "the church for a long time has been developing its theology along the patriarchal line of thinking which is very damaging for women because it denies the dignity of women as created in the image of God, just as men are. This is the theology of violence. Because it fosters the violation of women's right and it deadens women's spirituality."[281] Theology of violence buries women's potential, talent and creativity by binding them to the stereotyped roles in homes. Thus, women lose their freedom to live their lives as God's image and as God created them to be (Genesis 1:26-28). Instead, it puts women as subordinate beings, who are easily violated against. This theology seems to make man the fortunate human species, created to be fully human and gives him all the privileges including the privilege to have dominion over women.[282] As Daly also put it, 'The entire conceptual systems of theology and ethics, developed under the conditions of patriarchy, have been the products of males and tend to serve the interests of sexist society…women's critique is not a few passages but a universe of sexist suppositions.'[283]

As mentioned above, Christian theology thus over the centuries has dealt with the understanding of men and women as they are on the whole vary inadequately. Even in the history of the church, the concept and description of God as 'male' has been over-emphasized and therefore assumed. 'Female descriptions have been almost totally neglected and therefore today they sound rather shocking to most ears. Very often, following the most primitive creation stories of Genesis the woman has been seen as created very much as an afterthought, second and subordinate to the man. The man has constituted the norm and the woman a deviation from it. 'Maleness' and 'femaleness' have thus been polarized in the human situation.'[284] In the following discussion let us examine three theological assumptions on which man's superiority over woman has been erected. These assumptions are based on the Creation account found in Genesis 1and 2:

---

[280] Margaretha Hendricks-Ririmase teaches Old Testament at the Theological Faculty of the Indonesian Christian University in the Moluccas, Indonesia.

[281] Margaretha Hendricks-Ririmase, "Theology and Violence against Women" in *CTC BULLETIN: Bulletin of the Program Area on Faith, Mission & Unity* (Theological Concerns) Christian Conference of Asia. ed. Hope S. Antone (Vol. XXI, No. 3 December 2005), p. 6.

[282] *Ibid.*, p. 6.

[283] M. Daly, *Beyond God the Father: Towards a philosophy of women's liberation* (London: Women's Press, 2nd edition, 1986), p. 4., also see in Nicola Slee (2003), p. 115.

[284] Mary John Mananzan, *Women in Asia: Status and Image* (Singapore: Christian Conference of Asia, 1979), p. 48.

a) God's primary creation is Adam (man), not Eve (woman). Since woman was created from a man's rib, she is derivative and secondary ontologically. Thus, the priority of creation indicates precedence in a hierarchy and therefore women are given an inferior status. In some churches, a woman becomes a member only through her husband and not directly as an individual. On the other hand, some hold the view that Eve is created out of Adam's rib, not from the head, nor from the feet or some parts of the body, as a symbol of their mutual partnership.
b) Woman, not man was the primary agent of the fall, and therefore 'all daughters of Eve' are to be regarded with contempt. This assumption is used to limit the ministry of women in certain respects as against the ministry of men.
c) That woman was created for man and therefore her existence is instrumental and not fundamental. This assumption has led to the abuse of girls and women in every aspect.[285]

The Holy Bible is the supreme authoritative word of God to the Christian to which he/she has to conform. However, it implies that a Christian could use particular verses of the Bible for the justification of certain undesirable behaviour. There is no exception for gender relations in which Bible verses[286] were used for subjugating women in Christian context.[287] Let us analyze a few verses which are used as justification for the subordination of women by men in the Christian context, Genesis 2:4-3:24:[288]

> These are the generations of the heavens and the earth when they were created...then the Lord God formed man from the dust of the ground, and breathed into his nostrils the breath of life; and the man became a living being....The Lord God took the man and put him in the garden of Eden to till it and keep it...Then the Lord God said, 'It is not good that the man should be alone; I will make him a helper as his partner'.... The man gave names to all cattle, and to the birds of the air, and to every animals of the field; but for the man there was not found a helper as his partner. So the Lord God caused a deep sleep to fall upon the man,

---

[285] Elizabeth Leelavathi Manasseh, "Gender Justice: Evangelical Perspectives," in *Evangelical Fellowship of India Women's Ministries Department: Gender or Giftedness* (Bangalore: Vishranthi Nilayam, November 1, 2003), pp. 5-6.

[286] The verses or texts used are taken from the New Revised Standard Version. (NRSV)

[287] Natalie Yap Boon Kiat, "Religion and Gender Relations, with Special Reference to the Presbyterian Church in Singapore" in *Asia Journal of Theology*, Volume 11 Number 1 April 1997, p. 46.

[288] *The Holy Bible: The New Revised Standard Version Catholic Edition* (Bangalore: Thomas Nelson for Theological Publications in India, 2005), pp. 2-3 (only relevant verses have been selected).

> and he slept; then he took one of his ribs and closed up its place with flesh....Then the man said, "This is now bone of my bones and flesh of my flesh; this one shall be called Woman, for out of man this one was taken."...The man said, "The woman whom you gave to be with me, she gave me fruit from the tree, and I ate.

This portion of the text basically recounts the story of the creation and the fall of Adam and Eve. Adam, the representative of men was created before Eve, who represents women. It is the general assumption that the, preceding events or persons are considered to be superior, if not better. This suggests that men are superior to women, and thus it justifies the subordination of women.

Eve is blamed for being deceived first into taking the forbidden fruit and then instigating Adam to eat it as well. Thus she is the cause of the original sin, as there are different punishments for Adam and Eve even though both sinned. Adam was to till the ground for food whereas Eve had to bear several burdens. Her childbearing pains were multiplied. Her desire was for her husband. And more importantly, her husband would rule over her. Both ostracism and blame are directed more strongly towards women.[289]

Ephesians 5:22-30:

> Wives, be subject to your husbands as you are to the Lord. For the husband is the head of the wife just as Christ is the head of the church, the body of which he is the saviour. Just as the church is subject to Christ, so also wives ought to be, in everything, to their husband.... In the same way, husbands should love their wives as they do their own bodies. He who loves his wife loves himself. For no one ever hates his own body, but he nourishes and tenderly cares for it, just as Christ does for the church, because we are members of his body.[290]

The text here says explicitly that women are to be subjected to their husbands. As for the husbands they are asked to love their wives. In the case of women, the writer appears to be pointing fingers and firmly telling them that they must be submissive to their husbands. On the other hand, men are told to love their wives. This does seem like the work of a patriarchal society. This is the way our existing theology has been formed and interpreted. 1Timothy 2:11-15:

> Let a woman learn in silence with full submission. I permit no woman to teach or to have authority over a man; she is to keep silent. For Adam was formed first, then Eve; and Adam was not deceived, but the woman was deceived and became a transgressor. Yet she will be saved through

[289] Natalie Yap Boon Kiat, (1997), pp. 46-47.

[290] *The Holy Bible* (NRSV, 2005), p. 195.

child bearing, provided they continue in faith and love and holiness, with modesty.[291]

Here women are again told to be submissive. Above that, she should only learn in silence. Women are not allowed to teach and have authority over men. The text also ostracizes Eve who was deceived, and transgressed against God whilst Adam was not considered to be deceived. Therefore, women could only be saved through child-bearing practiced with faith, love and holiness with modesty in their lifestyles. Here the question is what about those who do not bear children and who remain unmarried? Can they be saved? Are the believers of Christ justified through Paul's permission alone in having authority over women? These are some key references used to justify men's superiority in Christian Religious Education.

1 Corinthians 14:34-35: "Women should be silent in the churches. For they are not permitted to speak, but should be subordinate, as the law also says. If there is anything they desire to know, let them ask their husbands at home. For it is shameful for a woman to speak in church."[292] In this case, women are asked to be silent in the church, and sad to say it is considered shameful for women to speak there. The writer also adds that the law requires women to be subordinated. If they want to know anything they can only ask their husbands at home.

The portions of the text mentioned above have one major theme in common. It is the need for women to be submissive to men. Above that they are not allowed to speak, to teach and to have authority over men. They have to bear the sin of Eve and the punishment for the sin committed. Today, these verses have become a convenient source for justification of the subordination of women in the Christian context. Thus, churches, its policies and theological implications/ interpretations based on such ideology have resulted in the unfair treatment of women.

The other issue we need to be aware of is the context of the written texts. That is, the Bible was written almost entirely by men.[293] In addition, the Bible was written in patriarchal contexts, where men's superiority was fixed according to the strength and authority they possessed based on gender.[294] These assumptions have also led people to misinterpret some of the controversial passages found in the Pauline epistles such as 1Corinthians 11:2-16; and thus have become barriers to creating gender justice in many spheres of life. However, Scripture itself clearly says that 'God created both Adam and Eve in God's own image' and held them equally responsible for the fall (Genesis 3:1-19). The Bible also affirms that all

---

291 *Ibid.*, p. 208.

292 *The Holy Bible* (2005), p. 176.

293 There is no certainty as to whether the books of Ruth and Esther were actually written by women. There could be a possibility that these books were written by men.

294 Lee Ye Ja, "Sexual violence against Women with Disabilities," *In God's Image: Journal of Asian Women's Resource Centre for Culture and Theology*, Vol. 25, No. 2, June 2006, p. 27.

human beings have the same dignity and value in God's sight (Genesis 1:26-27; Acts 17:25-26; James 3:9). Thus, 'men and women are created in the image of God,' means that any kind of damage to the wholeness and dignity of a person would be just like attacking and defiling the image of God.[295] The question to these texts is, do we listen to God who created human beings in his own image or obey a mere human being who needs justifications.

Our present theology therefore needs to be re-appraised in the light of the newer understandings of what it means to be human and made in the image of God. We need to recognize that all persons have 'male and female' elements and characteristics. And we find this a liberating notion in our relationships with one another. So, theology needs to use the whole range of description in its understanding about God and his actions towards his own creation.

Thus, examples are cited in the biblical-theological reflection including women who were negotiating their lives within a patriarchal context. Therefore, while recognizing the unique significance of the biblical records, theology needs to stress the importance of one's contemporary context and one's present experience of God. Because, the truths contained in the scriptures have been of vast importance in the past and they continue to be important. Therefore, the whole biblical texts need to be re-read and reinterpreted, reframing the theological thoughts in accordance with time and space, to understand God's intention in fulfilling His ministry in this universe.

As clearly examined above, Paul's Epistles have been interpreted in such a way as to cause confusion and misunderstanding about women, even causing discrimination and oppression against women. Thus, the existing forms of theology and biblical teachings are often oppressive and derogatory to the dignity of women. Even on subjects which are directly concerned about women, it is usually men who formulate the theory and begin to use them as norms. On the other hand, very often women too are ignorant and blind to realize and foresee the fact which hinders their freedom. Thus, those who are deprived of their living and cannot exercise their full God-given opportunities are living under violence. Women often must contend not only with vertical violence from the male-dominated systems in their society, but also with horizontal violence from other women or oppressive groups who take out their frustration and anger on each other.[296]

While interpreting gender-based violence from biblical perspectives, as a Christian what one needs to bear in mind is that, people who have grown up in the church have been taught a patriarchal, hierarchal model of relationships between men and women, and thus also the role of men and women within the church. Therefore, it is high time to correct it with proper education, based on

---

[295] Lee Ye Ja, (June, 2006), p. 28.

[296] *Discrimination Against Women: A Report of a World Council of Churches Consultation West Berlin 1974* (Geneva: World Council of Churches), pp. 86-98.

the biblical principles which reach every heart irrespective of gender, and this knowledge of truth could be imparted through Christian Religious Education. In this context, Faith Martin, one of the theologians points out that 'so much of what molds our lives does not come from written laws, but from customs taught through painful experiences and rejections-codes of civilization so powerful, so elementary, that we do not question their validity.' This shows how traditional teaching determines our religious beliefs and practices too. Within these traditional models, the function of women is restricted, whereas men are encouraged to function according to abilities, gifts and call.

Thus, as discussed elsewhere, the patriarchal social order, into which Christ came, is perceived by traditionalists to be the determinant form of Christianity for all time.[297] Thus, we are constantly challenged by all those cultural bondages by which women are placed in subjugation. As discussed in the preceding chapter, since biblical texts support women's submissiveness, men are considered as powerful to rule over their wives. So far, the Bible and the Christian traditional instructions have often ignored women's experiences. In the following work we would examine the inherent violence in religion.

Inferiority Status of Women in Scripture

Biblical texts emerge out of an ancient patriarchal culture and reflect patriarchal values and norms. Biblical texts themselves, then, are clearly problematic. But, it is not only the texts per se which are problematic; it is also the ways in which the texts have been used, interpreted and handed on to subsequent generations which constitute another layer of the problem. One of the feminist theologians, Nicola says, "The biblical texts have come down to us through thousands of years of translation and interpretation, a complex process almost wholly in male hands. We read the texts today 'through' this long tunnel, and this profoundly shapes how we hear and receive them."[298] Thus, this complex process of transformation and interpretation has functioned in a number of different ways to provide the biblical texts an oppressive edge for women. Therefore, in many cases, biblical texts and Christian traditions about women have been ignored and sidelined in preaching, teaching, and commentary and exegetical interpretations.[299] On the other hand, wherever women appear in the texts, it is clear that their status, position, service and values are largely assumed to be lesser than that of men. This reflects the whole patriarchal world-view of the biblical era, in which women were generally regarded as inferior to men, as infantile or incomplete persons. Phyllis

---

[297] Marilyn B. Smith, "*Gender or Giftedness: A Challenge to rethink the basis for leadership within the Christian community*, prepared for the World Evangelical Fellowship Commission on Women's Concerns (Bangalore: Vishranthi Nilayam, 2003), p. 7.

[298] Nicola Slee, *Faith and feminism: An Introduction to Christian Feminist Theology* (Wands worth High Street, London: Darton, Longman and Todd Ltd, 2003), p. 17.

[299] Nicola Slee, (2003), p. 17.

Trible summarizes the situation thus: Less desirable in the eyes of her parents than a male child, a girl stayed close to her mother, but her father controlled her life until he relinquished her to another man for marriage. If either of these male authorities permitted her to be mistreated, even abused, she had to submit without recourse...The narrative literature makes clear that from birth to death the Hebrew women belonged to men.

What such narratives show, the legal corpus amplifies. Defined as the property of men (Exodus 20:17: Deuteronomy 5:21), women did not control their own bodies. A man was expected to marry a virgin, though his own virginity was not needed to be intact. It was felt that a wife guilty of earlier fornication violated the honour and power of both her father and husband. Death by stoning was the penalty (Deuteronomy 22:13-21). Moreover, a woman had no right to divorce (Deuteronomy 24:1-4) and most often, no right to property. Excluded from priesthood, she was considered far more unclean than the male (Leviticus 15). Even her monetary value was less (Leviticus 27:1-7).[300] Thus, there are a number of texts both in the New and Old Testament which discuss women as subordinates as they received unequal treatment from the society.

But, when it comes to Jesus' ministry, he challenges certain aspects of the legal situation, as it is evident in his treatment of the woman caught in adultery (John 8) and his teaching on marriage and divorce (mark 10:2ff.; Mathew 19:3 ff.; Mathew 5:27 ff.). Throughout his earthly ministry, Jesus treated women with dignity and respect in a manner certainly unusual. Thus, women fare rather better in the New Testament, particularly in the gospels, where there are many incidents that centre on Jesus' meetings with women, has conversation and relationship with them. Since the Bible is regarded as the authoritative and normative witness to divine revelation in Christian tradition, it provides the Christian with its dominant narratives, images and symbols, and is a primary source in preaching, teaching, prayer, worship, doctrine and ethics. But, the Bible is also a deeply patriarchal and androcentric text.[301]

Thus, the Bible itself and its interpretations are problematic not only for women but even for the whole society because people assume that the Bible is the Word of God, a book with authority. We often question, how can women read the Bible as a liberating and empowering word of God? With that in mind various strategies for re-reading the scriptures have been developed by feminist theologians and sympathizers who critique this issue of gender-based violence. All these need to be incorporated in Christian religious education ministry if need be to impart a holistic attitude towards women and to overcome gender-based violence in society.

---

[300] Phyllis Trible, "Feminist hermeneutics and biblical studies", in A Loads (ed), *Feminist Theology: A reader,* (London: SPCK, 1990), p. 24 also see in Nicola Slee (2003), p. 16.

[301] Nicola Slee, (2003), p. 13.

Religion's Construction of the Concept of Women

According to Erich Neumann's theory, western philosophers and theologians from antiquity to modernity have constructed notions of women that allow the violence of male domination over women. They defined the male person as the norm for humanity, and the female person as the 'other.' Some see a woman merely as a 'womb,' an object to be used.[302] A few examples can be drawn from the philosophers. For Plato, 'woman is a fallen soul, an inferior copy of man who is the true human.' Aristotle also says, 'woman is weak in nature because she is a mutilated man.' Since woman's faculty is weak, he insisted that 'a man must rule over woman.'[303] It can be argued that their definitions are without any proof whether it is their own assumptions or out of their own creations out of frustration from women. These kinds of notions and constructions became stumbling blocks for the upcoming philosophers, building blocks of their negative thoughts about women thus misleading others. These statements are biased judgments on women. Therefore, today we could see those ideologies are in practice and made as norms, in which every female member in the universe experiences all sorts of violence, not only physical torture but mental, moral and economic disparity as led by gender bias.

Along with those above mentioned philosophers, G. F. Hegel too correlated the qualities of female and male genitals with mental abilities of human beings, and asserted that women's cerebrality is inferior compared to men. He further said, "The difference between men and women is like that between animals and plants."[304] This view can be challenged that, how can a human being's worth could be categorized with animals and plants which do not have the rational instinct. Since, by nature, plants can be eaten up by animals any time anywhere, so also a woman can be swallowed by man or killed. This kind of ideology was implanted from the very beginning of human existence. This could be one of the reasons why gender-based violence is continuing in every society whether it is in the patriarchal form of society or not. It could be argued that, since the present educational theories and theological exercises are based on those irrational and senseless philosophies, especially in regard to gender understanding from its inception till today, women are regarded as objects and categorized thus with different objects.

As elucidated, the philosophies which were handed down through different generations have fatally influenced the whole discourses of Christian theologians and their interpretations of the Christian traditions. As Muriel Orevillo-

[302] Muriel Orevillo-Montenegro, "Finding Our Voice and Subjectivity" in *In God's Image: Asian Women Overcoming Violence, Journal of Asian Women's Resource Centre for Culture and Theology,* Vol. 24, No. 1, March 2005, p. 12.

[303] *Ibid.*, p. 12.

[304] *Ibid.*, p. 12.

Montenegro[305] has rightly pointed out in her article 'Finding Our Voice and Subjectivity,' "Theologies in the past centuries tended to be anti-woman and misogynist."[306] Thus, the early Church Fathers and theologians had developed their theologies and philosophies about women's incapability and objectivity. Notable in this are St. Augustine of Hippo, Aristotle and St. Thomas Aquinas. For Augustine, women are only baby-making machines whose natural "use" is for procreation. He further believed that women would not attain salvation apart from their husbands. According to Aristotle (384-322 BC), "The female is a female by virtue of a certain lack of qualities-a natural defectiveness-a misbegotten male," he also calls women '*arren peperomenon*,' which means, 'a mutilated or imperfect male.'"[307]

As with Augustine, St Thomas Aquinas also developed the Aristotelian view and insisted that women are defective and lack wisdom. Thomas says, "women do not correspond to 'nature's first intention,' which aims at perfection (men), but to 'nature's second intention, (to such things as) decay, deformity, and the weakness of age'"[308] It is right to note that, it was on ly nine centuries after Aristotle's death, in the year 585 AD, a gathering assembled in a general council for all of France, the second Synod of Macon, forty-three Christian bishops and twenty men representing other bishops debated, among other things, a most peculiar topic; "Are women human and fully 'person' (*homo*)?" When a vote was finally taken, in the infinite wisdom of the males present, women were officially declared human![309] Thus Christian theology functioned for centuries as a potent culture force declaring women inferior beings, evil, defiling, dangerous and even grotesque.

Along with the philosophies of above mentioned theologians, early Church Father Tertullian (c160-230) also said: "Do you know that each of you women is an Eve?... 'You are the gate of Hell' ('the devil's gateway,' it is sometimes translated), 'you are the temptress of the forbidden tree', 'you are the first deserter

---

305 Muriel Orevillo-Montenegro is a Filipino feminist theologian. Her other fields of interest are ethics and ecumenics. She has been involved in church and non-government organizations that address issues affecting women and children in urban and rural settings in the Philippines.

306 *Ibid.*, p. 13.

307 Uta Ranke-Heinemann, *Eunuchs for the Kingdom of Heaven: Women, Sexuality and the Catholic Church,* trans. Peter Heinegg (New York: Doubleday, 1990), p. 187, also see Elizabeth Dodson Gray, "Feminist Theology and Religious Education" in *Theologies of Religious Education*, ed. Randolph Crump Miller (Birmingham Alabama, Religious Education Press, 1995), p. 202.

308 *Ibid.*, 188.

309 Gregory of Tours, *History of the Franks,* trans. O.M. Dalton (Oxford: At the Clarendon Press, 1927), p. 8, 20; 344-345; also Charles Joseph Hefele, *A History of the Councils of the Church from the Original Documents,* trans. William R. Clark, vol. 4 (451-680 AD) (Edinburgh: T&T. Clark, 1895), 406-409; *Theologies of Religious Education* (1995), p. 203.

of the divine law.'"[310] Echoes of Tertullian's words persist in Christian religious teaching of subsequent centuries, and till today many church's teachings refers to that kind of ideas while trying to justify the supremacy of men.[311] Thus, many a time preachers refer to the woman as the first human being who committed sin by eating the fruit in the Garden of Eden.

Likewise, one could trace the roots of gender-based violence in the philosophies and theologies developed by the early Church Fathers and theologians whose wisdom and philosophy were highly respected and accepted through out the generations, whose teachings were glorified and worshipped as powerful and authoritative. Every religion thus, has its share of perpetuating traditions that negate the personhood of women. Whatever then the traditions that continue till today, whether it is religious, socio-economic, cultural and political, they are based on the philosophies handed down from time immemorial. If that hinders the present society, this structural set up should be challenged in order to achieve a healthy atmosphere where every person lives in peace and harmony.

Theories of Motivation on Gender-based Violence

One of the important questions that are asked by feminist theologians, sociologists, criminologists, human rights groups and the public alike is: what causes men to be violent, abusive, and cruel towards women? Therefore, in order to answer those questions we need to analyze various types of violence against women and their varied patterns, which calls for examination of some of the theories. A well-known sociologist and prominent writer on social concerns, specifically on women and violence in India, Ram Ahuja[312] has identified several theories which he believes have some relevance for understanding violence in society and gender-based violence in particular. These theories range from intra-psychic theories to macro-sociological theories. They are classified on the basis of three levels of analysis: (1) psychiatric or psycho-pathological analysis, (2) socio-psychological analysis, and (3) sociological or socio-cultural analysis.[313]

---

[310] Tertullian, "On the Apparel of Women," in *The Ante-Nicene Fathers: Translations of the Fathers Down to A.D. 325*, eds. Alexander Roberts and James Donaldson (Buffalo: Christian Literature, 1885), vol. 4, 14.; *Theologies of Religious Education (1995),* p. 203.

[311] It is a tradition of the Baptist Churches in Nagaland to conduct a Women's service every Thursday, and once in the author's church while they were conducting a special thanks giving service, they invited one of the deacons to preach and surprisingly, he as the only male present in the worship had mentioned in his message that, "You women, you know why you are having this extra service? It is because Eve was the first person who committed sin in the Garden of Eden, you need to have one more service then for man and children."

[312] Ram Ahuja retired as Professor and Head of Sociology Department, University of Rajasthan, Jaipur in 1988. He has done extensive research on the topic-violence on women.

[313] Ram Ahuja, *Violence against Women* (Jaipur and New Delhi: Rawat Publications, Reprinted 2003), p. 201.

In sum, the psycho-pathological model focuses on the personality characteristics of offenders and victims as the chief determinants of criminal violence. This model also includes an analysis that links mental illness, alcohol and other intra-individual phenomena to acts of violence. Secondly, the socio-psychological model examines the types of everyday interactions which are the precursors of violence. Lastly, the sociological or socio-cultural model provides a macro-level analysis of criminal violence. This model examines criminal violence in terms of socially-structured inequality, and social and cultural attitudes and norms regarding anti-social behaviour and inter-personal relations.[314] Thus, gender-based violence is caused because of the socially-structured inequality or socially constructed imbalance and divisions between male and female.

Psycho-Pathological Theory

This theory gives two different explanations. According to one,[315] the causes of violence against women arise from the offender's psychological problems like depressive impulsiveness, uncontrolled emotions, etc. According to the other,[316] violence against women arises out of psychological problems of victims. However, there are no adequate data to support either of these points of views. It further says, "If women who are battered, raped, tortured, molested or kidnapped behave strangely, it is possibly the consequence and not the cause of being battered or raped or kidnapped."[317] Of course this theory may have reasons to say that violence on women arises due to psychological problems of the woman itself in some cases as cited above. But it could be responded that, both men and women face psychological problems as noted above, and in certain cases both encounter the same situation where they can be easily battered, tortured and molested by looking at their behaviours, but it is the men who take the chance to batter women due to the superiority complex which leads to gender-based violence.

Socio-Psychological Theories of Aggression

(1) Frustration-Aggression Theory

This theory first stated in 1939 by Dollard, et. al., derived many of its basic postulates from the Freudian theory. It explains the process by which aggression is directed to the source of frustration. The aggressive drive is an innate drive. It helps to explain individual violence because the individual is the focus of high personal involvement and of high frustration in the family.[318] It can be argued that

---

314 Ram Ahuja, *Violence Against Women* (2003), p. 202.

315 Ram Ahuja, (2003), see Kembe, Silverman, Steele, Droegemueller and Silver, *The Battered Child Syndrome,* 1962.

316 *Ibid.*, p. 202, see Snell, Rosenwald and Robey, *The Wifebeater's Wife*, 1964.

317 Ram Ahuja (2003), p. 202.

318 Ram Ahuja (2003), p. 203.

an individual's aggressiveness may not be totally an innate drive yet it could be from both the environment and inner instability which frustrates them when they encounter different situations. This is true according to John Dollar's assumptions.

> According to John Dollar, "whenever something interferes with an individual's attempt to reach some goal or end, he/she feels frustrated and frustration in turn leads to some form of aggression."[319] But it could be argued that, aggressive actions are not an automatic reaction as a consequence of frustration, and their occurrence depends upon numerous factors. This theory is criticized on the following grounds that: (1) the relationship between frustration and aggression is not innate, (2) a wide variety of responses may result from frustration, and aggression is not the only response, and (3) aggression may be an adaptive response and a rational choice of behaviour.[320]

Other criticisms against this theory are: (1) human behaviour is not an extension of animal instinct or innate behaviour but the product of a complex interplay of biological and environmental factors. An individual's social behaviour depends upon his/her social and cultural milieu; (2) responses to the frustrations are learned just like any other social behaviour and what is learned has a lot to do with the socialization practices which themselves differ from group to group and society to society; (3) people could do many things though they never do them, and hence receive neither rewards or punishments. Thus, people's own experience of rewards or punishments is not a necessary ingredient in the formulation of their behaviour patterns. Rather, they can anticipate whether a certain action will get those rewards or punishment by learning what is happening when others do it; (4) this theory overlooks the cases in which aggression can be an instrumental act for aims other than causing injury or pain; (5) this theory cannot explain the epidemiological aspect of the offence.

> In this connection, Berkowitz (1962) made a distinction between the reactive type of aggression and habitual and learned aggression which receive situational reinforcement and facilitation. In the latter case, aggression becomes customary, persistent and not just an ad hoc reaction. This learning and being exposed to aggressive modes of behaviour creates an aggressive view of the world.[321] This aggression-frustration theory vividly projects that, it is not innate behaviour but learned one which is enhanced by socialization, and becomes customary for a given society. Aggressive actions and frustration-thoughts are expressed in accordance with social norms and beliefs in which men's

---

[319] *Ibid.*, p. 203.

[320] *Ibid.*, p. 204.

[321] Ram Ahuja (2003), pp. 204-205.

superiority and inferiority of the female are maintained. For instance, if the society expects from every woman modesty in life in any situation and if the women/wives do not follow that, then it may also stimulate men's/husbands' attitudes leading to frustration and aggression.

2. Perversion Theory

Psychoanalysts explain violence on the basis of the Theory of Perversion (Gilles Pie, 1952) and the Theory of Symptom Formation. They do not regard perverts as constitutionally inferior people but maintain that perversion develops from instincts (Menachem, Amer, *Patterns in Forcible Rape,* 1971). According to Freud's early theory (1949), perversion essentially means persistence in the adult of infantile instincts and behaviour at the expense of adult behaviour. Violence can be the product of strong inborn drives or of pathological experiences in infancy or early childhood (Johnson, 1956). In the latter cases, childhood conceptions of the relations between the sexes as being aggressive and sadistic and the idea of pleasure as a negative process, essentially achieved by relief from a state of 'un pleasure' are carried into adulthood. This theory was considered important because it was supported by the clinically established fact that there is a higher incidence of perversion among males than among females.

Even though, this theory of perversion is based on the inborn instincts/drives or of pathological experiences, it could be argued that, violence might have been institutionalized and supported by the culture itself. As a person, whether a boy or a girl, from the very first hour of its birth itself, particular cultural formalities/rituals start depending on the sex of the baby. Thus, as persons grow up, they are nurtured with all sorts of norms and practices, which may turn out to be violent as they think they are superior.

3. Self-Attitude Theory

This theory maintains that in a society, a culture, or a group that values violence, persons of low-esteem may seek to bolster their image in the eyes of others and themselves by carrying out violent acts. (Gelles & Straus, 1979).<<<<< According to this theory, all individuals who use violence against women (that is rapists, abductors, murderers, and batterers) suffer from low self-esteem. But, there is not much support for this assumption. This theory could be challenged, as all individuals who use violence may not suffer from low-esteem alone, there could be some socio-cultural and economic factors too to use violence against women. There are ample examples for this. One of the best examples in India could be the violence embedded in dowry issues. Another universal example is due to power and authority vested in men due to patriarchy.

From the gender-based violence perspective too, this self-attitude theory can be accepted in a way as men think that they are superior to women in every aspect of their lives. A few instances could be-in terms of strength, as society has placed them in a higher level, in terms of intellectuals, as they are regarded as wise and capable. So, according to this theory, when a man thinks that he is unable to control a woman or feels low-esteemed, he turns out to be a violent person.

4. Motive Attribution Theory

This theory specifies the process used by actors to impute the motivations (dispositional state) of others. It explains how the structure of relations is such that there is a high probability of malevolent intent being attributed to the actions of other individuals, thereby setting in motion an escalating cycle of resentment and aggression. According this theory, cases of violence are not always stimulated, aided and abetted by others; a large numbers are the result of individual's own attitudes and social structures.[322] Thus, according to this theory, violence may be embedded through outside activities. It could be through the societal rules and laws which motivate certain actions set for a group of people in order to maintain traditions or standards in the given society.

Socio-Cultural Theories

(1) Structural Theory

This theory asserts that social groups differ in respect to their typical levels of stress, deprivation and frustration, and rely on the resources at their disposal to deal with these stresses. This theory thus explains an individual's action in terms of the ways it is shaped or determined by social forces of one kind or another. The offender's violence is seen as determined by the degree of his/her integration in the system. One consequence of accepting this position is that the action of individuals has nothing to do with their personalities and values, and that violence cannot be described in terms of conflict, suppression, sublimation, guilt, and so on. According to this theory, an individual's actions are determined and applied by the social structures, in which any person is obliged to accept. For example, the caste system in Indian society, where certain groups of people compel others to follow the dowry system, child marriage, and even restricting women in the decision-making process, etc.

(2) System Tension and Feedback System Theory

This theory was developed by Straus (a general Systems Theory of Violence between Family Members, 1973) to explain intra-family violence. According to this theory, violence is precipitated by factors such as stress and inter-individual conflict and is followed by consequences which maintain or escalate violence in the family and in society. Tension in the broad sense, of which stress and strain are manifestations under conditions of felt block age, is ever present in one form or

---

[322] Ram Ahuja, (2003), pp. 205-207.

another throughout the socio-cultural system-sometimes as frustration, aggression or normative deviation and sometimes as conflict and competition or upheaval and destruction.

According to this approach, aggression is recognized as a basic element in personality structure, personality as a factor in social relations among people, especially between the sexes. In relations between them, the male is perceived as aggressive and the female as passive, which may sometimes take the form of direct aggression of the male against the female.[323] Aggression is concerned thus with personality and not the result of the social system.

(3) Theory of Sub-Culture of Violence

This theory[324] claims that the life-circumstances of certain groups trigger violence as a relatively commonplace outcome of social interaction. It also asserts that values and norms provide meaning and direction to violent acts and thus facilitate or bring about violence in situations specified by these norms and values. In this context, anthropologist Oscar Lewis (1959, 1961, 1966)[325] has explained violence in terms of the culture of poverty. According to this view, the important traits of poverty are fatalism, authoritarianism and violence, as well as a sharp contrast between advocated and actual sexual conduct. This sub-culture of poverty explanation for criminal violence has been challenged on the ground that generally the poor are law-abiding and the affluent are not.[326] According to this theory, if the violators are from different social status, they will treat the issue according to their positions where weaker profiled one will be the victim in any case. As men are valued as superior by society, they overpower their female counterparts. On the other hand, particularly, when it comes to sexual actions, it is always the men who overshadow women.

(4) Resource Theory

This theory of intra-family violence developed by W.J. Goode[327] was in fact the first theological approach applied explicitly to family violence. Goode (1971), states that all social systems rest on some degree of force or threat. The greater the resources a person can command within a social system, the more force he/ she can muster. However, the more resources a person can command, the less the chances are that a person will actually deploy violence. Thus, violence is one of the resources that individuals' collectivities use to maintain or advance their interests. But violence is used as a last resort when all other resources are exhausted.

---

323 Ram Ahuja, (2003), p. 209.

324 Wolfgang and Pheracuti, *The Subculture of Violence,* 1967.

325 Finkelhor et al., *The Dark Side of Families*, 1983.

326 Ram Ahuja, (2003), p. 211.

327 W.J. Goode, *Force and Violence in the Family,* 1971.

Applying this set of assumptions to the family, Goode explains that the family is a power system in which four sets of resources are in operation to maintain stability: economic variables, prestige or respect, love, and force or threat of force. For example, when a child feels he/she is missing out on respect or love or faithfulness, force is the only resource he/she has at his/her command. Another example is that of a husband who wants to be the dominant family member but has little education, job prestige or income and lacks inter-personal skills, is likely to resort to violence to be the dominant person.[328] This perspective suggests that violence is more likely to occur when a man perceives his status to be inconsistent with his traditional power in the family which has been eroded because women's power has increased. He resorts to violence to compensate the loss of his power over his wife.[329]

(5) Patriarchy Theory

This theory developed by R.E. Dobash, and R. Dobash[330] maintains that throughout history, violence has been systematically directed towards women. Dobash's central theoretical argument is that patriarchy leads to the subordination of women and contributes to a historical pattern of systematic violence directed against females. Without further explanation one can assume that patriarchy maintains lower status for women and lifts up men's position, because patriarchy defines women as inferior. Therefore, in every patriarchal society, men control women and overpower their mobility, in which the powerless are compelled to listen to the one whom they assume to be superior to them.

Conflict and Control Theories

Scholars like Foucault (1975), Thompson (1977) and Rothman (1980) have presented a domination model of deviance. They have talked of rules imposed on the powerless by the powerful. Imposing varied restrictions on women and compelling them to remain dependent on men economically, socially, religiously and emotionally to make them realize that they are 'weak' and 'powerless' in all respects, stands as an example of this argument. Schur (1983) contends that male-control deviance-labeling results in their continued dominance in most spheres of life.

The constraints on women's rights can be interpreted as a function of the successful definition of women as different from and inferior to men. According to this theory, "Man talks of woman 'not in herself,' but as 'relative' to him. She is not regarded as an autonomous being. She is differentiated with reference to man

---

[328] Ram Ahuja, (2003), pp. 211-212.

[329] Madhurima, *Violence Against Women: Dynamics of Conjugal Relations* (New Delhi: Gyan publishing house, 1996), p. 44.

[330] R. E. Dobash, and R. Dobash, *Violence Against Wives*, 1979.

and not him with reference to her. She is the incidental, the inessential as opposed to the essential. He is the subject, he is the Absolute; she is the Other."[331]

This theory also says that sex-role norms clearly differentiate men from women. When these norms become internalized, they are accepted as facts and seldom questioned. Millet (1970) has said: "Because of our social circumstances, male and female are really two cultures and their life experiences are utterly different. Women live in such a different economic, cultural and social world from men that their reactions cannot be understood from a master model developed in male society. Thus, in every society, women are (1) declared as different, and (ii) defined as inferior, and (iii) women as stereotypes are justified, (vi) they are systematically deprived of rights, and (v) all attempts at change are restricted,"[332] Thus, women's mobility is controlled by men who are supposed to share their responsibility and privileges as their co partner.

1. Interactionist Deviance Theory

This theory explains family violence in terms of sex role or gender norms, i.e., differential expectations for values, attitudes and behaviours as a function of one's gender. These norms serve as important standards against which women and men are evaluated through application of various sanctions (Schur, 1984) >>>>>foot note). This is the real picture existing in every society, where every activity is designed and exercise-based on gender.

According to the prevalent sex-role norms, a husband expects a "good wife' to behave in a certain manner. She has to run the household smoothly, ensure children's well-mannered behaviour, avoid assertiveness and remain submissive to men folk and elders in the family. Any show of independence on her part would violate sex-role expectations for female behaviour. It also says that when women do not behave like the male's ideal of a wife, husbands use violence against them to make them conform to norms.[333] Thus, in some cultures, beating wives is the norm to teach them to behave correctly and obediently. This theory can be challenged from the biblical perspective where it is mentioned that God made both men and women in His own image, and as He shows no one is ever right to rule over someone in any case.

2. General Systems Theory

One of the theories very close to interactionist deviance theory is the general system theory. Though there may be better theories but for this research we will consider the theory which was formulated by Straus. Straus tried to apply a general

---

[331] Ram Ahuja., (2003), p. 213.

[332] Ram Ahuija, (2003), p. 15.

[333] Ram Ahuja, (2003), pp. 214-215.

systems theory approach to explain family violence.[334] According to him, family violence is a product of the system rather than of individual pathology. He argues that society expects a wife to be more committed to the marital relationship; this commitment represents a positive feed back loop that encourages violence in the future.[335] Therefore, whenever there is any conflict between spouses, it is always the wife who has to forgive and accept the husband's ill treatments and misbehaviours with instructions that the woman has to be humbled enough to accept her husband whatever the crime he has been doing against his wife.

Further, relative power of the husband and wife also becomes the source of conflict. If a husband feels that he should or must have power in the relationship, he may use violence to enforce that power. A husband may also use violence as a response to a wife's attempt to break off the relationship.[336] In a similar way, in the course of relationship when a girl proposes to break up the affair, boys spoil their whole life by throwing acid, killing (by using sharp weapons), or kidnap and take away to a far place forcefully.[337]

This theory also believes that if once a wife accepts violent behaviour of the husband, it provides positive feedback and there are chances that the incident will be repeated again. When a wife gives into the violent behaviour of the husband, her response represents the positive feedback to violence and it soon becomes an established pattern. When a battered woman gets any support from her informal or formal group, it will lead to a change in the basic rules of the system. However, when she fails to get any support, the pattern of violence is strengthened.[338] Thus, very often though a wife feels that she should bring to the public notice yet if the family members are not willing to support her, the same pattern continues and it becomes a system. The present social system where women are regarded as inferior and men superior has this at its beginning.

Different theoretical perspectives discussed above indicate that sociologists, anthropologists and psychologists, are seriously trying to address the problem of gender-based violence issues which engender violence on women. All the theories examined so far point to the innate survival, patriarchal and discriminative notions within especially among men which energized by gender bias give over to overt violence on women for power, prestige, recognition and so on as they are attested by culture, tradition, religion and biological differences.

---

[334] Madhurima, *Violence Against Women: Dynamics of Conjugal relationship* (New Delhi: Gyan publishing house, 1996), p. 48.

[335] Madhurima (1996), p. 48.

[336] *Ibid.*, p. 48.

[337] These incidents are a regular feature in every society. They are projected through the media and also many go unreported due to non-availability of the medium or due to threat from the exploiters.

[338] Madhurima (1996), p. 48.

No doubt, even the few theologians who are taking interest and are serious about the issues, have made it a core issue in the public deliberations. But, when it comes to church educational ministry, this issue is left far behind. Thus, it is imperative, to take this into account in the church educational teaching ministry, in order to educate people to make use of their God-given potentialities without exploiting others' personhood and relieve them from the traditional sex roles, in which women and girl child have been the most victims throughout the centuries.

Chapter 4

Gender-Based Violence in Nagaland

General Understanding of Nagaland Context

Every research analysis is done with a critical evaluation and examination of the given context, without which the findings and analysis will be vague. However, it is beyond the scope of the present research to explain the chosen context in detail, therefore in the following section the researcher examines the context of Nagaland in brief before further examination of the gender-based violence in the society. The State of Nagaland lies with an area of 16,579 sq. km. The State is bounded by Assam on the west, Myanmar on the East, Arunachal Pradesh on the North and by Manipur on the South, and it runs more or less parallel to the left bank of the Brahmaputra.[339] As mentioned earlier, there are sixteen major tribes in Nagaland, which constitute the Naga population in India. The population of Nagaland as per the Census of India, stood at 19,88,636 as on March 31, 2001, out of which 14,4,446 are males and 9,46,950 females showing an increase of 7,79,090 persons as compared to 1991 Census.[340]

Like other states in the country, Naga society is also a patriarchal society in which women are regarded as inferior and dependent. Owing to this patriarchal society in nature, Naga society is dominated by men in every aspect of their lives - socio-economic, political, and religious affairs, where women were allowed to play only the subordinate role in every aspect. In other words, patriarchy has permeated

---

[339] *Statistical Atlas of Nagaland 1991*, p. 8.

[340] Purtongzuk Longchar, *Historical Development of the Ao Nagas in Nagaland* (Dimapur: Print Home, 2002), p. 2.

all aspects of life and has been instrumental in defining gender relations based on the biological determinants of male and female, but not on God's edict of creation. Church hierarchy has allowed patriarchy to influence its interpretation of God's Word and has similarly sanctioned male dominance in its governance of the people of God.[341]

When women play a leading role, men feel that they are insulted, and thus oppose women's leadership. Thus, women's role is confined either to the home or private sectors. Till today under no circumstances a woman becomes an administrator of the village council, neither the executive secretary which is the highest post in the church ministry. Thus, as long as villages, towns and the churches continue to exclude women in the decision-making processes and negate the importance of their participation in shaping history, there is something amiss in their understanding of Christian principles. In this context Elsa Tamez writes, "A society in which women have an inferior status and are not partners with men in the struggle for justice and in the attempt to live as friends is also far from representing the Trinitarian mystery of God."[342] Thus, in Naga society women are deprived from involving in community decision-making and not allowed to inherit family and community properties like men. On the other hand, when it comes to getting education, they are not given enough chance to get higher education as their counter parts.[343]

Amidst these restrictions there is an increase in literacy rate, of late among women in Nagaland (40.39 in 1981-54.75 in 1991census).[344] Women's situation is becoming far better than before in many ways, especially for those who are in urban areas. Nevertheless, this does not mean that women have equal status in every aspect or have the same opportunity to access anywhere as their male counter parts. Still, there are ample of restrictions imposed on women in Naga society. What R. L. Hnuni has mentioned is applicable to Naga women too. She says, "The tribal women of the hills enjoyed freedom right from primitive days till today so far as mixing with the opposite sex is concerned. Their social

[341] Heshi Singson, "A Critical Analysis of Women's Role in Thadou-Kuki Church" in *No More Sorrow in God's Garden of Justice: Tribal Women Doing Theology*, ed. Limatula Longkumer Rajabari, Jorhat: Women's Study Department Eastern Theological College, 2007), p. 120.

[342] Maria Bingemer, "Reflection on Trinity," in *Through Her Eyes, Women's Theology from Latin America,* ed. Elsa Tamez (Maryknoll, New York: 1989), p. 79, see in *No more Sorrow in God's Garden of Justice: Tribal Women Doing Theology*, ed. Limatula Longkumer (Rajabari, Jorhat: Women's Study Department Eastern Theological College, 2007), p.12.

[343] It was till 1960s, women were not allowed to go for schooling, rather they were forced to work hard through cultivation and through other means in order to support their brothers. We could see very retired women in the state. Even today, especially in technical education very few women are involved.

[344] R.L. Hnuni, "Women in North East India: Vision for Tribes," in, *Women and Society: A Reader in Women's Studies,* ed. Nirmala Jeyaraj (Lady Doak College, Madurai: ISPCK, Delhi, 2005), p. 346.

freedom is often mistaken by outsiders specially those who come from Hindu and Muslim backgrounds." She further quotes the words of N. Chatterji about the condition of women that the interdependence and mutual appreciation of each other's position and responsibilities appears to point out that the 'condition of women in their society was in no way inferior to that of men and she suffered none of these derogatory and discriminatory treatment as may be found in some of the more advanced societies.'[345]

This is the view of an outsider who does not reflect on the real social life of the tribal people including the Nagas. The real situation about traditional practices which derogate women's whole life cannot be easily judged by others unless they attempt a critical research of that very context and prove the reality. Freedom in socialization and mixing with the opposite sex outside alone does not mean that there is no domination, subjugation or discrimination in the society. In every country and state there is a bias and mistreatment towards women from time immemorial due to the understanding of women as subordinate beings and sub-human as mentioned elsewhere.

Like any other state in the country, today Naga society is also experiencing a mixture of traditional and modern values. The Nagas have the belief that women must get proper education, employment, health care and more freedom of choice. They encourage and accept their entry into the professions and positions of power. On the other hand, the basic view of women as inferior and subordinate remains unchanged.[346] Women themselves have been entrapped by that understanding, adjusting to the traditional societal norms without realizing the fact that it derogates their lives. Some women even have opposed and showed disagreement to the ideology of women's liberation/women's empowerment from all sorts of gender-based violence with the comment they do not experience gender bias in the society. Although, throughout their life they experience deprivation in various ways, women are not sensitive enough to realize that they are trapped and deprived of so many privileges.

Due to that kind of perception and understanding, while talking about violence or gender-based violence in Naga society, people quickly refer to factional clashes and to the underground and military movement, where on several occasions women were molested, raped, harassed and manhandled and where men folk were beaten to death, tortured, and shot to death by the military and different factional clashes. On the other hand, gender-based violence is also referred to the situations in which wives were beaten by their husbands or by their

---

[345] *Ibid.*, p. 340.

[346] Without changing the basic view of women as inferior, servile, self-sacrificing and as essentially instruments of sexual gratification and reproduction, the problem of violence cannot be resolved.

male counterparts in the family and in the society.[347] The violence they experience in different forms is considered as a way of life because society taught them such is the way as men and women they play different roles. In following their roles as traditional norms maintain them, they suffered untold miseries both in the family and in the society. Although, Naga society comprises of different tribes, their mode of practicing cultural ethos and norms are almost the same. Therefore, every Naga understands that he/she should abide by the customary laws and traditional practices. In doing so, women are victimized in many ways. For this attempt, a few cultural practices would be discussed below.

Gender-based Violence Through Customary Law

From time immemorial, customary laws and traditional practices have governed the lives of the close-knit and numerically small tribal communities. It is believed that the Naga customary law originated and followed from their place of origin.[348] Nagas claim that in the beginning their ancestors were living together with God thus its violation was considered as violation against God. These laws were transmitted orally from one generation to another. With the passage of time, changes were made according to the needs of the community. The customs and laws were considered to consist of truth, justice and public utility and were observed by people as moral, religious and social codes. As such it still holds great relevance for the Naga community.[349]

These unwritten laws serve as a code of conduct for members of any tribal community. Any member who violated the social and religious norms was liable to be punished and fined or excommunicated from society.[350] Traditionally, the important offices and positions in most of the social organizations have been given to the males-as chiefs, chieftains, headmen, priests, witch-doctors, land-owners and managers.[351]

As mentioned earlier, custom is an unwritten law established by usage that has transcended time. Custom is a stereo-typed system. People were guided by customs in their activities-social, religious and ethical life and, with this as their

---

[347] Ironically, one of the respondents (Questionnaire No. 5), mentioned that there is no gender-based violence at all in Nagaland. He further says, "We should not make a mistake-'The Forest to a Tree," For him, violence is something which involves guns and arms, killing and fighting between different groups or nations. Therefore, he says that, it is unwise to do research on gender-based violence which is not relevant in Naga context. There are many more who have expressed themselves in the same manner. Therefore, a study to challenge the gender-based violence in Naga context through Religious Education is worth exploring.

[348] Interview with Sademmeren on 29th June 2006 at Mokokchung, Nagaland.

[349] Tajen Ao, "Naga Customary Law and its Influence on Legislation," Unpublished paper, date and year are not available, p. 3.

[350] Saral K. Chatterji, *Society and Culture in North-East India: A Christian Persprctive* (Delhi: The Christian Institute for the Study of Religion and Society, 1996), p. 22.

[351] *Ibid.*, p. 22.

background they ran and maintained their social organization.[352] Thus, Nagas still believe that, 'if one custom is broken, all customs will be discarded. And if one part goes wrong the whole system becomes ineffective. If a custom is not observed and is discarded there is no alternative to substitute it,'[353] Thus, the Naga customary law has been legalized by the rules of Administration of Justice and Police Act 1937, article 371 A of the Indian constitution and the Village Council Act 1978.[354]

When critically examined, in the customary laws of the Naga society, women's rights are not included in many areas where as more rules are rather imposed on women. It was only in 1998 a Memorandum was issued by the Land Revenue Department of the Government of Nagaland, under No. Lr/1-1/94 stating its concern for the development of women in securing them justice and making them equal participants. Yet it also mentions that the government will not interfere in the traditional customary law concerning land and its transfer.[355] It shows that even the state government cannot do anything, either to revise or change the traditional practices which were made as customary law. Thus, even today, Naga society strictly follows their cultural practices in which, women are the only victims. Men have been in control and power by virtue of the position they hold. In many cases, women are kept in control more than men, in the form of punishments or social ostracism. For example, a promiscuous female in the traditional Naga society is punished by shaving her hair. But a promiscuous male is not punished in any form.[356] Thus, from time immemorial those kinds of unequal treatment were assigned as a sign of punishment for women.

It is worth mentioning that, one of the priorities after the establishment of the village was to elect and organize a village council, comprising of representatives chosen from the dominant clan in the village.[357] The main duty of the council was to lay down laws and regulations for the social and political administration of the entire community members. Village councilors were elected (male) from each clan.[358] Women had no place at all in the village council. Women could not participate in any public debate. Thus, women had no part in village

---

[352] Tajen, Ao, N*aga Customary Laws,* Mokokchung: Aowati Imchen, 1980 x.

[353] *Ibid.*, p. xi.

[354] Akang Ao, *Practicing Naga Customary Law* (Dimapur: Modern Press, 1999), p. 3

[355] A memorandum Issued by the Land Revenue Department of the Government of Nagaland 20th March 1998. 'The development of women forms an integral part…it will intervene to secure gender justice and empower women so as to make women co-equal participants and partners…The ownership and transfer of land in the traditional holdings are governed by the respective customary laws…Government does not consider it prudent or expedient at this stage to intervene in the matter."

[356] Saral K. Chatterji, *Society and Culture in the North-East India.*, p. 23.

[357] Imti Aier, *Ao Naga Social and Customary Genealogy* (1967), p. 4.

[358] *Ibid.*, p.5.

administration or in the decision-making process. Though both men and women were members of the community, they did not have a right to raise their voice but simply to follow the rules made by men. It is true women got maximum customary restrictions but less customary privileges.[359]

It is very encouraging to see administrative privileges of women in the other states when talking about Naga women's situation. A staff correspondent of the Government of Himachal Pradesh which appeared in the daily news paper with the heading-'Empowering women in Himachal Pradesh.' The reason for quoting this is to show and to encourage women in endeavoring their dreams as equal partners. Especially it is quite appropriate to present for the people of Nagaland, where women are not recognized in the administration both in the church and state. It says,

> For empowering women in the hill state, the new government here has declared a 50 per cent reservation for them in all Panchayati Raj Institutions and Urban Local Bodies, claimed an official spokesman here on Saturday. He said the governments' decision to enhance the social security pension from Rs. 200 to Rs. 300 a month would benefit at least 68, 455 widows in the State. As much as Rs. 11,001 is being provided to poor and helpless girls as marriage grant under the Mukhya Mantri Kanyadaan Yojna and Rs. 25,000 grant to young widows for their re-marriage. A financial assistance of Rs. 1,000 a year is being provided to widows, helpless and divorced women to bear the expenses of two children. The State Government is spending about Rs. 30 crore every year on various programmes aimed at welfare and upliftment of women of the State. The spokesmen said that the Government has announced to generate employment and self employment avenues for unemployed girls and women in order to make them self dependent.[360]

Literally speaking, the Naga tribe as a whole did not have a political organization, but their respective village organizations were similarly based upon the clan[361] they belonged to. In spite of changes that have taken place at the higher level, village communities follow the same pattern of government even today. The male inhabitants are regarded as citizens of the republic, and they perform every role of citizenship. Women inhabitants are not regarded as citizens, especially when it came to decision making. Even though every citizen contributed his/her share of duties and services for the common welfare of the republic, women are not seen as having this responsibility in the same way as the male.

---

[359] In Naga society, women are not allowed to involve in decision making nor in the community administration board which are in practice as in others states of India.

[360] *The Hindu,* Sunday, March 23, 2008, p. 7. (Bangalore).

[361] Clan is a distinct family belonging to a common ancestor. Every Naga belongs to a certain clan.

Today, many of the liabilities including debts are liquidated by women left by men but they are not entitled to inherit landed property. All these make their social position different from men, and it makes them inferior and subhuman, because every human being has equal rights before God. This may be one of the reasons why voices of women in protest are emerging in the society. Women want to be treated as equals and want the society to give them the opportunity they give to men. According to the customary law, men are given more opportunities in the society. For instance, the sons carry the family name and are authorized to do certain rituals and responsibilities. Assuming that once a daughter gets married she will leave the family, enter another's house or become others' property. That is the reason women are denied properties and other rights. Though women are deprived of getting their share and are counted as subhuman and subordinate, once their parents become old and unable to manage themselves, daughters are the ones who take care of the parents till their last breath.

Unless, women are given the same privileges and responsibilities without gender discriminations as men before and after marriage, women will never have freedom and they will continue to suffer more under rigid cultural practices. Therefore, customary law needs to be re-examined and restructured and if necessary totally discarded which does not have any meaning in this post modern context. We need an atmosphere whereby every human being irrespective of sex may feel full personhood without any prejudices. Issues like property rights, different sex role and gender biased rules of community administration, etc which affect the rights of women, must be taken into consideration with seriousness, and sensitivity.

Gender-based Violence and Inheritance

Under the Naga customary rules of inheritance, property devolves upon the heirs by succession. Inheritance is always in the male line, sons, brothers, nephews, cousins etc. Thus, customary laws in patriarchal Naga tribal cultures recognize only male ownership and right of inheritance. Culturally they believe that, the daughter after her marriage comes under the care of a different clan and family, and as such is not entitled to own the properties of her father. Thus, among the traditional Naga societies, women are not entitled to any share in the ancestral property. In succession of property, sons, brothers, nephews, cousins, etc are the order of preference for inheritance. The son takes precedence over the brother; the brother takes precedence over nephew; the nephew over the cousin and so on. The sons inherit the property of their father jointly and the grandsons join with their fathers in the property of their grandfather.[362] Among the sons, the eldest son gets more preference in the property of the father. In the absence of the son, the brother or uncle or the nearest kinsman takes preference in succession.

---

[362] Imti Aier (1967), p. 73, Mills, J. P., *The Rengma Nagas,* (Guwahati: Spectrum Publications 1980), p. 143.

Among the kinsmen, the choice of the heir is preferred to a person who is the descendant of the eldest son of the ancestor.

At the time of the extinction of a clan, the man who is the last soul of the clan can adopt a minor boy for heirship.[363] In this situation, though the man has so many daughters, in order to maintain the continuity of the clan and to preserve the ancestral things, he adopts a minor boy who comes from any clan of a different place or other linguistic tribe. Thus, the adoptee can inherit the property including ancestral property, and is entitled to get other social privileges leaving aside the real daughters. Though the system of adoptation is not so common these days in Naga society as before, when it comes to inheritance, daughters have no share at all. Thus, while examining the inheritance system in Naga society, one could see the biased treatment given to women in the family.

When examining about the Sumi customary law, Ms. Zhimomi (1989) states that, women can possess only moveable property in absolute ownership, if they have bought it. However, women who have bought land cannot bequeath it as they please, since the sons and other male heirs will claim the land. In the absence of sons or other male heirs, the property and inheritance of a man will revert to the man's nephews or to the sons of his clan rather than to his daughter.[364] Thus, beside her tireless job for the family throughout her life, still women find themselves very insecure in the family, and as a woman she has no decision-making power or the right to claim properties. Because in the traditional Naga societies, the wife or a woman is hardly consulted for taking major decisions, especially those relating to land and property. All the above mentioned bindings are imposed on women according to the unwritten customary law laid down by the village decision-making body. When we talk about the gender-based violence in society, Sheetal Sharma comments in this way:

> Historically, world over, either by law or by custom, the status of women is determined by asymmetrical power relationships in decision-making, personal and social rights, access to resources and entitlements. Women in many countries still lack rights to inherit property, own land, get education, obtain credit, earn income or work outside home; they are still widely under-represented in involvement in decision-making at the domestic or social level. The reality of women's life in India is not different. Women most of the times, are even deprived of some of the fundamental human rights and this denial is justified often in the name of tradition."[365]

---

[363] Imti Aier. (1967) p. 80.

[364] Juanita War, "Status of tribal women in North-East India: Perspectives and Realities" in Saral K. Chatterji, *Society and Culture in North-East In Dia* (Bangalore: The Christian Institute for the Study of Religion and Soc iety, 1996), p. 9.

[365] Sheetal Sharma, "Women's Education: Key to Prosperity" in *Women's Link: Women and Education,* Vol. 13, No. 1. January – March 2007, p. 2.

Thus, many times, while talking about the restructuring and changing the condition of women, many express that the existing tradition cannot be changed, as if tradition is something very rigid and unshakable. In other words, even though people seem to be aware that women are in need of social upliftment, the traditional practices remain unchallenged and unquestioned.

Gender–based Violence in Traditional Marriage

The Nagas consider marriage as a vitally sacred institution of society and ordained for the procreation of children for the continuation of the social unit. There is no written literature so far on Naga marriage system but they follow a well established canon. Marriage practice is guided by the un-written customary laws. They have been following this from generation to generation. Clan system is the fundamental social fabric of the Nagas. Every aspect of their custom and culture is normally based on it. Thus, in every Naga society, marriage is well defined, according to their culture, religion, custom and tradition.[366] Marriage within the same clan is strictly prohibited as they believe that they are from the same blood which is closely related. The couple violating the clan code is restricted from the community established activities.[367]

Most of the Naga tribes practice both arranged and love marriage. Of course some Naga writers have mentioned that both boys and girls enjoy considerable freedom in choosing their partners, but it is not applicable in all cases. In certain cases, girls have to listen to their parents or relatives in choosing their husbands. It is heart-rending to note, that in a few cases, girls have to accept without any question their life partners against their wishes if their parents have commitments to the boy's family when they were still young or if her parents and boy's agree. On the other hand, proposing for their life partner from the girl's side is regarded as 'shame' in the Naga society therefore, even if they admire or have interest, girls cannot approach in the first place the boys, where as boys can propose to any girl any time they wish. Likewise, when it comes to girls or women there are so many norms and restrictions.

The best example in this regard is from one of the tribes in Nagaland. It will show how many women were under the bondage of traditional marriage practice, especially under can the *Ang* system. *Ang* means King or Chief of the village. It is the real picture of marriage among Konyak Naga tribe, it says, "The Konyak *Ang* can have many wives. *Ang* can marry from the same clan from other villages for maintaining the purity of royal blood.The children of *Angs'* concubine can get married from other clans. Marriage is often arranged by parents when the girl is still young and very often when she grows up she is compelled to accept

---

366 N. Talitemjen Jamir and A. Lanunungsang, *Naga Society and Culture* (Mokokchung: Nagaland university Tribal Research Centre, 2006), p. 173.

367 Interview with Takasangyu on 23rd June 2006 at Mokokchung, Nagaland.

her husband against her will. The *Angs* can marry more than 50-60 times."[368] If an *Ang* selects a girl to marry she cannot refuse and she is compelled to marry him whether he is an old aged person or not. The girl has to obey the *Ang*.[369] Some of the native writers thus say, "When a Naga woman marries, she goes out of her father's family and comes under the authority of her husband. It is also mentioned that, in the contemporary society, the husband is the custodian head of the family, whereas his wife is the administrator-manager of the family. She controls the entire family affairs."[370]

It can be argued that, the above mentioned statements are not true in many cases. When it comes to family planning, decision-making, sharing of property, financial and children's education etc., the wife's suggestions are hardly taken or she is totally controlled by the husband.[371] In some communities, women lose their family name or clan identity after the marriage even if they want to retain it due to cultural norms.[372] Wife takes her husband's title after her name but that is not the same case with the husband. The researcher feels that by taking the husbands' family name or title, the wife loses her family identity and becomes the husband's property. For instance, for the Ao Naga, one of the major tribes in Nagaland, in case of inter-marriage, the husband's family chooses a guardian (god father) for his wife from his own village, even though her real father is still alive, but in the case of the husband, that is not required.[373]

Thus, this is the existing women's situation in regard to marriage practices in which women have to observe certain norms in the name of culture. The situations are gradually changing among the educated women but a majority of women are yet to come out of that cultural practices. Nagaland being one of the few Christian majority states in the country yet, has failed to present the gospel message against all these ill treatment meted to women. Here the question is, 'Doesn't the church have no right to fight against social evils?' or whether the church's educational ministry has anything to do with the issues of gender-based violence?

Gender-based Violence through Traditional Religion and Church's Teaching

The native Naga religion is basically similar to the type of religion found among the tribes throughout India. It was an animistic religion, with nature believed

---

[368] S. Eunice, "The Status of Konyak Women Under *Ang* System," in *No more sorrow in God's garden of justice: Tribal Women Doing Theology*, ed. Limatula Longkumer, Jorhat: Women's Study Department Eastern Theological College, 2007), p. 76.

[369] *Ibid.*, p. 75.

[370] *Ibid.*, p. 216.

[371] Questionnaire., No. 10, 11, 12.

[372] Questionnaire., No. 28.

[373] Questionnaire., No. 29.

to be alive with unseen and mysterious forces.[374] Nagas believed in a vaguely-conceived supreme spirit[375] which they imagined to have created the world and the ancestor of the human race. They also recognized many minor deities, ghosts and spirits of trees, rocks, rivers and even hills as their gods.[376] The Naga people believed in the spirit world and they understood their whole life to be surrounded by these spirits both good and bad. The Nagas believed that spirits are extremely hostile to human beings. Spirits can reside anywhere and in any shape. They can take the shape of a tiger or a snake. They can come down in the form of lightning or as floods. Therefore, Nagas believed that all illness is caused by evil spirits, of which there are legions. Thus, to avóid any misfortune or harm, they made sacrifices and set up a number of rituals. In the ritual ceremonial functions, women were not allowed to come to the common altar.

In other words, women could not become the religious head of her family, clan, or the village, and was debarred from performing religious rites and sacrifices.[377] Based on the traditional religion, Nagas believed that having sex with women on the day of fishing/hunting makes them unsuccessful. Women's chastity is seen as the condition for safety during fishing/hunting in the river/forest. Thus, sexual control is enforced by catching/hunting and in turn the catches of fish/animals are dependent on women's faithfulness. Thus by maintaining control over women's bodies, men continue to subjugate women to a great extent.[378]

In line with traditional religious teachings, Christianity also contributed a lot towards gender biased teaching. One cannot deny the fact that missionaries who came to Nagaland also came from the patriarchal church traditions who brought along male biased theology and teaching. Therefore, they were not aware of the cultural exploitations towards women in the society. Without realizing the context they established churches and structured the church administration in the same pattern of village administrative system. No doubt, the subservient attitude towards women, among Nagas, is primarily cultural, and it is further endorsed by a defective understanding of Christian priorities and values in the church administration itself.

Thus, church administration also appropriated the clan-based male village administrative pattern in the church, in which for example, the pastor is like the head of the village council and the deacon board like the council members.

[374] *From Darkness To Light:* A Publication of the Nagaland Baptist Church Council on the occasion of the celebration of 125 years of Christianity in Nagaland (Nagaland: Nagaland Baptist Church council, 1997), p. 15.

[375] Each tribe has its own name for the Supreme Spirit, few example-For Ao, *Lijaba,* for Angami *Kepenvopfu,*, for Sema, *Aluho*, etc., which is believed to be a 'Male God.'

[376] *From Darkness To Light* (1997), p. 15.

[377] N. Talitemjen Jamir and A. Lanunungsang, p. 219.

[378] Ellen, "Role of Women in Naga Jhum Cultivation" in *Building upon Traditional Agriculture in Nagaland,* ed. Amemba jamir (Bangalore: NEPED and IIRR, 1999), p. 163.

Deacon board is considered as the highest decision making body of a local church which is constituted by men. Thus, women were not included in the deacon board till 1990s. But with the negotiation from the Theologically Trained Women's Association, a few women have been appointed in the urban churches only. Thus, from the very beginning of Christianity, women were considered as inferior there, and not allowed to exercise their God-given opportunity.

An Overview of Gender-based Violence Situation in Naga Society

Without analyzing the situation properly, many writers and people in common think that there is no gender-based violence in Naga society, since Nagaland is a Christian state. As mentioned, it is said, "The coming of the gospel has radically changed the Naga society, particularly women. The gospel has liberated Naga women from the bondage of sin, ignorance, and suppression. The gospel has opened the eyes of Naga women and brought them from darkness to light."[379] Naga society follows the patriarchal and patrilineal system, where women are regarded as inferior to men in society and in the family circle because of their feminine characteristics by the power and authority that they hold. Women are not entitled to co-ownership of property with men. In regard to naming, a girl can be named only after her father's family, and not by any chance can she draw the title of her mother or she can name her children after her mother.

As noted elsewhere, in Naga society, women are regarded as subordinate to men and many derogative terms, which are used for women reflect the low regard given to women. Very often that kind of word hurts their sentiment and they think that they are low esteemed. The conventional form of categorizing women and children, for example, the Ao Naga has phrases, "*sungochung-a* bunch or '*tetsur tanu, for women* children,' Kuki tribe has such sayings as, "the words of women and the horns of female *Mithun* are of no use"; "the speaking of women is like the chirping of birds at night."[380] For the *Phom*, one of the tribes considers women as "feathers of cock or hen can not be used in the hat."[381] Likewise, each Naga tribe has its own saying in regard to women in the society. On many occasions, in order to defame women, men folk use the sentence likes 'what do these women children know about'? The usage of the above-mentioned terms is no doubt, a derogatory term to all women irrespective of their status, background, position and age.

Today, one can easily speak of women as highly honored, well recognized, and respected in public life, but it is not true as people think. When it comes to the issues like ownership system and the law of inheritance, women are not accounted for. They are not given their share, they are deprived of their rights. Of course, a

[379] *Op. cit.*, p. 133.

[380] R.L Hnuni, "Women in North East India: Vision for Tribes", in *Women and Society: A Reader in Women's Studies*, ed. Nirmala Jeyara, (Lady Doak College, Madurai: ISPCK, Delhi, 2005), p. 341.

[381] This was informed by one of the pastors from Phom Naga to the author on June 2006.

handful of women may have the opportunity to get little properties and a piece of land which was acquired by their parents, or may hold some high positions out of their efforts and intellect. Yet in general, women are shunned from all privileges. One of the sociologists says, "No doubt, women enjoy a considerable amount of privileges and rights, unlike other communities in India yet, when we compare their status with that of the status of men, it is not encouraging to see the reality of their position even today."[382]

In the field of socio-cultural and religious relations, Naga women are still far behind men. They can not come to the front in the field of socio-cultural affairs especially when it comes to leadership. Though many male scholars have mentioned in their writings that Naga women were never treated as inferior to men, because of her sex, women were restricted in many ways. In this, one of the Naga scholars, Panger Imchen has 'mistakenly' mentioned in his book, *Ancient Ao Naga Religion and Culture,* that "The Ao woman was never treated as inferior to men. From earliest times an Ao woman could obtain all basic education just like the men and could be consulted, especially for traditional songs, history, art and culture etc, festivals and even religious affairs. But because of her sex, a woman was restricted in some ways, politically and socially:

(1) She cannot participate in public debates or discussions but can consult and advice her husband at home to a certain degree.
(2) She is not entitled to fame and title but much reference and praise is made of her in songs sung at merit feasts performed by her husband which is the highest social and religious meritorious sacrifice for the community.
(3) She cannot inherit property-that is landed. She is not liable for any debt of her ancestor or her heirs.[383]

When it comes to church activities, women are not given a chance to hold the position of the Executive Secretary or Pastor.[384] In recent years, due to many theologically trained women, they have been given a chance to hold leadership in the youth and children's ministry. They are also designated as associate pastor for taking care of women's fellowship. Though there are a number of theologically trained women working as full time ministers, during the pastor's absence in the

---

[382] N. Talitemjen Jamir & A. Lanunungsang, *Naga Society and Culture,* p. 217.

[383] Panger Imchen, *Ancient Ao Naga Religion and Culture* (New Delhi: Har-Anand Publications, 1993) p. 116.

[384] There are more than 1500 churches and around 25 Church Associations and Conventions in Nagaland. But so far there are no women pastors or women executive secretaries. No woman deacon in the local churches exist except for a few women deaconesses in the urban churches. See also questionnaire nos. 21, 22.

church, one of the lay deacons takes the pastor's place.[385] Though women are more sincere and devoted in church activities, just because of their femininity, they are denied recognition. Therefore, not only in political and social but even in the church circle, steps need to be taken to improve gender-based violent condition. Male chauvinism is still in full control of ecclesiology. As the researcher has identified above, women have no status, no leadership, and no decision-making roles as their male counterparts. Thus, to address patriarchy in the church implies that patriarchs have to ask themselves in order to bring emancipation to half of their congregation. The problems lie, when one has to address oneself. It is not just social and ecclesiastical improvement we need but self-improvement.[386]

Setting up of 'State Commission for Women' in Nagaland

Even though gender-based violence is rampant everywhere, there was no 'body' in the State level as such to protect women from all forms of violence in the Naga society, except for a few women's organizations in the name of social welfare groups. But till recently, there was no Women's Commission to protect women from gender-based violence. Thus, every incident of rape, harassment, and molestations or denying rights to women beginning from marriage issues to inheritance and also right to exercise their potentiality, were kept in secret except for a few which came to the public eyes. Taking for granted that Nagas are fun loving people, freely mixing with the opposite sex outside, they didn't realize that they need a constituent body to protect women and to fight against gender-based violence in society till recently.

Nagaland boasts that it is a State with Christian majority. But, they appear to be living in denial about their status in the society. So where are the Christian principles in their teaching ministry? The rejection to set up the State Commission for Women in the first place by the Government was on the basis that "atrocities against women are relatively unknown in the state and problems such as dowry system, child marriage and caste distinction etc., as prevalent in some of the states are not practiced in the state.[387] But in reality, there are many young girls, below

[385] According to *Baptist News,* Volume 58 Issues 2, April – June, 2007, p. 14, there are 20 associations and 1347 local churches with 454349 Baptist members in Nagaland. Still there is no single woman Executive Secretary or Local Church Pastor at present. In the past years a few women pastors were given chances. Even if they have been given the responsibility, it was noted that, men folk did not cooperate and ignored their leadership, by commenting that 'women can not take the men's place'.

[386] R.L. Hnuni, *Women and Society: A Reader in Women's Studies*, (2005), p. 351.

[387] Letter by the Chief Secretary to the Government of Nagaland addressed to the Chairperson of the Government of India, National Commission for Women, "Why the Government of Nagaland does not require a State Level Commission for Women?" http://kuknalim.com/modules,php?name =news&&sid=2123&mode=&order=o&thold=o, accessed on 1st December, 2005.

the legal age,[388] who get married, and even more serious, becomes mothers outside of marriage. Then what about the preference for male child, and the denial of patrimony to female children? Are these issues not serious than the child marriage in rural Hindu society? Are such gender based discriminations on the basis of one's cultural tradition any different from the dowry system and the caste system in some States?. There are many instances of unseen incidences of gender-based violence in the name of cultural traditions.

It was only in August, 2006, when eighteen leading women submitted a memorandum to the Nagaland Governor Shyamal Datta, urging him for immediate setting up of a 'Nagaland State Commission for women' (NSCW) and adoption of 'State Policy for Women' (SPW), a concrete move took shape. The memorandum stated, "It was disheartening to note that, till date, the state government has not set up the mandatory body for the protection of women in the state. There has been an alarming rise in violence and crime against women and children in state, which more often goes unreported, and policies and guidelines for protection of women's rights have been ignored and violated."[389] Thus, after much deliberations the memorandum was accepted and for the first of its kind in Nagaland, a department was created for "women's development"[390] under the able Secretary Mr. Sukhalu and Joint Director Mrs. Betty Angami, under Nagaland government. Also, "State Commission for Women" was set up officially in April 2007, under the designate President, Mrs. Sano Vamozo, Mrs. TCK. Lotha as Secretary and Ms. Alen Konyak as a member.[391]

Throughout the centuries, control over women and the exercise of patriarchal authority have resulted in various forms of gender discrimination in Nagaland as cited earlier. Life-long discriminations have increased their oppression and made them to suffer from triple injustices-excess workload in the family and outside, less wage, no status both in private and public life, depriving their rights. They are continually oppressed at home by their husbands and sons, in the institutions by their male counterparts through different means discrimination from their seniors. Thus, gender-based violence in different forms affects women's active participation and discourages them from active involvement in political affairs and in church ministry.

Nagaland being a Christian State every community member is regarded as a believer by birth. As members they were taught that every believer must go to

---

[388] It is a fact that, two of the author's sisters got married at the age of 17, they were compelled to accept the proposal due to family pressures.

[389] Xavier Rutsa, "Appeal for Women Commission," in *Eastern Panorama: News magazine of North East,* September 2006, p. 42.

[390] This source has been published by the directorate of Information and Public Relations, Nagaland: Kohima, 22, 2007.

[391] Interview with Dr. (Mrs) Rukhono K. Iralu and Dr. (Ms) Buno Liegise, on May 29 2007, Bangalore.

church regularly, should give tithes and offering, maintain good moral life which is acceptable before God and fellow beings. Of course, affirming faith in God, proclaiming the gospel and extending charity work in the name of God is regarded as a priority. However, when it comes to social issues with regards to ethical lives like gender justice, churches are hesitant to raise their voice and unable to stand firmly what they preach and prophesy. Amongst them, issues on gender-based violence are not at all included in its preaching and teaching ministry.

It is worth mentioning here as we assess the gender-based violence situation in Nagaland that, in the recently concluded Nagaland State General Assembly Election' held on 3rd March 2008, for the first time in Naga history, four women contested from different constituencies representing different national and regional parties.[392] As per their life history, they were all educated, financially sound, government officials and involved as social workers with good reputation, but it is quite discouraging to know that none of them were elected. The voters viewed them 'as not fit for politics,' How can the whole community survive under the leadership of a mere lady who does not have equal status as men? (This information was received through one of the main agents of a lady candidate through telephonic conversation by the researcher.) As mentioned in the preceding chapter, never in the history of Nagaland women were in the State Legislative Assembly, even though women are more in number. Thus, the gender based violence in Naga society situation may not be same as in other parts of states, yet, in a different way gender biased treatment is quite obvious both in church and State. This is a great challenge to the Christians whose teachings emphasize equality, justice and tranquility as followers of Jesus.

In sum, setting up a State Commission for Women, making Laws for the protection of domestic violence and implementing Acts for the welfare of women at the national or state level alone will not solve the problem of gender-based violence. So long as the society considers that gender-based violence is a private matter, which has to be solved within the family circles, especially issues relating to domestic affairs, or the customary laws as it is in any circumstance, discriminations against women will persist not only in Nagaland but in every society. The age old traditional understanding of female inferiority and male superiority in every aspect need to be corrected by educating people based on the biblical principles. It is imperative, thus, Christian Education could be one of the best means to bring awareness to its faith community.

---

[392] Four women who contested in the Nagaland State General Assembly Election held on 3rd March 2008 are: Mrs. *Zennieslie. Angami* (BJP), Mrs. *Rhakile, Yimchunger* (NCP), Mrs. Rosemary, *Ao,* f.

Chapter 5

Field Research on Gender-Based Violence

Analysis and Interpretation

Introduction

In research work it is mandatory to gather a good amount of resources through the library as well as from field research. Since, by nature of the study, Christian Education comes under 'practical theology,' its credibility depends on how good the first information is and how best it is used for the specific topic. Therefore, in order to get valid and appropriate information about gender-based violence, an empirical research was conducted among the Nagas in Nagaland. This was done with a view to explore the age-old hidden issues of gender-based violence among Nagas who never consider those matters as important while half of its population suffers from gender-based violence.

Since it is beyond the scope of this study to cover all the Nagas settled in different parts of the country and elsewhere, this study concentrates on Nagas in Nagaland only. Although there are more than 16 tribes living in Nagaland, speaking different dialects, having their own independent church administrations, yet they function under one political administration. It is interesting to note that, even though they are from same state, they cannot understand each other as they speak and use different dialects. They could however, be easily identified through their accents, dresses, community festivals, or even by looks. Besides, each tribe has certain characteristics which keep them alive with their identity. In spite of these differences, their traditional practices or the observance of cultural norms are almost the same and they could easily complement each other's practices, especially with regard to maintaining customary and inheritance laws, cultural activities, church administration systems, and the system of family set up, etc.

Empirical research involved both interviews and the questionnaire. Interviews were held with people who were holding certain responsibility in the community both in church and society. In other words, they were those who have had some knowledge about decision-making and public administration. Questionnaires were distributed to people of different walks of life representing different fields: theologically trained men and women, political leaders, village council members, church leaders, academicians from different disciplines, Christian educators, parents and children. Besides, views were also sought at women's seminars and conferences held in different places during 2004-2007 in which the researcher herself participated.

As discussed earlier, empirical research was conducted in three district head quarters during June-July 2006. Since, there is no common language for the Nagas, English language was used as the medium of correspondence, and the ce, the questionnaire was prepared in English. Since the intention of this research is to respond to the challenge of gender-based violence through Christian Religious Education, in this following discussion the writer wishes to critically analyze the situation of gender-based violence as it prevails in its different forms considering the socio-cultural, religious, and political conditions in the Naga society.

Thus, a critical analysis and evaluation of the different structured situations with regard to gender-based violence is the method of research, which tries to understand women's struggles and their positions in the family, in the church and in the society. This attempt to describe and interpret the data collections relate to the empirical research findings emanating from the questionnaires and interviews administered to the respondents. For this study, we need to keep in mind the following purposes: (1) to understand the existing pattern of political administration and leadership structures; (2) to know the church structure with reference to gender-based leadership; (3) to examine the role of sex both in the family and in the society; (4) to determine how gender-based violence issues are taken seriously in Naga society, (5) to find out how gender-based violence issues are taken up in the church educational ministry, (6) to analyze the Naga cultural norms which impacted gender-based violence, and (7) to figure out how best it could be incorporated in the educational ministry in the church.

Choosing the Places for Empirical Research

There are eight (8) district head quarters and more than 16 major tribes in Nagaland; but for the current research, the researcher chose three towns, considered to be the most populated areas in the State, viz, Kohima, Mokokchung and Dimapur.

Kohima: Kohima is the Capital of Nagaland. This is the place where all the tribal groups are represented and it is the administrative centre of the whole state. More than half of the empirical research was done in this place. The main administrative office of the Nagaland Baptist Churches Council (NBCC) is located here; through which all the local churches are directly involved in their responsibility through their associations. In fact, one can see many churches belonging to each tribal community in this capital town.

Mokokchung: Mokokchung,[393] is the second biggest district in the state, from where the researcher hails. This place marks the advent of Christianity and where for the first time the impact of Christianity was felt. According to recent research, this district is declared as 'Nagaland's most advanced District,' with 1004 females for every 1000 males, it has the 7th healthiest sex ratio among the 538 districts of India in the 0-6 age group population.[394]

Dimapur: Dimapur,[395] is the last to be declared as a district according to the government administration, yet the biggest and a fast developing place in terms of economic, educational, and business enterprises in the state. It has connectivity with other parts of the country through different means of transportation and communication. One can see many non-governmental organizations in the name of Mission and a number of theological and Bible colleges in this town. Since this is a commercial place, one can also observe numerous social evil activities day by day.

In the above mentioned towns, questionnaires were distributed personally, to those representing different tribes and peoples' groups: political leaders, village council members, Christian ministers, social workers, parents and children, in order to obtain primary information about the prevailing situation of gender-based violence in the Naga society. After collecting the data, the researcher analyzed the data and interpreted the issues according to the data collected through questionnaires and interviews.

Altogether three hundred questionnaires were distributed in the above mentioned three places, representing different groups of people from various churches and localities, two hundred eighty seven responded with duly filled questionnaires which were quite encouraging and informative. Yet, in order to give a clear percentage/figure, tabulation was worked out to a round figure and tabulated for three hundred respondents.

As the research area was too vast covering the wide range of issues on gender-based violence in Nagaland, the analyses and interpretations were grouped under three major headings namely - gender-based violence at Home (family), in the Church and in the Society. Again it was classified accordingly as they appeared

---

[393] Mokokchung is the district where the first Christian Missionaries from the West (American Baptist), established and from where they evangelized other districts in Nagaland.

[394] Most Advanced district. Sources accessed from the Internet; accessed on 23rd April, 2007.

[395] Dimapur is a commercial city not only for the people of Nagas but for the whole of North East and for other states. It has more than twenty seven theological and Bible Colleges, mission centres for different churches and non-governmental organizatons here.

in the questionnaire in order to obtain a clear situation through the opinions expressed about gender-based violence in the Naga society.

Background of the Respondents

Before analyzing the gender-based violence situations in detail, it is appropriate to give the respondents' general descriptions with the help of a table. The logic behind this description is to indicate the actual representations from different peoples groups, their places, educational status, their professions, and sex representation in the empirical research.

Background of the Respondents

Sex		Age		Marital Status		Education		Place	
Male	136 (54.67%)	18-25	50 (17%)	Married	187 (62%)	Degree and Above	122 (41%)	Mokokchung	90 (30%)
Female	164 (45.33%)	26-40	86 (29%)	Unmarried	113 (38%)	Up to Pre University	162 (54%)	Kohima	130 (43%)
		41-55	116 (40%)			Basic Education	16 (5%)	Dimapur	80 (27%)
		56 and above	40 (14%)						

Table 1 indicates the detailed representations of respondents. Out of the 300 respondents, 30% are represented from Mokokchung, 43% from Kohima and 27% from Dimapur. Regarding the ratio of sex, 54.67% participants were male and 45.33% were female. They were divided into four groups according to their age with a view to know specifically their opinions according to time/age and their experiences. 17% respondents were in the age group of 18-25. The second group was (29%) between the ages 26-40. In the third group, 40% were between the age group of 41-60 and the fourth and last group 14% were from 61 years and upward. About the marital status, 62% respondents were married and 38 percent were unmarried.

With regard to their employment, the respondents had varieties of jobs based on their educational qualification. It is difficult to categorize every job holder, therefore only their educational qualification was taken into consideration. It was divided into three groups: basic education; up to Pre University and Bachelor degree and above. Only 12 percent of the respondents had only basic education, 54 percent had up to pre university degree, and 41 percent were in the category of degree and above. Except for a very few of them almost all the respondents were educated people (this is important since the questionnaire is written in English which is the second language of the respondents). This table shows that empirical research was done in a variety of groups of people covering a large area reaching out to different categories representing different walks of life in Nagaland.

Understanding of Gender-based Violence

Violence surrounds a woman's life from conception to death, and it has become a routinized affair in all societies of the world since innumerable centuries. However, people are not conscious of the gender-based violence, and many times though they are in the midst of those endemic dangerous situations (embedded between sexes from time immemorial) they rather considered it as a way of life. This may be so as the nature of patriarchal society guaranteed men as rulers, proprietors, protectors, and exploiters which made them to think that they are physically stronger and regard themselves as protectors,[396] bread winners and decision makers. Therefore, women remain silent even though they experience untold miseries through various forms of violence from their male counterparts. In order to ascertain whether people are aware of their gender-based violence a suitable question was posed to them. Accordingly, indicated that 86% (158 women and 100 men) had heard about the gender-based violence while only 14% (16 women and 26 men) of the respondents were of the opinion that they had never heard about gender-based violence. Although a majority of the respondents said that they had heard about gender-based violence, they were not aware of the real issues involved therein. A few of the respondents expressed surprise that 'there is no gender-based violence at all in our society.' On the other hand, those who said 'no', too were not so sure about the issues but out of their answers it is indicated that they were little aware of the discrimination done on women in society.

After ascertaining their awareness about gender-based violence, it was necessary to visualize their understanding of gender-based violence by giving various options to get their opinions. Each respondent ticked the sentences whichever he/she considered comes close to his/her understanding. Thus, a

[396] It is interesting to observe that whenever a couple go to the jungle or to the field, the wife would carry all the food stuff and implements to be used in the field which is heavy enough for a person, and the husband would follow her by holding a Tao and Spear in his hands so as to protect themselves from wild animals or enemies.

majority of the respondents understand it as a 'fight between husband and wife.' 90 respondents were in support of 'quarrel between men and women for specific rights.' 248 respondents were of the opinion that gender-based violence is physical assaults, 'beating of wife by husband.' 186 respondents also agreed that gender-based violence includes 'talking ill about the opposite sex in order to make them angry.'102 respondents supported the idea of 'spreading harmful gossip about the opposite sex.'112 respondents agreed to the opinion of 'depriving someone's rights and oppressing others.'160 respondents said it also includes 'pulling down someone's dignity and worth.'143 respondents were of the opinion 'injuring someone's sentiments by putting forwards false comments.'227 respondents were also of the opinion, that it includes 'denying opportunities just because they are of the opposite sex.'

When asked to give reasons for their answers, some respondents understood that the gender-based violence is anything related to physical abuse by men on women, and all of them related it to physical injury through fighting specifically by the opposite sex. On the other hand, many of them opined it as any harm purposely done on the opposite sex just because he/she is a male or female. However, very few of the respondents mentioned that there is any gender-based violence in the Naga society.

Awareness of Gender-based Violence

Nagaland is one of the three Christian majority states in the country. Without any doubt, it can be mentioned that 90 percent Nagas are Christian. Very often outsiders and Nagas themselves think that there is no gender-based violence in the church and in the society. On the other hand, people in general assume that Christians enjoy peace and harmony without any fighting, beating, killings, destructions, corruptions and such related problems. But, when we examine these Christian states it is found that they are no better than those states where Christians are a minority. It is found that generally in the patriarchal context no place is free from gender-based violence, although each situation may vary from one place to another.

Based on the cultural tradition and general perceptions about violence, when we talk about violence in Nagaland, people unknowingly refer to the violent situations that occur between the Indian army and the Naga underground factions, also the fights and clashes between different Naga underground groups. Thus, when one discussed about the gender-based violence, most of the people thought that it is a physical assault on each other.

Gender-based Violence Through Media Projection

Gender roles are determined through different societal norms and traditional practices which were there from time immemorial. In the recent past, it is also mediated through different characters as portrayed in the media. As people are taught and practice what they see and hear from the different sources they handle, it is undeniable that, half of the media presentations are around killings, wars, extortions, unstable political crises, quarrels, uncompromising situation in the family, in the society and also in the church, etc. In all those above mentioned scenes, women have been projected as the objects used for commercialization, and to discipline women in the family or in society, exposing their vulnerability for different purposes. Although, those mentioned scenes have been witnessed throughout the century, people are less conscious about gender-based violence through all these presentations.

Therefore, in order to find out how much people are conscious about what they are watching and reading, and also how the media plays a role in regard to gender-based violence, a question was asked, 'what kinds of gender-based violent scene have you seen in the television and newspapers? Please give a few examples and explain why you consider them to be gender-based violence.[397] For the above mentioned questions except for a few who could not watch television and read news papers, almost all the respondents expressed that 'in many of the television programmes women are used as objects to attract or please the opposite sex, more over it presents the situation in terms of dowry related harassment, prostitution, rape report, sex selection, exposing women's body (pornography) and many more. These are a few opinions expressed by the respondents out of their experiences through different media. Majority of the respondents, 70 percent were of the opinion that by watching TV and reading newspapers they have witnessed gender-based violence. Media presentation does not simply attract viewers but it also motivates people to act it out. Respondents expressed that they learn a variety of new techniques both bad and good. Thus, on many occasions women are the victims. Very surprisingly, 30 percent of the respondents had not come across gender-based violent scenes in the media. It is assumed that those respondents are not even aware of the issues regarding gender-based violence or seldom read news papers or watch TV. It is quite possible that those who use TV just for entertainment or to pass time may not observe gender-based violence.[398] No doubt, a majority of the respondents expressed their opinions that then media presents a lot of information on gender-based violence which encourages viewers.

Gender-based Violence in the Family-Acquired

Gender-based violence begins in the womb and continues till the tomb. Since, the home is the first learning institution in the world, whatever a person learns at home through different activities is imprinted on his/her mind and continues to exercise its influence till the last breath. Thus, a person develops attitudes as she/he grows day by day and gradually adopts behaviour and working system from their

[397] Questionnaire Nos. 5 & 6.

[398] Very few respondents had mentioned that they use TV for entertainment and for educational purposes.

parents and elders with whom they mingle and live with. In other words, gender-based violence is learnt by observation and absorption from childhood, and that the learning process continues throughout their lives till death. Therefore, how a person relates to another and how he/she is treated as boy and girl, as husband and wife, as men and women starts from home and extends to greater society where they belong. In order to obtain details of gender-based violence in the family a few questions were raised: (a) who controls the finance in your family? (b) Normally, who does the household chores besides outside duties? (c) What is the normal practice in your family about sharing property and family land, who gets the major portion?[399] The following information uncovers the situation of gender-based violence based on the opinions obtained from the respondent's answers.

13 percent of respondents were of the opinion that household work is done by men. While 27 percent respondents say 'by women' and 60 percent respondents expressed that 'by both husband and wife'. When examined carefully, it is found that those who support this idea are those where both husbands and wives are employed. On the other hand, a majority of the respondents have mentioned that household works are done by women without any time limitation.

Marriage Related Issues

It is universally true that there is no strict and fast written law regarding marriage on how husband and wife should behave. Even then, there are certain cultural traditional practices which compel both husband and wife to adopt during and after marriage. Generally, in regard to marriage arrangement, in the process of planning for marriage, there is always a tendency to follow the traditional practices which were used as norms, in which the boy and his family members take the initiative to bring up the proposal where the girl has very little option to give suggestions. Of course, opinions and suggestions are sought from the girls' side too for necessary arrangements. Therefore, in order to determine the gender-based violence in relation to marriage the following question was asked: 'whether there is gender discrimination in the traditional marriage practices.'[400] Almost all the women agreed to the question and a few men respondents too put forward their opinions that there is a bias in the traditional marriage practices. Because, in some cases, the girl has to accept the boy her parents have selected for her even though she does not like him.[401]

---

[399] Questionnaire Nos. 8, 9 and 11.

[400] Questionnaire No. 34.

[401] It was in early 1990s, one of the researcher's close friends was forced to marry a person who had lost his wife after long illness leaving behind three children. After much discussion the parents forced her to say 'yes' to the proposal because that husband was rich enough to influence the girl's parents and had a good job too. After the expensive wedding celebration was over on the third day she ran away with her boy friend with whom she was in love for the past few years.

From the data collected, 32% of the respondents expressed that there is gender-based violence in the traditional marriage practice and 3% said that there is no gender-based violence. And a majority of the respondents did not answer at all in this regard. In the traditional marriage, usually the boy spends for all the expenses. Therefore, the girls have nothing much to say in the arrangement unless the boy's family asks them to share the responsibilities between them.

Except for a few, a majority of the respondents disagreed with this statement. They expressed that, women should preserve their identity and dignity by retaining their family name, should not force the wife to adopt their husband's title or name against their will. The reason behind this question could be, some tribes have the practi ce of changing the wives' family name (clan) after their marriage, though many wives are not willing to change their original family name. They are compelled to change and ask her to use her husband's title.[402] Today, due to change of time and the nature of educational and professional paradigm shift, either of the parents' names is accepted and used for the children. In this, the Central Board of Secondary Education (CBSE) has given the option for the child to mention either the mother's or the father's name or both in the school records.[403] In this regard,

20 percent of the respondents are willing that the wife should adopt the husbands' name or title after marriage. Whereas 62 percent of the respondents are not in favour of the idea of adopting husband's name by their wives. In other words, they don't accept the statement/idea of accepting their husband's name or the family title thinking that they may lose their identity which was inherited from their parents. 18% of the respondents did not give their opinion; a few of them mentioned that they are not aware of this kind of practice.

One of the respondents expressed that she had a very grand love marriage, though her parents opposed in the beginning for their relationship; gradually both the parents came to the consensus to go ahead with their marriage. The real problem arose when her husband and his family members asked her to adopt her husband's family name.[404] Since she was so adamant to use/accept that and continued to use her family parents' family name, as before, gradually mistreatment started and the in-laws began to ignore her suggestions whenever there was a family get together, and discussed family affairs. Today, the situation is slowly changing especially among the educated people but still it is continuing in some of the tribes which regard it as the tribal norm and cultural pride.

Issues Related to Work Load

Generally, no one is idle as no one is exempted from any kind of work. However, I would like to categorize work in to two types. First, the out-side work whether

---

[402] Questionnaire No. 28.

[403] *TheTimes of India*, Bangalore, Friday, July 13, 2007, p. 12.

[404] Questionnaires No. 28.

paid or unpaid and the second one is the household work without pay. Out-side works are normally limited to certain hours depending on the nature of the work. On the other hand, household works are unlimited continuing from morning till night. There is no reward or salary as such for household chores where as whether big or small out-side works are paid ones, some times there are promotions and rewards too who ever deserves it.

Though there are a number of people living together, there seems to be a difference in assigning routine work for both men and women. Therefore, in order to identify the work-load among family members, specifically between men and women besides outside professions, a question was asked, 'who does the major household chores in the family?'[405]

The data analysis indicates that 13% of respondents were of the opinion that a man does the household work. 27% of respondents say 'by women'. 60% of the respondents were of the opinion that household chores are done by both men and women. When the questionnaires were analyzed it was found that, 40 respondents who mentioned that men do the household chores were the ones who are not working or hold a regular paid job, thus have enough time to be with the family. The respondents who have mentioned that it is done by both men and women were mostly employed ones, working outside as well.

Issues in Sexuality

When asked whether they are sexually abused by their spouses,[406] none of the men responded that they are abused by their wives, where as some women respondents boldly mentioned that they are occasionally sexually abused by their husbands, especially in a situation like-when they don't respond to their demand immediately and when their husbands are drunk. It is also mentioned that, not only wives but female relatives and maid servants, and those who are helping in the family too are abused. A few respondents mentioned without any hesitation how their husbands sexually abused them, their sisters and maid servants during their absence.

Among those, one of the respondents answered the above question without any reservation by pouring out her untold miseries and agony which she had experienced, defaming all her family members in this way: "yes, many times I feel like a victim of his sexual appetite. I am often thinking that he wanted only my body from the very beginning, I was so ignorant of it, only to realize it now after he swallowed me."[407] Again, when asked, 'has your spouse hurt you psychologically? If yes, in what way?' She further says, "Yes, he molested my two younger sisters culminating in raping one of them. Many times I thought of divorce but due to

[405] Questionnaire No. 11.

[406] Questionnaire No. 30.

[407] Questionnaire No. 30. The respondent is a house-wife. Her application for church ministry was 'detained' several times because she is burdened with small children.

many reasons I could finally forgive the crime."[408] As there are such incidents, as expressed by the female respondents, it indicates that, though they are not bold enough to express the incident in order to save the family honour, many women are going through sexual violence from their spouses and their male members inside their home. Sexual violence is not only between husband and wife, but also among many female members in the family including maidservants and even female visitors. Therefore, in order to ascertain the reality a question was asked- have you come across any sexual abuse from your spouse.

In this, 15 of the respondents (5%) expressed that, they experienced sexual abuse from their spouses. Those 15 respondents were all female. 34% of the respondents said they never came across sexual abuse from their spouses of which, 12 respondents were women and 22 were men. 61% of the respondents mentioned 'No answer,' out of which 101 respondents were men and 82 were female. Out of the 300 respondents, only 15 respondents mentioned that they came across sexual violence from their spouses. It shows that there exists sexual violence among married couples or even among partners though they did not respond to the question. It is assumed that though they experienced sexual abuse they wanted to keep away from the public eye or accepted it as traditional norms/ practices.

It is natural and cannot be denied that once a normal and a healthy person whether male or female undergoes sexual abuse, automatically it will also affect him/her psychologically or morally. It is thus a life-threatening game experienced in human society. Though people are going through such psychological crises, very few people feel that they need to confront it openly and squarely. Of course, sexual abuse is not the only factor that amounts to psychological violence as there are other related factors which produce psychological trauma. For this, a question was asked 'whether they have experienced psychological violence from their spouse.'

Analysis shows that 29% of the 300 respondents were of the opinion that they were abused psychologically by their spouses. While 10% of the respondents were of the opinion that they experienced psychological abuse from their spouses, on the other hand a majority of the respondents amounting to 61% responded with 'no answer.' It seems 86 of the respondents who experienced psychological abuse were wives, while 31 respondents were husbands. According to the responses, they were psychologically abused when they received derogatory comments from their spouses whom they trust. That is, whenever they experience sexual assault or when their partner is flirting around with the opposite sex, whenever their ideology differs, and whenever they are insulted in the public by their spouses.[409]

---

[408] Questionnaire No. 32.

[409] One of the male respondents mentioned that one day in a wedding party his wife hit him with an umbrella in front of others. He was hurt very much. He said, it is not only we men who oppress women, but women too harass and mistreat their spouses.

Distribution of Property in the Family

From the very beginning of Naga history, it is noticed that the customary law taught about the right to property and land ownership, automatically binds the sharing of properties among children/sons and daughters. Since, there is a history of inheritance laws, all the respondents referred to the 'customary law' when they discussed traditional issues. Thus, according to customary laws, women are not entitled to inherit the land and properties of immovable ones like - house, fields/ farms, etc. In some rare cases, if a parent acquired land out of their joint-venture among family members, only those plots may be shared a little with the daughters, but not the same as sons. Otherwise, in general, daughters get a minimum share like ornaments, clothes, weaving instruments, and a few household things, a piece of land or house in the case of a rich family. However, giving properties to daughters vary from family to family. Whereas for sons there is a major share, beginning with the house and land from their parents and even from forefathers which are inherited through the ages.

Therefore, in order to obtain their opinion on property-sharing among sons and daughters, a few questions were placed before them: 'what is the normal practice in your family about sharing of property? Please explain.[410] A majority of the respondents expressed that women have very less chance to acquire family properties which is very unfair. On the other hand very few respondents had mentioned that daughters also should get their share. A few opinions expressed in the questionnaire[411] by the respondents are:

(a) Society being patriarchal in nature, women should not claim any rights in case of landed properties except if supported by an affidavit.
(b) Daughters are also the bonafide members of the family so they should get the share as sons.
(c) Contrary to the above opinions, some of the respondents mentioned, cultural traditions cannot change, because it was there from the very beginning. Rather people should retain that rich cultural heritage and abide by what the customary law says.
(d) As per Naga culture, sons have all the rights for landed properties, whereas the daughters can enjoy their family rights as long as they remain single. That is, if she gets married, those properties will go back to her fathers' family.
(e) To show that all humans are equal, it is fair to give a share of the family land to the daughters, they too have the same responsibility, and to create the feeling of belongingness. Giving the family land away may also create a feeling of oneness even after daughters are married. Again

[410] Questionnaire No. 12.

[411] *Ibid.,* No. 12.

a question was asked 'who gets the major portion of the property in the family.

A majority of the respondents said that a major portion of the parents' properties are for the sons, whereas daughters get only a little, which includes ornaments and some household things. Therefore, when one is denied what he/she is supposed to get, that is against the human rights principles too. Because every human being irrespective of whether female or male (sons or daughters), has the right to own and to live one's life according to one's choice.

Financial Management in the Family

Economic stability is required for a sound and healthy family life, in which economic responsibility should be properly shared between the spouses, and there is a need to have transparency in handling money. Everywhere irrespective of the family structure, whenever there is no proper financial stability and mishandling by one spouse, it creates problems in the family. Thus, in order to figure out the instability/inequality in economic position in the family, especially between husband and wife, the following question was put forward: 'whether they have experienced economic abuse from their spouse.'[412]

Though most of the respondents were not willing to express the violent situation in the family in order to protect the family honour or name, it is to be noted that gender-based violence exists in the family. One of the best examples of it could be in the preference for a boy-child in every family so that he can inherit from his father where as daughters cannot. Therefore, better attentions are extended to boys than girls among the children. This kind of treatment could be seen easily through certain responsibility allotted to them on the basis of sex. A few female respondents said:

(a) Since I am not earning anything my husband does not give his salary to me, every time I go for shopping for domestic purpose he makes a list and hands it over to me, again after return I have to explain to him every penny that I spent. He used to purchase even my dresses too without my knowledge. I cannot buy anything without his approval.

(b) Another respondent said, 'my husband only goes to the bank. How much money is in the savings and how much he draws from the bank I am not sure, many a time I am hurt by the way he mishandles the money. Whenever I enquire about it he gets angry and replies that it is out of my earnings. Although, I am educated he does not allow me to work saying that if I can teach our children their lessons that is enough.'

(c) One of the female respondents expressed that her husband never supported her financially, "she alone had to take care of the children

[412] Questionnaire No. 33.

> and other family affairs. He spends all his earnings in drinking and gambling. Especially during children's school admission when my salary could not manage to pay the fees I really need his support, but whenever I talk about financial problems he gets angry hits me."[413]

Thus, in regard to economic abuse, the total respondents were of the opinion that they were economically abused by their spouses, that a majority of the respondents who experienced economic abuses were women.

Gender-based Violence in the Church Ministry

The church is the people of God, the believers in Jesus Christ, under the rule of the Holy Spirit. The church is where God rules and it is intended that His believers live in a situation where the Holy Spirit guides and where people live in peace and harmony without any prejudices. Though every church stands in that faith and on the principles of equality, peace, partnership, justice and harmony in terms of church activities, yet, they themselves create a contrary atmosphere by exercising all forms of violence based on gender. In order to find out the gender-based violence in the church's ministry, specifically in its leadership, decision-making process and church ministerial activities, a few questions were asked, and out of their answers, the researcher categorized the issues in the following way:

Gender Sensitization Programmes

There is a regular Women's Fellowship both in the Association and in the local churches. At the Association level, there is a separate women's department headed by the Women's Secretary. At the local level, there is a women's department under the leadership of 'Women Leader' or 'Associate pastor for women.' Under the initiative of the women's leader, women's services are conducted regularly once a week, every Thursday. Besides, many activities are taken up by the women's fellowship like, conducting seminars on different topics, house visitation, charity works and evangelism covering different institutions, hospitals, rehabilitations, and prisons, etc. One of the valuable tasks taken up by the women's fellowship is in the raising of funds for the fellowship and for the local church in general by different means, like doing manual work, through charity or through well wishers' contributions. Moreover, women's fellowship extends its concerns by conducting awareness programmes educating community members. Thus, with the active initiatives of the women's fellowship, churches conduct various awareness programmes throughout the year.

In order to obtain how seriously gender-based violence is considered in the church's ministry-what kind of awareness are imparted to women in order to

[413] This situation was expressed to the researcher by a working woman during a personal interview. She has five children, but her husband never extends his help financially. Whatever money he gets he spends it on drinking and gambling.

empower them, and what type of issues are discussed in the seminar, a few questions were asked-'How often does the church conduct seminars or consultations on women's issues?[414]

From the 268 respondents' answers, it was noticed that the churches conduct programmes two to three times in a year. Some churches conduct only once in a year. The type of programmes they conduct for women are on the topics of child care, family and financial managements, women empowerment programme, sex education, and HIV/Aids education, etc. Very surprisingly, no respondent mentioned programmes on gender-based violence/issues or Christian education for violence on women. A few respondents mentioned that, 'we are so fortunate to be in our church because our church conducts seminars for women every year on several topics like-how to be a good house wife, how to keep accounts properly, learning about sex education, HIV/Aids awareness, career guidance education, co-curricular activities, and Bible study'. These responses may clarify the real situation about women in general. However, it may be mentioned here that unless the society reviews the traditional practices which hinders women and deprives theirs rights in sharing privileges and responsibility, among the sex (Naga) women will remain 'eating in the same bowl, which is serve by others.'

2. Issues in Leadership

The church structure is somehow little different from that of the state government. In the Association and Convention level, the highest post is the Executive Secretary. Every association has its own Executive Secretary, under which there are several Associate Secretaries for different departments. For instance, there are departments for dealing with women, youth, Sunday school, child evangelism and mission etc. At the local church level, there are different department too. Each department is run under a full time minister. Therefore, in order to obtain information, how the leadership opportunities are shared in the church's ministry and what kinds of leadership are taken up by women, a question was asked, 'what according to you would be the suitable ministry for women in the church?'[415]

Analysis indicate, 11% of the respondents were of the opinion that pastoral ministry is suitable for women, while 67% of the respondents were of the opinion that women can opt for the post of Associate pastor in the church. 72% said a woman can be a youth director, 93% were of the opinion that she can be a child director, while only 1% of the respondents were in support of her being a church secretary, 55% of the respondents of the opinion of a missionary, 68% of the respondents were in support of the evangelist, and 6% of the respondents were of the opinion that a woman also should be given a chance to be the Executive Secretary at the Association level.

---

[414] Questionnaire No. 15 and 16.

[415] Questionnaire No. 17.

As the above presentations clearly shows still the church has an understanding that certain leadership position are set aside for men only, therefore, a majority of the respondents were not in favour of women's leadership in the church's ministry. Thus, it indicates that all the highest posts like the Executive Secretary (Bishop) and Pastor are for men while the lesser and minor or assisting posts are for women. Very interestingly, still churches are of the opinion that women are good only for the children's and youth ministry. With that understanding, whenever there is any vacancy in the church's ministry, always the first preference will be for the male candidates.

Decision-making Process in the Church

It is mandatory to appoint deacon board members (Pastorate Committee) in all the local churches in Nagaland. The appointment can be for certain years, and it varies from church to church. It is like a supreme body which discusses the overall activities of the church under certain guidelines, for all the departments. The pastor and the secretary act as ex-officio members of the meeting. This is the highest decision-making body in the church circle. Therefore, in order to obtain information regarding women's participation in the decision-making process in the church's ministry a question was asked, 'whether women are allowed to attain membership in the church decision-making body.'[416] From the responses it is found that, there is no consistency in the answers given due to different patterns of church administration. In the recent past, a few churches (Urban areas) have appointed women as the deacon board members.

From the answers it is seen that even though women are allowed to attend the meeting, their representation is only 20-30%. Moreover, their suggestions and opinions are not taken as valid. One of the respondents mentioned in this context, that 'even though we want to express our opinions we are compelled to be away from the discussion while preparing refreshment, again another woman who is a deacon board member expressed that 'since women's representation is just 20%, our opinions are always sidelined.' Thus, in regard to decision-making in the church's ministry, it is men who lay down the guide lines for the whole of church's activities.

Role of the Church in Liberating People from a Culture of Violence

In a state like Nagaland, the church is one of the most important platforms to enlighten the people in several aspects. The church is the right place to provide a platform to address all kinds of issues which infringe peaceful living, inequality and discrimination, and oppression. The age-old cultural practices which denied certain sections of the humanity, and whose lives are surrounded by various forms of violence need to be liberated from the culture of violence. Therefore, in order to obtain opinions about the churches' role towards liberating people from a

[416] Questionnaire No. 41.

culture of violence, a question was asked, 'what could the church do to liberate people from the culture of violence? Please suggest ways.'[417] Opinions expressed by the respondents were numerous:

(a) Churches should preach the message of equality and justice.
(b) The Church must provide a platform to address all forms of violence which negates the wellbeing of the society.
(c) The Church should appoint persons on the basis of qualification and abilities rather than on gender.
(d) The Church should incorporate women in the church and state administrations as men if one is capable.
(e) Traditional mindsets of the people need to be changed where there is a wide distinction between men and women in every aspect of life.
(f) The Church should without any reservation be ready to fight the most dreaded social evil issues like sexual violence, domestic violence and economic violence which a woman considers as taboo to be discussed in her teaching ministry.

Thus, in order to liberate people from the culture of violence, every church needs to be focused not only on preaching alone but should keep in touch with the situation of this fast changing world, the context where every human lives, and the rigidity of customary laws need to be transformed in accordance with the context. One of the respondents expressed that, 'though churches preach about equality, justice and peace, rather they themselves encourage inequality, do lots of injustice and practice all sorts of corruptions which creates disharmony.'

Gender-based Violence in Social Life

A person is very much determined by the societal norms and its structures from where she/he comes from. In other words, irrespective of whether one is male or female, rich or poor, high or low or even educated or un-educated, a person is bound by the traditional cultural practices. It cannot be denied that, there is a wide distinction between male and female with regard to social norms in every society, based on the power and authority, weak and strong, as this creates all forms of violence specifically gender-based violence in the society. Thus, keeping those points in mind, several questions were formulated which considered imperative in order to obtain opinions concerning the crises situation faced by the women in the Naga society. Out of many mentioned, there are a few important issues which hinder women to get their rights as citizens. They will be examined below.

1. Right to Inheritance

All human beings have the right to live and enjoy the fullest as implicitly mentioned in the constitution and also from the human rights perspectives.

[417] Questionnaire No. 47.

Denying someone's rights is against the Human Rights Principles. Therefore, in order to obtain the practice of right to ownership and distribution of properties among men and women in Naga patriarchal society a question was asked, 'What is the normal practice regarding the right of parental property for daughters in the family?" In response to the above questions,

48% expressed that movable properties should go to sons and immovable things should be distributed among the children according to sex, while 46% respondents suggested that whatever properties that the parents acquired should be equally shared among the children, irrespective of sex. The reason behind that was so because they were all from the same parents, therefore there should not be any partiality among children. Further, they expressed that denying equal share to daughters is a crime. In regard to property-sharing, another question was asked, "Do you feel it is fair to give a share of the family land to the daughters?"[418]

In this, 19% (28 men & 32 women) of them opined that daughters also should have the right to own the family land, while 68% (men 150 & 68 women) respondents said daughters have no right to claim the family land. 13% (30 men & 12 women) of the respondents did not share their opinions with this issue. They expressed their opinions, why they feel that way. A few could be mentioned here:

(a) From time immemorial in our society women are not allowed to inherit land, it is against the customary law if our society allows daughters to inherit the land. Need to preserve our rich tradition.

(b) Women cannot take care of the landed property because it involves physical strength to clear up the place which is not possible at all from the side of women.

(c) If a daughter is given her share of land it will go to others because once the girl gets married it will be under her husband's care and it will be become some others' property eventually.

(d) Women should not claim equality with men in sharing properties because from the very beginning there is a clear indication who will take or get what kind of things.

(e) Women are men's property, without men they are incomplete, as long as they are with men they don't need separate land; whatever their husbands bring or get that is for both of them.

Contrary to the above mentioned opinions, it was also expressed that equality should be maintained in sharing property because:

1. Both daughters and sons are from the same parents if one sex is denied to get their share that is against biblical teachings.

[418] Questionnaire No. 25.

2. Treating children differently according to sex is against the Human Rights perspective, equality should be maintained.
3. Gender factor should not come in while dealing with property sharing, it should be based on equality, and daughters also should get what they deserve.
4. Daughters too can preserve family identity by maintaining land and other assets if given an opportunity.
5. No distinction should be made between sons and daughters in distributing parental assets including land because both sons and daughters are equal in the eyes of the law.

2. Participation in Decision-making

Matters relating to the community well-being and development, setting out guidelines, rules and regulations, legal laws or customary laws based on certain principles or traditional practices are discussed in the public meetings, which is held annually, occasionally or whenever a need arises. Every community comprises of both male and female citizens. Responsibilities and privileges should be shared among community members in order to maintain tranquility in every sphere. Therefore, in order to know the representation in the decision-making and in public meeting, questions were raised, 'do Naga societies allow women to participate in the State decision-making process? If no, why are they not allowing them, what are the obstacles?[419]

Except for a very few, a majority of the respondents expressed, even though there is no restrictions for women not to attend in the decision-making meeting, yet from its inception men only took the lead. Further, it was mentioned that it was so because men are more open/frank, expressive/outspoken, capable of handling the critical situations, whereas women are 'good for nothing, very talkative, not knowledgeable, and full of inferiority complex.' With this understanding women are deprived of many opportunities even after being exposed to many awareness programmes by NGOs.

Table 18: Women's participation in decision-making

From the analysis it shows that 66% of the respondents (111female and 86 male) were of the opinion that women are not allowed attending the decision-making meeting. While 34% (5 female and 97 male) expressed that women too are given chance to attend every community meeting. When asked about the obstacles (for not allowing women to attend), respondents have mentioned that 'public places are for men, if women are allowed the whole meeting would be disturbed, 'they are not knowledgeable to come out with the concrete decisions.' One of the male respondents expressed in this way, 'though the church and state have their own perspectives and policies to function according to the context yet culture plays a dominant role in society, our culture is patriarchal and so it limits

[419] Questionnaire No. 41.

women's participation.'[420] Another female respondent explained, 'these days the government encourages women representation in the Village Development Board so whenever there is a public meeting in the village we are also invited but we are entrusted to make tea or to serve food, so our opinions are not included in the agenda.'[421]

From the above discussions it is clear that women's participation in decision-making is very obscure, where men folks decide, make rules and regulations for the whole community. In doing so, in many cases, a woman is deprived, discriminated and her position is misinterpreted which lead to gender-based violence.

3. Gender-based Violence in Public life.

Every human being has the right to live and exercise his/her choice according to his or her own ability. But in most of the patriarchal societies, women are not considered equal to men. They are treated as subordinate beings, making them dependent on men. A few instances out of the questionnaires may be mentioned here:

Whenever there is a public meeting it is meant only for men. As cited earlier, women are invited but they are assigned other work like preparing refreshments, cooking, shopping, which deprives their attendance and participation in the discussion. So, men in their own interests do all the decision-making. Whenever women put forth a few suggestions or advice contradicting their opinions, men stop them half way by commenting 'women/children take your seat or keep quiet, "don't interrupt the matured men's discussions." On the other hand, when women's issues are brought for discussion, they are discarded by saying 'it is a private matter.' Therefore, in order to obtain their opinions towards gender-justice, a question was asked, 'what would be the appropriate place/platform to talk about gender justice?[422]

34% of the respondents were of the opinion that the Church is the right platform to discuss gender justice, 9% mention Political Bodies, 17% respondents say Village Council, 20% respondents have mentioned NGOs, 20% respondents were in favour of Women's group, 5% of the respondents supported that the state government is the appropriate platform to discuss gender-justice.

Findings of Field Research on Gender-based Violence

As the pioneering research in this issue of gender-based violence in Naga society from the Christian Education perspective, the author has noted many important findings through interviews and questionnaires. Since, people in general and specifically women folk had understood that violence is some action which causes physical injury due to fighting between spouses and more recently as atrocities

[420] Questionnaire No. 42.

[421] One woman Village Development Board member has mentioned so in her response, and it is true in many cases.

[422] Questionnaire No. 20.

done to women and children by military regimes, in the initial stages, when the author approached the respondents, they were somewhat reluctant, irresponsive, and also defensive by saying that, there is no valid case to do research or there is nothing much to explore regarding gender-based violence in Naga society. People further responded that unlike in other parts of India there is no beating, fighting between husband and wife, no practice of dowry harassment due to it, no suicide cases owing to torture and harassment of women. Rather, they opined that Naga women enjoy every facility like their male counterparts in the family and outside. They are given education as with both sons and daughters. Moreover, as military oppressions are not so serious as before, these days women are given enough chances to accommodate them in every field both in church and society, etc.[423] Therefore, according to source the study could be just a waste of time, and as it is not related to the church's educational ministry it is not worth researching on this very topic.

Besides, there were various criticisms from different walks of life; people made comments saying, 'Naga women have a better opportunity than those of other states.' One of the reasons for suggesting this could be their natural friendly disposition, their ability to mix freely with those of the opposite sex and their readiness to socialize. But, a critical appraisal of the real situation of the Naga society, and its analysis as in the data supports that along with its social structure and traditional practices, it falsifies this assumption. The rigid customary laws and patriarchal tradition among the Nagas have however deprived women of their opportunities for participation and mobility, keeping them silent for a long time. After a critical evaluation and cross-checking of the empirical data, the author found out that there are several inconsistencies in the respondents' answers. For instance, opinions vary between the older people and the younger generation on matters relating to the issue of gender and gender-based violence. Given below are a few major findings out of the over-all analysis of gender-based violence situation in Nagaland:

1. Patriarchy and Gender-based Violence

As mentioned elsewhere, Naga society is patriarchal, where the father or a male member of the family controls the family, properties, politics, religious rituals, and economic affairs. He has the last word on matters of decision-making in the family and in the community. Thus, men dominate the socio-economic, religious, political and family life, while, women play only a subordinate role. Since patriarchy articulates structural and institutional relations of dominations, authority and power relations between women and men, women's freedom of choice and their behaviour, action, and thought are restricted.

[423] These are the comments and expressions received by the author in the beginning of her empirical work. To respond to those kind of criticisms and comments are quite challenging.

2. Gender Roles in the Family and in Society

Patriarchal ideologies generally lay down some distinctive roles and social norms for both men and women, and this applies to Naga society as well. The concept of 'gender' describes the socially given attributes, roles and activities, and the responsibility connected with being a male or a female in a given society. As mentioned earlier, the traditional stereotype roles define that, a woman must be humble, feminine, motherly, caring, soft spoken, hardworking, etc. Therefore, the roles and the functions in a society are defined according to the sex of a person. Thus, gender identity determines how one is perceived, and how one is expected to think and act as a woman or man, because of the way society is organized.[424]

Gender also determines how power is distributed between the sexes. In Naga society, therefore, the home and family life are regarded as a woman's place while public life and politics are that of a man. Thus, women's role is confined to homes, especially to domestic affairs. Their main roles of motherhood and the task of housekeeping have been maintained as the vocation of the woman and the yardstick for gauging her usefulness. What the sociologist Tapati points out is also fitting and could be applied to the Naga women too. She says, "Woman has but one resource-Home. The end and aim of her life is to cultivate the domestic affections, to minister to the comfort and happiness of her husband, to look after and tend her children and exercise her little supervision over domestic economy."[425] It is this mindset that discourages a girl for example, who is trying to pursue higher studies. One often hears from others including her family members ridiculing her and saying, 'it is enough as long as you are able to take care of your husband properly and mange to teach your children in their home work, no need to learn more and spending time and money over that.'

Thus, in the accepted norms of Naga patriarchal society, household work and nurturing children are exclusively the woman's responsibility. A strict adherence to this norm can be observed in some tribal groups even today. Especially in the rural setting, gender roles are very obvious. No wonder then one can see women carrying babies with a load (bamboo basket contains fuel, clothes, implements and food stuff) on their back, while going to the field, whereas, the husband will simply followed her holding a *Dao*[426] or stick.

Thus, a majority of the respondents are in the opinion that, household chores are mostly done by women. No doubt, from this one can assume that from the very beginning society understood women's place to be in the kitchen, while all the household work nurturing the children and serving her husband/all female members in the family are her lot. Therefore, in Naga society if a woman

---

[424] Candida March, Ines Smyth and Maitrayee Mukhopadhyay, *A Guide to Gender-Analysis Framework* (Oxfam GB), p.19.

[425] Tapati Chakravarty, "Women's Education and Employment: Uncertain Future," in *Women's Link 8/3* (July-September 2002), p. 4.

[426] A big knife used for cutting trees or clearing jungles.

does not know cooking, weaving, knitting, etc, she is considered a tomboy. For instance, even an under-aged Naga girl knows how to cook and to take care of small babies and doing household work when other elder brothers and father are around doing nothing. In fact, women have the triple burden, as breadwinners, child-care workers as well as the servitors of their husbands and male members. Though women spend countless hours putting a lot of efforts in domestic affairs, it is hardly acknowledged or counted as work because it does not involve money and as it is based on their sex, it is considered as their assigned role in society.

3. Gender-based Violence in the Political Arena

Although, Naga women have a very rare chance of participating in the political life of the society, especially when it comes to decision-making, it has not been a reality as yet, because in the rural set up, the village council is the highest political administrative authority consisting of only men. Except for a few, most of the tribes follow a gerontocratic form of polity where male elders from different clans are nominated. Similarly, in the urban areas, the political administrative authority consists of select male members, although the pattern of administration is democratic.[427] The village council that comprises of male members has the overall authority in every community.

In spite of the new developments, the system of Naga villages' council administration continues to follow the old pattern even today, where a woman is not allowed to become the Village Administrator or Representative under any circumstances. Today, these traditional practices are somehow changing due to the new development scheme where women are given a chance to be in the Village Development Board (VDB). Although, women are allowed to attend the meeting, they cannot contribute anything to the discussions. Only a few selected women can attend and they are as servitors, throughout the meeting. Even if they get a rare chance to express their thoughts their speech will be cut short by saying, 'women and children do not disturb mature men's discussions.'[428] Thus, when asked whether women are allowed in the decision-making, a majority of the respondents have mentioned that they are not allowed. Almost all say, women are not given any chance to take part in the community meeting. As Elizabeth Moore says, "The public sphere is the arena for male and the private sphere is the arena for women and children."[429]

Thus, public matters in Naga society are regarded as men's activities and women's roles are located at home. This patriarchal attitude still dominates the

---

[427] Tajen, Ao, *Ao Naga Customary Laws* (Mokokchung: Aowati, 1980), p. 114 ff.

[428] This was expressed by a woman respondent in the questionnaire, being one of the Village Development Board members, out of her experiences. Likewise there are several occasions where women receive this kind of comments.

[429] Mary Elizabeth Moore, "The Unity of the Sacred and the Public Possibilities from feminist Theology," p. 206.

socio-political, economic and religious life, where the voices of women, for justice go unnoticed in the society. It regards only men as rulers, administrators and policy makers in the society and it cannot accept women as administrators. Never in the history of Nagaland there were any female State Ministers or members of Parliament, Chief Secretary, nor Village Council Member.[430] It seems that only in 2005 October, the first Naga lady Head *Gaonbora* (Village elders/municipal member) was appointed under Dimapur Town Municipal in Nagaland. However, many different organizations, peoples' groups and Goanbora association, etc., and their members themselves opposed this.

Very surprisingly, more criticisms were raised from the women's organizations, by saying that never in the human history a lady who is supposed to be at home and taking care of household responsibility, had been given this kind of chance. The candidate Mrs. Pangichila Pongen expressed this,[431] when the author interacted her.[432] This was so, although the selected candidate was a knowledgeable and well-established person financially. But, just because of gender differences, this was so, as the society is trying to justify men's ruler-ship and strength. Though, a majority of the respondents claimed that Naga women have better positions in the society, yet not so, in every aspect of life. The real situation arises when the time comes for women to hold the position of responsibility and privilege. Though in some of the respondents' answers it was mentioned that there is no discrimination and exploitation towards women in Naga society, it is very obvious that in many ways gender-based violence is seen and meted out through various forms of violence as already discussed elsewhere. Unless these kinds of traditional attitudes and practices are totally wiped out, gender-based violence would remain active and continue to flourish in every society in general and in the Naga society in particular.

4. Gender-based Violence in Property-sharing

In every given society sharing of property becomes a problem to everyone in the family, and to the wider community members, whether it is inherited or not, whenever somebody dies. The right to properties becomes a crucial issue in Naga society today, as this consciousness is more obvious among the educated and especially to those who are exposed to the outside world. One of the main goals of several women's organizations is to claim the right to inheritance and fairness in property-sharing among the children irrespective of gender. Although, this issue was one of the topics in every women's gathering it is sad that till today it has not been resolved, and many good citizens are deprived of their rights due to this age-old cultural practice where women are the worst victims. Most unfortunate

[430] Interview with V. Achumi, a government official, Kohima, Nagaland, on June 14, 2006.

[431] She is the first lady *Gaonbora* appointed by Dimapur Municipal body, Nagaland.

[432] The opinions in a way of complaint towards the selection of woman *Gaonbora* appeared several times in the daily news papers and was also discussed in several public gatherings.

groups are those who are in the rural areas who are solely depending on land-resources, and are under the mercies of their parents for life sustenance. They face untold miseries owing to certain norms, which they have to abide by and accept those customary laws.

In this connection the respondents' answers and opinions were analyzed and the findings were formulated accordingly. Based on the respondents' opinions and discussions about property sharing, opinions can be divided into three different types of inheritance or property rights in the Naga society:

1) Clan-owned Property

Whatever property it may be as owned by the clan, it was never given to women. Almost all the respondents feel that the land or property which belongs to the clan should not be given to women because when they get married their children will take only the father's title and automatically she too will become a co-sharer with her husband's property as long as they live together as husband and wife. It is clear then that, a woman does not have her share in the clan property on her own merit. Even though, a woman does not have her own, in the case of the widow or unmarried, she can make use of her clan land for cultivation, construction and for other purposes.[433] This is the practice from the very existence of Naga society. Therefore, it was the opinion of all the respondents that women do not have any share in the clan property.

2) Family-owned Property

The property that is passed down from the forefathers to fathers either as land or things, they are owned only by sons. Immovable properties like lands and houses are reserved for sons/men. For instance, a house or a plot of land owned by the father from his parents as his share is never given to daughters. Only the sons inherit it. But in the case of unmarried women, they can make use of the land for cultivation or farming, construct houses but if she gets married or if she dies it will go back to the family again. She cannot dispose it off as she likes to any one or for any purpose. In this inheritance issue, the researcher was told by her own mother that "in all the naming ceremonies for the first five daughters till her naming was performed, it was just by killing a cock/hen among the family members as a celebration of their birth. But when the sixth boy-child was born, your grandfather was overjoyed and had a great celebration for his naming, by saying that 'now my inheritor has come.'"[434] It is clear that, women do not have a share in the family owned property. Till today, women are thus denied property rights in the Naga society.

[433] Interview with Mr. Satemmeren, Head *Dobashe*, Mokokchung Nagaland, on June 26, 2006.

[434] Interview with Mrs. Sowainla, Mokokchung, Nagaland, on June 23, 2006.

3) Parents-acquired Property

The properties that are acquired by the parents during their life as husband and wife come under this category of property. In this, both the moveable and immovable assets are included. It is the norm that all the immovable assets go to sons and out of the movable things too a major share of the property goes to sons. Daughters get only a minimal share, as a token of her parents. In most cases, things like weaving instruments/sewing machine, ornaments, clothes, agricultural implements in the case of rural agricultural settings, are given to daughters. In the urban areas, a few parents who are rich enough, having multiples assets with fewer sons or blessed with only daughters start sharing among the children but the major share goes to sons. If there is no son in the family, nephews of uncles inherit the properties.

In sum, according to the Naga customary law, daughters cannot inherit family properties, only sons can. In the absence of a son, it is the nearest kinsman of the father who becomes the recipient. In this connection, the researcher is a witness to an incident where, one of the church ministers admitted that, on the death of his brother (who does not have a son), he was asked to occupy his brother's house and other properties even though he was reluctant to accept them. The wife and daughters had no choice but to accept the decision.[435] As Jeuti Barooah says in his article, "A widow has no right over her husband's property, she remains a guardian and her eldest son is *de jure* head of the family."[436] The plight of the spouse after her husbands' death or that of the daughter after her fathers' death is deplorable indeed, for they have no share in the property.

Human Rights and Gender-based Violence

According to the United Nations Human Rights Commission (UNHRC), "Human rights are the essence of man. They are what make a man human. That is why they are called human rights. Deny them and you deny man's humanity."[437] Thus, the United Nations publication[438] states that human rights could be generally defined as those rights, which are inherent in our nature without which we cannot live as human beings. The same publication also states that human rights and fundamental freedom allow us to fully develop and use our human qualities, our intelligence, our talents and our conscience to satisfy our spiritual

---

[435] Interview with Rev. Imna (pastor), on 15th September 2006, Bangalore.

[436] Jeuti Barooah, "Property and Women's Rights in the tribal Areas of the North east," in *Changing Women's Status in India: Focus on the Northeast,* ed. Walter Fernandes and Sanjay Barbora Gauhati: North Eastern Social Research Center, 2002, p. 105.

[437] *Understanding Human Rights*, Metro Manila: Structural Alternative Legal Assistance for Grassroots, p. 111.

[438] Human Rights: Question and Answer, United Nations Department of Public Information p.4, 1987. in *Understanding Human Right*, p. 1.

and other needs. They are based on humankind's increasing demand for a life with dignity and worth whereby a human being will receive respect and protection.[439]

The above mentioned Human Rights Commission has been made and used, sometimes modified according to the context and applied to specific needs to protect certain rights for human goodness. Thus, every nation-state has adopted the commissions' decisions and modified them and even reframed them to suit its own country. Even laws have been made in every country based on the human rights commission. Yet, in many places, this human rights issue is kept aside and a decision is taken according to its community customary laws, especially, when it comes to gender issues, the issues on property or inheritance. Nagaland is one of the states in India, which ignores Human Rights Commission's decisions and strictly follows its own traditional Customary Laws.

The Customary Laws of Nagas as examined earlier, does not have a written code as a legal law or regulation as such, yet they are used as cultural norms and guiding principles wherever necessary and suitable. Sometimes they are called as moral laws to discipline community members for certain matters. Therefore, a majority of Nagas is not aware that, gender-based violence is a violation of Human Rights. Especially, when we talk about 'Human Rights issues,' no wonder, many people refers only to the situation where people are killed, harassed, tortured, abused, mishandled, and where women are raped by the military, innocent people killed during the fight between different Naga underground factions and between Army and underground people.[440]

Thus, no adequate awareness has been given so far from the Human Rights group towards gender-based violence as 'human/women rights problem,' rather it was considered only as a private or a community responsibility when the situation like rape, divorce, ill-treatment on women in the family and in public places, inheritance and property issues between sons and daughters arose. It is heart-rending to witness the rejection, mistreatment, injustice done to women on many occasions and people in general as they are yet to be educated to fight against all sorts of injustices done to more than half of its citizens by making use of the statements laid down by the Human Rights Commissions.

While talking about women's rights, the author feels that people of India in general and Nagas in particular, need to learn from our leaders' words. Two examples suffice from the writings of Mahatma Gandhi. He says, "I am uncompromising in the matter of women's rights. I should treat the daughters and sons on a footing of perfect equality."[441] Also the first Prime Minister of India,

---

[439] *Ibid.*, p. 1.

[440] These are the opinions expressed by the fellow Naga citizens to the author while discussing the issue 'gender-based violence is a violation of Human Rights.'

[441] Pratap C. Gine, "Women's property rights: An Issue of the North East India Christian women," in *Women's Issues in the 21st century*, ed. Narola Imchen (Jorhat: Women's Study Centre eastern Theological College, Jorhat, Assam, November, 2001), p. 151.

Pandit Jawaharlal Nehru, addressed the same issue from a different perspective. He said, "The status and social position of the women indicate the country's character more than anything else."[442] If a nation is to progress further, it is imperative that women's rights need to be recognized and respected. Women's rights would only then be recognized when their rights to property and leadership are recognized, because there hangs the dignity and identity of women.

Gender-based Violence in the Church's Ministry

From its inception, church's administration in Nagaland was appropriated on the lines of village administrative pattern. One can easily observe the patriarchal form of government even in the church administration. In other words, patriarchal ideology is found very vividly in the church's ministry too. The church remains one area throughout the world where patriarchy persists and where women, being half of the population are alienated. No church is free from patriarchy.[443] Thus, the present Naga churches' structure is very much patriarchal especially in the rural congregations. So, the present church administration structure is nothing different than the pattern set for the village council, where the pastor is like the head of the village council and the deacon board members are like the elected village council male members.

According to the church tradition, the Deacon Board (the Pastorate Committee) is regarded as the highest decision-making body of the local church. In the past, women were never appointed to this committee assuming that women are subordinate beings and weak in decision making. But, owing to the feminist movement and awareness on this issue, gradually deaconesses were appointed in few churches, especially in the urban churches. Though women were given the designation as deaconess, their participation was hardly recognized. Their suggestions were hardly taken, and in many cases their male counterparts in every decision-making overpowered them. Even now men occupy the pastoral ministry, the deacon board and almost all the high administrative posts in the church ministry. Thus, the whole structure of the church is like a reproduction of the village administrative system. The patriarchal structure of the church administration excludes and denies women's participation from all major leadership roles.

The churches in Nagaland have a very rigid church structure restricting women's mobility, with a gender-based discrimination. On the other hand, along with the men's patriarchal ideologies, women are also ignorant about their deprived condition, and without realizing their potentialities they keep on compromising with the age-old cultural practices which dehumanizes their personhood. Rather

[442] Brigalia H. Bam and Lotika Sarkar, *New Perspective for Third World Women* (Bangalore and Madras; CISRS & CLS 1979), p. 36 Quoted from *Women's issues in the 21st century*, p. 151.

[443] R.L. Hnuni, "The Role of Women in the Church," in *Transforming Theology for Empowering Women* (Jorhat: TSC, ETC, 1999), p. 68.

than trying to appropriate their situation, they say that 'we should not compete with men, men are men, and we have to depend on them throughout our life.'[444] While women often speak out and comment, in this view, still they accept this kind of ideology. On the other hand, men also claim that they are the masters, owners as they are in charge of the over-all church activities.

In the Association/Synod level leadership positions, like the Executive Secretary, President of the Council, and the Chairperson of Deacon Board, they are always reserved for men. Never in the history of Nagaland have churches or associations had a record of these kinds of privileges claimed by women. Therefore, while discussing about women's leadership for the above mentioned posts in the church's ministry, one of the long-time ordained woman ministers, Rev. Dr Noksangchila[445] remarks that, "we even could not discuss or try it and (we thought) it may not happen in reality during my life time, I suppose, but you dedicated youngsters should take up the challenges, don't give up, because God is the God of equality.'[446] She shared this with the author out of her long experience in the church's ministry, serving for more than 55 years in different capacities. Her experience was based on a misconception and general assumption that, women are incapable of holding the above mentioned high positions because people presume that women are weak, limited in understanding political issues and are unable to give the right judgments.[447] It is the opinion of the respondents that the church is one of the institutions where all forms of gender-based violence are embedded.

While finding out the existence of gender-based violence in the church's ministry it is fitting to mention about the statistical report of Nagaland Baptist Churches Council, 2005. There are more than 2000 women theological graduates in Nagaland and the number is increasing year by year.[448] It is undeniable that, though both men and women study in the same institution with prescribed syllabi and finish with the same degree, yet, once they come out of the theological studies, the issue of 'women being subordinate to men' arises. The patriarchal church structure rather decides their ministry, not by the virtue of their theological qualifications, capability and ministerial experiences, but on

[444] It is interesting to note that, in almost all the churches in Nagaland there are separate seats for the Deacon Board Members near the dais. While clarifying the matter regarding the separate seats for them, one of the deacons replied to the researcher without any hesitation that, 'Men are the Masters of the Church,' so they need to sit in the front and watch out what is going on in the worship.

[445] Rev. Dr. Noksangchila is one of the pioneers in theological studies among the Naga women and the first woman to be ordained minister from Nagaland, ordained in 1991. She was also the first woman pastor in a local church for a few years and the former Chaplain in the Christian Medical College, Vellore, Tamil Nadu.

[446] Interview with Rev. Dr. Noksangchila on May 30 2004, Impur, Mokokchung.

[447] Questionnaire, No. 19.

[448] This was informed by the Nagaland Baptist Church Council Women Secretary, Kohima, to the researcher on 2nd July, 2006.

the basis of gender. Sadly, many of the able Naga women theological graduates end up teaching in schools, serving NGOs, and work in government offices, and stay at home as mere housewives. What F. S. Downs[449] once mentioned in his article is quite appropriate. He said, "Women students in theological field are preparing themselves only for roles that are traditionally reserved for women- either as women workers in the church or as teachers."[450] Thus, only 25% of the theologically trained Naga women are in the church's ministry today in Nagaland and the rest, 75 percent are in the above-mentioned ministries. Even a few of them are working in the Call Centers in cities.[451]

When talking about the appropriateness of ministry for women in the church, many of the respondents both men and women supported the (secondary) assisting roles of women.[452] Thus, women are totally denied their worth and identity, at the same time, they themselves don't realize yet what injustice is being done to them. Today, a majority of women are conscious about their subordinate state and, how traditional patriarchal practices have made them to take up subordinate roles both in the church and in the state ministry. Thus, a majority of the respondents expressed that women face deprivation, discrimination, and rejection in the church's ministry.

Programmes on Gender-based Violence

With regard to programmes on gender-based violence, except for a few respondents almost all the respondents mentioned that the churches conduct programmes on women once or twice a year. All the programmes are arranged by the women folk themselves like raising funds, locating the resource persons, programme arrangement, etc. While conducting such a kind of programme, many a time men folk comment that 'it will be just a waste of time as, women's discussions are of no use, unnecessarily spending time neglecting household work', etc. With regard to the topics in seminars, issues like management, stewardship, sex education, how to educate children, the role of wives, housekeeping, health caring, HIV/ Aids awareness, women's empowerment, status and role of women, etc, are given importance. However, those issues on gender justice, gender-based violence and

---

[449] F. S. Downs is one of the teaching missionaries from American Baptist Churches Mission, USA, who has been teaching for several years in Eastern Theological College, Jorhat, Assam and the United Theological College, Bangalore, and has done extensive research on North East Indian Church history.

[450] F. S. Downs, "Women's Issues in Theological Education: A Historical Perspectives," in *Transforming Theology for Empowering Women,* ed. R.L. Hnuni, p. 77.

[451] This information was available when the researcher inquired from the youngsters working in the Call Centers in different places. When asked for reasons,they opined that they opted for this as they might as well find themselves useful in secular jobs, where their skills are recognized. Since they are not going to get into the ministry what they desired for according to their degrees and interests. This is the situation prevailing in the church's ministry in Nagaland.

[452] Questionnaire No. 10.

relationship between men and women are not taken into consideration. The author feels that bringing awareness among women-folk alone cannot bring any change. This may be the first step. If we need transformation and justice in the society, both the sexes need to be equally educated in every aspect. In other words, gender-based violence/situation can be improved only when both men and women are educated, and success in life can be achieved only when both learn to respect each other as equals.

Gender-based Violence in Traditional Marriage

As elucidated in the previous section, there is gender-based violence in the traditional marriage system too. In regard to choosing a life-partner, compared to women, men are given more importance and they have more chances to choose what they like, and in doing so in some cases girls cannot say 'no' even though they do not like the person.[453] Again when it comes to marriage celebration, the husband's side takes the major decisions where the wife has no opinion in the overall marriage matters. Besides, when it comes to expenditure for the marriage, the husband spends for almost all the marriage expenses, which are very burdensome for the husband's family members during that time, and in return the husband's family takes advantage of deciding other matters too, or does so without the wife's family opinions. Eventually, the situation is changing among the equally educated couples. This is applicable only to a very few people, especially in the urban settings. There is thus an urgent need however, to create an atmosphere where both could work out the issues with mutual understanding respecting each others' worth and dignity as husband and wife.

Opinions Drawn from the Respondents

Through the empirical investigations, it is clearly figured out that, the opinions expressed by the respondents vary according to age group. The respondents who are in the category of 50 years and above, 58 female and 63 male, are of the opinion that traditional practices based on customary laws are good enough for the whole community, and they further expressed that it should not be changed in order to preserve each of the rich cultural practices. They also suggested that every citizen should abide and preserve his/her rich cultural heritage where there are certain norms for both men and women in the society. Moreover, they opine that 'since we have been practicing those norms since time immemorial, it cannot be replaced and interfered by the modern practices.' It is also observed, among this age group there are quite a few who are more open and adaptable, and they expressed that the Naga society needs to be changed towards newer applications

---

[453] Among the Naga tribes, the *Konyak* tribe has a 'King system,' in which the King has the freedom to choose his wives as many as he wishes. In that case, once he selects a girl, she and her parents have no choice but to accept the proposal. In this situation some girls are deprived of their wishes.

by discarding the discriminatory practices based on gender, and allow equal opportunity to everyone irrespective of sexes.

On the other hand, respondents in the age group of 50 years and below, 77 male and 102 female respondents are more flexible and open to outside world opinions. Except for a few, a majority of the respondents in this age group expressed that, the present traditional practices based on the customary laws hinder women's lives and their mobility in various ways. A few examples could be mentioned here, like denying leadership roles, not allowing in the decision-making both in the church and society, depriving their shares, restricting their movements, exploiting their bodies, rejecting their opinion, etc. No doubt, Nagas are the people who strongly hold on to their traditional practices and preserve their rich cultural heritages as cited earlier. By following that, they often fail to realize the oppressive actions toward half of its members in the society. Thus, they play according to the distinct gender roles, which only victimize and torture women in several ways, as it enhances gender-based violence in the society.

It is worth noting that, along with the traditional cultural restrictions on women, the Christian religion has also played a significant role in restricting women's place by interpreting biblical texts, quoting the references where it is mentioned about women's submissiveness even up to the extent of saying: women are the bearers of sins, unclean and the weaker sex. One of the main hindrances for subordination of women in Naga society could be due to the separate women's services as a formal gathering on a specific day, in which it is assumed that, since they are the first of the humans to fall into temptation, they need to confess their sins.[454] In this case, the researcher feels that, the present regular women's' service conducted on Thursday in every Naga faith community need to be debarred in order to have uniformity in their beliefs. In other words, the present traditional practices in the church administration need to be reconstructed where everyone could maintain equal participation. Therefore, unless the Naga society breaks some of the traditional practices in the church and society, it has to go a long way to achieve justice and equality.

The reasons behind all sorts of gender-based violence are no other than the issues of superiority and inferiority complex among the people. We have already witnessed those pictures from the multiple theories discussed in the preceding sections. It is high time for the Nagas to come out from the aged old traditional customary laws, which considered women as inferior and subhuman, depriving their birth-right as equal partner with men-folk. Without any hesitation, the writer would like to comment in this way: 'Nagaland is regarded as one of the most backward states of the Indian Union, not only in economic and political fronts but it also suffers mostly from social backwardness and it is reflected very sharply in the Status of women in the state.'

---

[454] This kind of comments are often made by men folk whenever they see women having a separate worship/service apart from common fellowship.

Chapter 6

Educational Ministry of the Church on Gender-Based Violence

Introduction

In a constantly changing socio-cultural, economic, political scenario and religious outlook in today's society, Christian faith is challenged to address many realities. The challenge is to determine what kind of Christian educational system church need to impart to meet all those challenges. That is the main concern in this chapter. In order to meet those challenges in the society, specifically in the faith community, one needs to give serious thought to these realities in order to bring changes, transforming the traditional understanding which is not rational/ helpful and relevant in the present context, and to liberate people from all forms of violence specifically gender-based violence existing in the church and society. Therefore, while talking about the gender-based violence one of the great Christian educators John Westerhoff's opinions become meaningful as we analyze the present educational ministry of our churches. To quote, "a call for radical reformation of the ways we approach the educational ministry of the church needs to be taken seriously."[455]

In order to do this Christian educational ministry needs to be very critical, exploring the reality about the faith community and the people around them. Healing a broken society created by status-quo, gender differences, racism/ ethnic differences, exercising power and authority in the human society, should be the aim of the church's educational ministry. But, many a time the Christian

[455] John Westerhoff, *Will our Children have faith* (New York: Seabury Press, 1976), p. 6.

community understands this task very narrowly, in the sense that they consider this only for a certain group of people. In the following discussions we would see how the Christian community understands the Christian education traditionally.

Contextual Understanding of Christian Education

The traditional form of Christian education programme in the church in many faith communities, has failed to address many social issues/problems, taking it for granted that those social issues are civil matters which are not appropriate to be discussed in the church. In common terms, the churches' educational programme is understood as intentional biblical instructions, which are given to only children through Sunday School, Confirmation classes and sometimes through some, set programmes like the Vacation Bible School. Those instructions were followed by conducting examinations by grading scores and recognized by awarding gifts and certificates. But this remains an intellectual exercise, which remain only for a short period of time concentrating on particular age groups in the church. It does encourage and benefit some and for many a kind of formal education, which ends up with a certain biblical knowledge, yet not a faith development. As the emphasis is mostly on children's education, many adults are left without any activity for faith formation except in Sunday services. They are more an informative exercise than a radical transformative programme. They are not only blind to the reality around but also lop-sided in its interpretation and applying the radical biblical propositions to remedy the issues.

Thus, Christian education was understood just for the limited age groups, an education mainly for the children alone and for the specific time. When we talk about the understanding of Christian education programme in the church through Sunday School, what one of the Christian educators, Anne Streaty Wimberly has mentioned in her book-*Soul Stories: African American Christian Education,* seems instructive: "she said, I have gone to Sunday school almost all my life. It seems that it's always been a habit to go to everything the church offers. Over the years, Sunday school has become an important part of my life, though. Right now, I go for the interaction. This allows me to get something different than it's possible to get in church services."[456] In the following discussion we will see the reasons and inspirations where she felt the Sunday school is important in imparting Christian education. She says:

> I go to Sunday school to tap into the richness of the Bible. By doing this, I get spiritually fed and my faith gets renewed and strengthened. I enjoy the study. Really, I'm hungry to find out what is in the Bible, I want to know what God's will is for my life. I want to see what the Bible has to

[456] Anne Streaty Wimberly, *Soul Stories: American Christian Education* (Nashville: Abingdon Press, 1994), p. 18

say for what I need to do with my life and how I can face all of the things that come at me every day.458>>>>>>>

Being involved in Sunday school and Bible study groups has been freeing for me spiritually and in other ways too. That's what I want. That's what makes me feel good about going. It is not always what the teacher teaches that makes the difference. I get a great deal out of talking to other persons and hearing what others have to say. I can remember a particular time when we shared about persons we knew who were in need. We got into a discussion about the Bible had to say about Christian responsibility. We talked about what we thought we ought to be doing. This led to our deciding on specific things to do. We made plans and carried them out. Isn't this what it's all about? Developing relationship? Sharing with others? Studying the Bible? Doing for others and knowing why we're doing it? I think so.[457]

It is important for me to be able to talk about the problems and the concerns I face every day and to come to some idea about how to handle them. We don't always do this. But, when we do, it helps me. I see attending Sunday school as a time when I can draw strength from what the Bible has to say. I come to find answers to questions I have about what to do. I need to hear the words and the messages that can take me a step beyond where I am. I need to be able to see that I'm going to make it in spite of whatever problems I am facing. This is why I come. 459.

On the other hand, the traditional church's educational ministry seems to be concerned more on individual salvation and one's own spiritual development, and provides no opportunity to wrestle with Christian faith in relation to the existing issues in the society. Therefore, whatever programmes are conducted by the churches in regard to certain prevailing social issues are not regarded as church's educational progamme. Thus, in general, Christian religious education is mostly confined to and within the biblical narratives, teaching about the stories of Jesus' life and ministry. There is no much room for dialogue on certain social issues, other faiths and surroundings, narrowing it down to a specific teaching for specific time. Therefore, Christian education instruction need to base its exploration on Bible principles, at the same time this includes people's life stories both their problems and difficult situations and also expectations and wishes too.

The Sunday school should equip and enable the students to cope with the times in reality from a biblical perspective. Students need to focus and sharpen their minds to discern and analyze the situations that disrupt faith communities. They need to view objectively the situation of injustice, exploitation, discrimination, etc., in society from a biblical perspective, using relevant illustrations from the

[457] Anne Streaty Wimberly, (1994), p. 19.

Bible. They also need to learn to discern the hand of God in working out his freedom, harmony and peace in a multi-religious and multi-cultural society.

Thus, as mentioned earlier, Christian religious education is understood as an educational activity for certain stages of people with a syllabi within a limited timing. In other words, Christian religious education is understood as the institutional routine teaching ministry of the church for the children and for the faith community alone. With this understanding, the churches' educational programmes become very superficial, a programme just for one or two hours of teaching ministry held once in a week. There is little place to discuss those social issues which are encountered in day to day life. This calls for a rethinking, reframing and re-analyzing of the religious educational ministry programme in the church.

Knowing the reality of the context, a leading Christian religious educator from India, comments in this way, "there is no justification for continuing the traditional types of Christian religious education, which actually support and nurture normative-exclusives and maintain the Christians' alienation from the cultural kinship, instead of encouraging the Christians to participate in the process of human culture in India. Traditional Christian religious education negates the fuller human life by propagating exclusion from the culture of the context."[458] This is appropriate when we analyze the whole context of the educational ministry of the church today. For instance, many prevailing issues like gender-based violence or gender justice and terrorism, etc., are not integrated in the church's ministry. Therefore, in the following section an attempt is made to understand Christian education, its purpose and how important it is in dealing with different issues in the society.

The Philosophy of Christian Education

As cited in the preceding chapter, Christian education is the process by which a faith tradition is passed on from one generation to the next. Therefore, for the faith community, it is a process in which teaching and learning about the Christian faith takes place not for a certain stage in life but through-out one's life. Thus, it is an educational task of the church for the church, and without Christian education, the formation of persons within a given tradition, the church has no future.[459] Thus, Christian religious education is not only an education which emphasizes the relationship with God alone but education for all humanity; fellow human beings, irrespective of sex, colours and faiths, and also with nature around them. Thereby, Christian religious education does not concentrate only on and within the faith community but goes beyond that understanding.

---

[458] Samson Prabhakar, *Towards an Indian Christian Religious Education*, (1990), p. 25.

[459] *Concilium: Religion in the eighties, The sexual Revolution,* Baum, Gregory and John Coleman, (Edinburgh: T&T. Clarks LTD, 1984), p. 16.

Moreover, Christian religious education arises from a person's action or ministry experience. These actions and experiences become the bases for people's reflection, and thus produce transformation-their own persons, cultures, the churches, and the societies. Thus, Christian religious education is a process of spiritual and social transformation, transformation in every aspect. It requires a socio-cultural transformation leading to religious, economics and political transformations in society.

In the line of above definitions, Christian religious educator Sherill has expressed that, "Christian education is the attempt to participate in and to guide changes which takes place in persons in their relationship with God, with the Church, with the other persons, with the physical world and with oneself."[460] Another well known Christian educator in India who has contributed much towards Catechetical education was D.S. Amalorpavadass. He defined Christian education as "the dynamic procedures in which a group of believers are guided with due respect for their freedom, to meet and discover God in the midst of their life situations and understand God's designs through the instructions and interpretation of sacred scripture.[461] When the writer says "a group of believers" he does not mean children or people at certain stage of their lives but those who have a heart to change the existing tradition which diminishes their whole being. Freedom from the social structural practices, which created the situation of the oppressed, and the oppressors, may be due to patriarchy or certain societal norms. On the other hand, when a certain group of people exercise their power and authority against another group or between men and women, education is the best means to provide consciousness about their situations, empowering them by giving appropriate awareness, and therefore Christian education needs to play its pivotal role by educating its faith community.

Christian education is all about leading people towards building up a new humanity in the midst of their struggles and educating them with the right biblical interpretation. In this context, Samson Prabhakar says, "Christian Education needs to be a spiritual process that motivates the learners to build a new ethos of mutual trust, mutual respect and mutual learning and thereby move towards a wholistic spirituality."[462] He further says, "Christian religious education activities need to be understood as those activities of the Christian community through which she intentionally attempts to create an inclusive community, which consists

[460] Anto Amarnad, "Religion and Education for life," in *Journal of Dharma: Religion and Education, Dharmaram College Golden Jubilee Commemoration* Volume, April – June 2006, Vol. 31, No. 2, p. 241.

[461] D. S. Amalorpavadass, *A Survey of One Decade of Catechatical Renewal in India,* (Bangalore: NBCLC, 1973), p. 7. in *Anto Amarnad, "Religion and Education for Life,"* in Journal of Dharma: Religion and Education, Dhamaram College Golden Jubilee Commemorative Volume, April – June 2006, Vol. 31, No. 2

[462] Samson Prabhakar, *Together with People: Essays in Honour of Rev. D. S. Satyaranjan* (Bangalore: South Asia Theological Research Institute, 2004), p. 98.

of communities that respect the integrity of each other and open to differences of each other. Christian religious education needs to be understood as a means to bring transformation in all aspects of community life."[463]

One of the leading Christian educators, Thomas H. Groom's understanding of Christian religious education supports the preceding thoughts expressed by different educators. According to him, "Christian religious education is a political activity with pilgrims in time that deliberately and intentionally attend with them to the activity of God in our present, of the story of the Christian faith community, and to the vision of God's Kingdom, the seeds of which are already among us." Christian education, like all education, is rooted in experience; all experience contributes to the understanding of life. The ministry of religious education, thus, should relate to the past, present and the existential realities of life.

Christian education is also holistic, because teaching and learning takes place within the community of faith. This means, education of the whole person is not an individual endeavour but it is something that happens within the community of the church. The teaching-learning process involves the active participation of the whole community in dialogue, and in co-operation amongst the members. Therefore, Christian religious education must open spaces where people can learn the faith tradition, engage that tradition with issues of life and seek to live in a way that are faithful to God. As Sara Little, an educationist has rightly mentioned, "through Christian religious education we face into the world, explore the deepest meanings of our lives, engage one another, and partner with a God seeking wholeness and meaning for all life."[464] Thus, Christian education should enable people to assume various roles of responsible citizens and should help them to develop their attitudes, making them aware of their rights and responsibilities in the community.

In this, what Elizabeth Dodson Gray, a feminist theologian, says is pertinent: "I want a Christian education which focuses on the historical Jesus and his startling message of liberation and diversity and inclusion, because that message and example would be relevant in a positive way to our contemporary struggles with racism, sexism, heterosexism, classism, and speciesism." She further mentions: "I also want a religious education that is body-affirming and sexuality-affirming. And I would also like us to honour the body of the Earth."[465] She also quotes the words of Joanne Carlson Brown and Rebecca Parker, who say: "We do not need to be saved by Jesus' death from some original sin. We need

[463] Ibid. 85.

[464] Jack L. Seymour and Donald E. Miller, *Mapping Christian Religious Education Approaches to Congregational Learning* (Nashville: Abingdon Press, 1997), p. 118.

[465] Elizabeth Dodson Gray, "Feminist Theology and Religious Education,' in *Theologies of Religious Education,* ed. Randolph Crump Miller (Birmingham, Alabama: Religious Education Press, 1995), p. 225.

to be liberated from the oppression of racism, classism, and sexism, that is, from patriarchy."[466]

Therefore, Christian education or Christian religious education needs to explore the dignity of all humanity where every part of creation has its own world to cultivate without any binding and control. Thus, the purpose of Christian education is to challenge the social structure, which oppresses people based on their sex/gender, which dehumanizes half of the God's creation and to promote peace and justice, freedom and harmony in every aspect in the society irrespective of sex.

Education in General

While attempting to understand Christian education, it is appropriate to examine the purpose of education in general too. The very word 'education' implies by its compound composition that the task and purpose of education is 'to lead out and guide through.'[467] Education can be nothing less than an impetus for change from one state to another. If one who is "educated" has not changed, then no "education" has occurred at all. Yet, education is more than change. It is change that liberates one from an unevaluated way of living. True education is liberal education that which leads from the shackles of an unexamined life to the freedom of intentional and productive patterns of thought and behaviour.[468]

The intention thus, of this section is not to discuss 'education' in detail but to understand how education plays an important role in bringing justice, peace, equality and transformation in the given society, because the faith community cannot be separated from society. It is universally true that whatever problems or crises arises it is through the wisdom acquired by proper education that settles the issues by providing proper guidance and awareness. Different people may have their own way of expressing about the word 'education'. Let us consider a few of the definitions given by different educators.

According to Gary D. Borich, 'there are three domains that come under any education programme: cognitive behaviour (mean to develop intellectual abilities and skills), affective behaviours (to develop the attitudes, beliefs, and values), and psychomotor behaviours (dealing with co-ordination of physical movements

[466] Brown and Parker, "For God so Loved the World?" p. 27, in *Theologies of Religious Education*, ed. Randolph Crump Miller, p. 226.

[467] "Education" is a derivation from the Latin compound verb "educo," meaning 'to lead forth or bring out.'See Glare, ed., *Oxford Latin Dictionary*, p. 587, in. *Does the Church Really Want Religious Education*? Ed. Marlene Mayr (Birmingham, Alabama: Religious Education Press, 1988), p. 144.

[468] Timothy Arthur Lines, "A Plea for Authentic Religious Education: A Southern Baptist Perspective", in *Does the Church Really Want Religious Education?*, ed. Marlene Mayr (Birmingham, Alabama: Religious Education Press, 1988), p. 144.

and bodily performances).'[469] Education is, thus, an act of integral growth. Every educative process is something that leads to self-discovery and a discovery of the divine within human beings.[470] No doubt, education is equally employed for the sake of liberation and well being of oneself and the society. In other words, education is meant for liberating individuals and the society from all forms of violence, it is also education, which enables the development of one's intellectual faculties, abilities, attitudes and beliefs system.

According to Anto Amarnad,[471] only when the educational system becomes an authentic service to humanity in building up the higher and transcendental needs in one, we can expect a real solution to the existing challenges of our time. The higher and transcendental ideals and values must stay not only in the domain of religion but also in every venture of the human, particularly in the field of education. Therefore, for him religion and education are the decisive dimensions to make humanity ascend the higher horizons of genuine divine-human integration. He further says, that when education is meant to 'lead out' from ignorance to knowledge and wisdom, religion is meant to 'lead into' the inner realm of the human and, thus, to reach the heights of immortality and eternal bliss. While education fundamentally leads to the joy of enlightenment, religion is the way to live the wisdom in inner happiness. Both education and religion have their abilities to refine human consciousness and, thus, to perfect the ultimate meaning in human life. Therefore, education within a religion should be seen not as a simple story-telling romance but must be all the more an integration of creative and dynamic instructions and formation on divine and human realities to achieve profoundness of human vocation. Therefore, all the issues around one's life in the society need to be included in religious education.

Christian Education as a Transformative Praxis

The term transformation means a process of discernible and significant change in the form, structure, system, function and condition of society.[472] These changes always affect the life of the people. Such changes may be either the result of a plan for conscious effort by individuals and groups, or may be the result of unexpected events. It can be argued that, culture and theological dimensions are social constructions, and can be changed and transformed by human intervention.[473] Thus, our society is patriarchal. It is a system in which women's position within

---

[469] Borich G.D, *Effective Teaching Methods* (New York: Macmillian Publishing Company, 1992), P. 119, in Anto Amarnad, *Religion and Education for life*, 2006, p. 241.

[470] *Ibid.*, p. 242.

[471] Associate Professor of Pastoral Theology and Catechetics in Samanvaya Theological College, Bhopal and Dharmaram Vidya Kshetram, Bangalore.

[472] *The Oxford English Dictionary*, 2nd Edition, Vol. XV111 (Oxford: Clarendon Press, 1989), B. Kuppuswamy, *Social Change in India* (New Delhi: Vikas Publishing House, 1989), p. 43.

[473] *Ibid.*, p. 43.

the structure and duties towards the family precede their rights as female. These structures are tightly woven but always there is scope for modification, rectification and transformation, and education is the key for restructuring, so also Christian education as in a faith community. Thus, Christian education needs to be understood as a means to bring transformation in all aspects of community life. That is the sole purpose of the Christian education while dealing with the gender-based violence issues.

Further, in this process, the context in which education is carried out becomes important. Therefore, biblical and theological re-interpretations are very important in the given context. The society still trusts the Christian message. Even when it was interpreted in a patriarchal mentality, through re-interpreting that message, it has the power for transformation, since it is done with the realities of the context. In this event, following the reinterpretation exercise then, the biblical texts which derogate women in exclusive language need to be reinterpreted and reframed as not to hurt anyone but rather to feel the wholeness as they read and accept it as an inspiring God's Word. Unfortunately, many of the Bibles extensively used are the old edition which still uses exclusive terminologies. Thus, if we want our educational ministry of the church to be successful, they should be willing to adopt the re-reading of the Bible with a new eye, which endeavor the ministry of liberty and freedom from oppression. The following are some of the ways to deal with gender-based violence in the present context:

1. Raise consciousness among women about their real oppressive and institutionalized situation in a patriarchal society.
2. Women need to break out of the culture of silence. The patriarchal system always has gaps that one can break into and work for transformation through Christian education, through self-esteem and the empowering process.
3. Women are the largest group to suffer from economic, political, religious and social discrimination; therefore women need transformation in order to come out from discriminative attitudes.
4. Transformation of a person implies the improvement of the status of that person in the family, in the community, and in the society. On the other hand, it should enable one to identify the factors of violence, and empower the people to respond in such a way that they become agents of eliminating gender-based violence both at home, church and society.

No doubt, education is basically a means to realize and enhance one's true potential, in its multiple dimensions. It should be an instrument in the discovery of one's identity, which is basically found in nature and culture. Education should enlighten the individuals to continuously discover the meaning of life. It should also equip the learners to face life's challenges and assert themselves and stand against any kind of aggression and oppression. It should help in building up one's self-confidence, character, and personality, becoming a creative human of the living society. No education is meaningful without a reference to society. According to Ahmed (1995), education is an instrument towards a new society. Therefore, any education that alienates a member of a society from its culture and its tradition is no education at all.[474]

Therefore, Christian education should transform and liberate women to achieve many social, psychological, economic, political and religious privileges which are denied to them customarily. On the other hand, Christian education would make men conscious of their roles for and attitudes toward women, considering their subjectivity. The issues and reasons behind gender-based violence are not legal but rather structural and attitudinal. Therefore, mere policy measures are not enough to stop gender-based violence. In this context, Sheetal Sharma says, "A change in attitude across sections is required in order to enhance consequent socio-economic, political and religious status of women in every place."[475] Centuries after centuries of traditional understanding on objectivity of women considered them as dependent, someone's property, and subhuman, inferior and incomplete persons without husbands or men. These kinds of outlook, feelings on women, positioning their conditions, negative thoughts and mindsets, need total transformation. Unless, the whole human society experiences freedom from which they live in, there would not be a complete life at all. Christian education needs to struggle towards those transformative actions.

Furthermore, in order to bring gender justice, the church would need to do critical reflection on the opportunities for service that are offered to everyone in the given society without any distinction between sexes. But, many a time people fail to realize that they were in a state of subjugation by doing certain roles even in the church activities. In this, Mary Elizabeth Moore has rightly mentioned by saying that, "If women are only serving in traditional women's roles and men in traditional roles for men, something is wrong. Liberation and transformation are possible only when communities live and model a role of flexibility, it is also possible only when all persons are able to discover and use the variety of gifts in ministry."[476]

---

[474] Rais Ahmed, "Perspectives in Higher Eduaction" in N Kuberol, (ed), *Professional Competency in Higher Education* (Delhi: CPDHE, University of Delhi), 1995. See also in Gregory and Jancy Gregory, "Role of Education in Tribal Development: Issues and Cocerns," in *Social Action: A Quarterly Review of Social Trends,* January-March 2007 Volume 57 No.1., p. 20.

[475] Sheetal Sharma, "Women's Education: Key to Prosperity," in *Women's Link: Women and Education,* Vol. 13, No.1 January – March 2007, p. 3.

[476] Mary Elizabeth Moore, "Women and Men in the Social Order" in *Religious Education as Social Transformation,* ed. Allen J. Moore (Birmingham, Alabama, 1989), p. 88.

Christian Education as a Liberative Action

According to Daniel S. Schipani, "A liberative Christian education cannot be simply a tool in the hands of theology, for the latter is no longer practiced in an ivory tower divorced from the world. The relationship between a liberative Christian education and the theology of liberation is dialectical in nature. Here theology is education, and education is theological."[477] Therefore, a liberative Christian education must lead to an encounter with Jesus Christ in history and the liberation struggle. What Christian education is concerned with is not knowing but living, not only knowledge but action, not only interpretation but transformation. Christian education is an evangelical praxis too—a process of action-reflection-action based on the liberating.activity of God.[478] The liberative activity of God need to be interpreted through the educational ministry of the church in which, the church becomes a unique context for doing religious education in a liberative mode. The above mentioned author writes regarding the liberative actions of Christian education, thus: He says,

> One key dimension of the overall purpose of Christian religious education is promoting social transformation for the sake of freedom, justice, and peace. This specific goal of concern with and involvement in society's political and socio-economic realms; such a goal also calls for taking into account the system and structures of those realms even when focusing on the special realities of persons, groups of people, or interpersonal and communal relationships. The forms and manifestations of power, the expressions of oppression and suffering as well as the quest for justice and peace, the role of ideology and interest, and the dynamics of social conflict, including political and educational strategies, must be included in a committed and contextualized religious education.[479]

Therefore, in order to promote the liberative action in the context of Christian education, one needs to be liberated from the traditional way of understanding of Christian education and from the structural oppressive condition where people are and what role they played and are being anticipated now. In this, Paulo Freire, a famous Educator has argued that 'for oppressed people to be free, they must first recognize the condition in which they find themselves.' One of the primary ways in which the oppressor controls the actions of the oppressed is by restricting the thinking of the oppressed. The oppressed look at the world and perceive the reality in terms that are determined solely by the oppressor. Thus, this constricted

[477] Daniel S. Schipani, "Liberation Theology and Religious Education," in *Theologies of Religious Education...*, p. 286.

[478] Matias Preiswerk, *Educating in the Living Word: A Theoritical Framework for Christian Education*, trans. Robert R. Barr (Maryknoll, N.Y.: Orbis, 1987), pp. 109, 112-113.

[479] Daniel S. Schipani, "Libeartion Theology and Religious Education"..., p. 304.

world-view prevents the oppressed from claiming their freedom.[480] Thus, unless a person comes out of that understanding, he/she is still under the bondage of the oppressors, which needs liberation.

Again, Paulo Freire asserts that the oppressed need to recognize the situation in which they find themselves before liberation can become a reality. This process of coming to an informed knowledge of one's condition, and the accompanying process of developing the necessary tools for liberation, has been termed by Freire as 'conscientization.'[481] In many societies for centuries women were regarded as inferior beings, and they had taken subordinate roles. They were also discriminated and oppressed. The subjugation context made them to think they are unable to think for themselves unless someone decides for them, and being unable to do what their counter-parts are doing, they went along with the existing system by accepting the norms set by the community which is purely governed by men.

In this, one of the best examples is the theory which is expounded by Freire, 'Banking system' where women folk have to accept whatever men folk have decided and designed for them, without further question or examination, because they were treated as 'Inferior by the Superior.' For, instance, since women are not allowed to attend in the decision-making body, whatever men folk decide, women have to accept and adopt that norm. In that situation, women are deprived of their rights by not being able to express what they feel for themselves and for the whole community members.

Thus, women were ignored, victimized, segregated, oppressed and, abused through different means, as such many a time they were deprived economically and morally and tortured physically, emotionally and spiritually. Women were thus subjugated to heinous acts before and after birth, and denied their personhood. In order to come out from those situations, women who were oppressed required a profound knowledge which needs to be acquired through proper and timely Christian education as living in the faith community. To arrive at that knowledge, one needs to acquire critical education, as Paulo Freire rightly brought out the word, 'conscientization.' Therefore, in order to bring changes in the existing oppressive stage in human society and to bring liberation from all sorts of oppressions both in the church's ministry, family and social situation, liberative education is the need of the hour, in which Christian education needs to play an important role, based on the biblical principles which teaches equality and justice.

While talking about the education for liberation in the context of Black Christian education, one of the leading Black theologians and writers Shockley says, "The center of education for liberation occurs when persons are able to utilize their capacities of self-transcendence to evaluate reality, and as subjects, of

[480] Paulo Freire, *Pedagogy of the Oppressed* (New York: Herder and Herder, 1970), p. 31.

[481] Paulo Freire, *Education for Critical Consciousness* (New York: Continuum, 1973), pp. 18-20.

naming the world instead of being named by it."[482] It can be worth mentioning here that, unless the women themselves discuss and have dialogue among them, change and transformation will not come. They need to critically analyze their crisis situations, and bring changes, instead of waiting for the changes to come through the male hierarchical order. They ought to decide and evaluate their past and present situations. The real consciousness will happen when a person is given appropriate knowledge and to acquire that, a person needs proper education through which she/he can decide for himself/herself.

While discussing the liberative Christian education for the faith community, along with other Christian educators, Anthony G. Reddie, one of the Black liberation theologians and Christian Religious Educator in Britian, rightly commented that, "Education is either designed to maintain the existing situation, imposing on the people values and the culture of the dominant class (i.e. domesticating people values, as one tames an animal to obey its master's will) or education is designed to liberate people, helping them to become critical, creative, free, active and responsible members of society."[483] Thus, in the context of civil society, where women are discriminated through different forms of violence just because of gender, lowering their status, devaluing their contributions, Christian religious education can be used as the tool to educate people about their right living, their place, responsibilities, shares, and their rights. Thus, Christian education is the right way to facilitate the search for personal meaning and, in helping to find God's redemptive purpose for life, which can certainly suggest answers to their problems. As Warren S. Benson has said, "Christian education exists to give persons a liberating perspective on life, one that helps them make sense out of a troubled and perplexing world."[484]

People face different life's situations in their day to day lives. On many occasions they are confused when they experience violent attitudes from whom they trust and ought to be cared, they are hurt when someone whom they think trustworthy exploit them and deprive their personhood. Christian education is the appropriate means of responding to that situation, whose principles teach equality, sanctity, brotherhood and sisterhood by the galvanizing work of Jesus Christ. In this, as a called-out community to be witnesses of Christ, churches have to play a prophetic role. Gender-based violence is only one aspect of violence, yet that is the core issue of all social problems in the society. Because almost

---

[482] Anthony G. Reddie, *Nobodies to Somebodies: A Practical Theology for Education and Liberation* (Werrington, Peterborough: Epworth Press, 2003), p. 87.

[483] Anthony G. Reddie, (2003), p. 85, see also, Anne Hope and Sally Timmel (illustrated by Chris Hodzi) *Training for Transformation: A Handbook for Community Workers*, in 4 volumes (Gweru, Zimbabwe: Mambo Press, 1999). P. 8.

[484] Warren S. Benson, "Seeking a Biblical Base: An Evangelical Protestant Perspective" in *Does the Church Really Want Religious Education?*, ed. Marlene Mayr (Birmingham, Alabama: Religious Education Press, 1988), p. 202.

all human related issues like, war, HIV/AIDS, inequality, power and authority directly and indirectly are related to this and it affects women's life.

Church's Role Towards Gender-based Violence

As mentioned elsewhere, Christian education is one of the church's most enduring weapons against evil, ignorance, and injustice. The church is called to witness against all those by spreading the gospel, by teaching their congregation how to love and respect themselves and others, and how to fight the forces of violence. The church has to show concern and take action wherever it sees need, hurt or wrong. The church has a great deal to do by way of improving its activities through Christian education. In this connection, Warren S. Benson[485] says, "Christian education is commissioned to engage in the formation of a Christian person: one who thinks christianly and acts Christianly.[486] He further pointed out that the church and the ministry of Christian education has four functions: evangelism, edification, worship, and social concern. The heart of the ministry of the church is the gospel. The church must work in all these four areas to be faithful to our Lord.

All the above cited concerns cannot be achieved or may not be successful unless every church member is treated without any distinction and prejudice. Therefore, when examining the Christian education and the role of the church in the educational ministry of the church, it is not only the biblical exposition alone and leaving not enough avenues to interact and meditate on the truth that is still found in the Bible, but rather, letting believers to come to know the understanding of God's intention on earth through the teachings of His words, which could be made possible through Christian religious education. In other words, Christian education needs to be concerned with life, and with the growth of eternal life within the human limitation. Christian education need to be concerned with the progressive transformation of the behaviour toward the character, values, motives, attitudes, and understanding of God himself, where every church member feels God's abiding presence both in their personal and in social lives.

Many churches have failed to develop proper facilities for educational ministerial resources. At the same time, their understanding of the overall Christian education activities are narrowly understood as cited earlier. Therefore, Christian education activity has become a routine work, just to fulfill the requirement of the annual activity, where students were graded and awarded according to how much

---

[485] He was a minister of the Evangelical Free Church of America, professor and vice president of academic administration at Trinity Evangelical Divinity School. He was the Co-author of *Christian Education* (Moody Press, 394 pp.), and co-editor of *Youth Education and the Church* (Moody Press, 478 pp.). See *Does the Church really want Religious Education?: in Ecumenical Inquiry*, ed, Marleen Maye, Birmingham, Alabama: Religious Education Press, 1988), p. 200.

[486] Warren S. Benson, "Seeking a Biblical Base: An Evangelical Protestant Perspective," in *Does the Church really wants Religious Education?* Ed. Marlene Maye (1988), p. 200.

marks they have obtained during the exam. For instance, as mentioned earlier, every church has a structured Sunday school lesson, through which she instructs people.

As James H. Harries, a Christian educator, professor of Practical theology, has clearly mentioned in his book, *Pastoral Theology: A Black-Church Perspective:*

> Christian religious education strengthens our faith and equips us with the tools to fight injustice and indifference. It is a major tool to be used in the battle against the evil that is so much a part of the social and political system. However, it is also a critical and necessary ingredient in the battle toward self-understanding, self-criticism, and the development of an education programme that will help to usher in the day of freedom for the Black and those of us who practice ministry.[487]

Christian education can be used as a major tool to fight the gender-based violence too, which is a burning issue everywhere by educating the faith community, by bringing awareness, and looking at the traditional stereotype gender roles, not merely by making women study it as an academic exercise alone. When examining the church's role in rooting out gender-based violence, one important area we should consider here is, sharing of privileges in terms of leadership in the church's ministry, because the church should be the agent to pave way for the secular world. Yet very sadly, in many cases, women church ministers end up their life in frustration and in some cases face abusive situation from their male counterparts/ministers. As a result, it is the women who have to bear all the blame, by receiving the comments that she is not capable of holding that responsibility, and cannot discharge the responsibility as male ministers.

It is undeniable, that women are also called and gifted by God to be pastors, priests and teachers, and it is a fearful thing for the organized church to block women from that ministry. Richard D. Kahoe, a psychologist, who has done research on sexism and the human personality, has revealed that "it is psychologically unhealthy for both women and men to favour female subordination. Conventionally submissive women tend to be self-protective, risk-avoiding, resistant to change, and maladjusted. Men who oppose equality for women tend to be more authoritarian and non-conforming, higher in general neuroticism and need for power, and less reflective and self-reliant."[488] He further raised two questions-Can a church be justified in denying equality to its women? Or...Can a church be healthy that denies women, their human equality? Or...Can a male-female relationship be healthy which proceeds on the carnal pattern of dominance and submission? And he concluded that, the mutual submission and

---

[487] James H. Harris, *Pastoral Theology: A Black Church Perspectives* (Minneapolis: Fortress Press,1991), p. 103.

[488] Virginia Ramey Mollenkott, *Women Men and the Bible* (Nashville: Abingdon, 1978), p. 136.

mutual service of male and female is the best road to psychological health and positive human relationships.[489] Though, women ministers or women in general may not react to the treatment meted out by men, their sentiments have been hurt and they feel low whenever they face discriminatory situations.

While acknowledging the gifts and capability of women in the church and society, Ivone Gebara, a feminist theologian from Latin America also comments, many women are especially gifted with a deep intuition about human life and are able to counsel, and to express their problems, to give support, to propose solutions, and to confirm the faith of many people.[490] It can be argued that, both men and women are equally gifted and also both have limitations and in capabilities, yet women are generally considered as inactive, unversed, illogical, and weak, who cannot be counted able as men. Thus, there are situations where women experience rejection and devaluation. In other words, women were kept silent under the traditional structures which made them to accept whatever comes in their way, without questioning and arguing (culture of silence). If we ought to fulfill God's mission where human beings have a place to speak out from their condition, and stand against those unfair treatment meted out to them, then there is hope for humanity-women, from oppression and exploitation.

Therefore, the church through its Christian educational ministries should provide the Christian community its support, and partnership, to uphold equality, mutual respect and self consciousness, making them to picture the God who is always on the side of the neglected ones in society. God calls the church to live beyond the norms of a culture tainted by the fall, to provide a community where each person can become all what God intends for him or her to be.[491] While talking about the church's educational ministry, one has to bear in mind that, the education ministry in the church is the process and content of teaching about the life and teachings about Jesus Christ and applying these concepts to every phase of the church's ministry, teaching people to respect themselves and others. Christian educational ministry in the church is responsible therefore for bridging the gap between the teachings of the Bible and the socio-economic and political reality in the faith community.

Christian Educators' Role in Responding to Gender-based Violence

Mary Elizabeth Moore says,

> If Christian religious educators are to be true to their inheritance, they will assume responsibility to lead people out (e-ducere) from the

[489] *Ibid.*, p. 136.

[490] Ursula King, *Feminist Theology from the Third World: A Reader* (London: SPCK/Orbis Books, Second Impression 1996), p. 49.

[491] Catherine Stonehouse, "The Church: A Place where all God's children grow?" in *Christian Education Journal* Autumn 1992, Volume XIII Number 1, p. 44.

> limitations and life-destruction of a sexist social order to the freedom and life-nurture of an inclusive social order. This includes drawing out the deepest hopes that people hold for the social order and leading people to share their hopes for the sake of a communal vision and communal work. Within the context of a religious community, this educational enterprise is carried forward in relation to the community's tradition and vision.[492]

Therefore, it is appropriate to mention that, the task of Christian educators is not simply to play a domesticating role, making people to accept traditional norms, acting upon that and fitting into the social order which is continuing generation after generation, but rather making people realize their potentiality and also limitations and guide people to understand that men and women are equal partners in the society. In other words, Christian education is nothing but to bear new hope a new understanding, this involves teaching and learning. That means creating a spirit of search, critiquing the old thoughts, leading to a new vision and actions which bring change in the whole humanity, and it should be the intention of the church's educational ministry. In this context, what a feminist theologian Elizabeth Dodson Gray has mentioned in her article is relevant. She leaves a few questions to be considered while responding to the challenges of gender-based violence through Christian religious education. She says,

> Can we invent a religious education which does not assume, and therefore teach, hierarchy (men over women, humans over other species, humans over nature and the planet, God overall)? Can we discover the "creation-based value" of every species, which is established in that covenant with the entire creation, a creation of which we are only a part and not its Lord and Master? Can we climb down from the high illusion we have of ourselves as "king of the castle" and in "dominion" over all the other species? Can we write some curricula filled with real biological data about our Earth and our life-partners on it, as well as with some genuine theological humility about our place in the divine scheme of things? We talk about humility as a Christian virtue, but it has seldom been practiced in our theology! Can we teach Jesus in religious education in a way that would make it obvious to our children that they should be "in solidarity with the poor?

In turn, the role of the minister in shaping and envisioning a prophetic role that promotes liberation and transformation amongst the people of faith is

[492] Mary Elizabeth Moore, "Women and Men in the Social Order: Challenge to Religious Education,' in *Religious Education as Social Transformation,* ed. Allen J. Moore (Birmingham, Alabama: Religious Education Press, 1989), p. 85.

highlighted.[493] It could be argued that, in many faith communities women are not given their due share in the church's ministry, they are denied their God-given potentiality. Even though both men and women are trained for the church's ministry, spending the same amount of money and time in the same institution and instructed by the same trainers. But, when it comes to employment in the church's ministry, women are last to be counted in the list or sometimes excluded from certain ministry.

Proposed Suggestions to Improve Gender-based Violence Situation

In order to avoid gender-based violence and to achieve wholeness and equality between male and female as co-partners in God's creation, to acquire peace and harmony among human beings without any distinction and prejudices, we need certain things to be kept in mind. Hence, every responsible Christian should strive towards these goals:

1. Change of Attitude

Attitudes of both men and women need to be changed. Men have to see women as equal partners in all walks of life, partners who can help the society as a whole, achieve what it desires whether it means an over-all development or political, economic, social, cultural or other changes or the promotion of human rights in various fields. On the other hand, women also have to accept their new and suggestive role as responsible citizens by adopting new methods of working system and changing their traditional attitudes. It cannot be denied that, unless both men and women are willing to change their attitudes of stereotyped patriarchal sex roles, gender-based violence will remain the same.

2. Equal Partnership

The ideology of superiority and inferiority between men and women based on their physical structure needs to be corrected. So, long as a person responds to the needs of their fellow beings they are capable and unique in their own way. The question of superiority and inferiority should not be the way for creating gender-based violence. As Brian Wren, a theologian from the West expressed his thoughts regarding the need of the change in the traditional understanding of theology which taught about superiority of men, "Male dominance is a theological problem because God creates us in two coequal genders and does not intend that one should subordinate the other. A civilization built on male dominance and female subordination is a profound distortion and sin, but not immutable. It has arisen in our history and prehistory, so can be changed and be superseded."[494]

---

[493] Anthony G. Reddie (2003), p. 118.

[494] Brian Wren, *What Language Shall I Borrow? God-Talk in Worship: A male Response to Feminist Theology* (Britian: SCM, Press, 1989), p. 4.

3. Unique Individual

Contrary to the above opinions, it can be argued that, God does not 'do' theology but we do theology in our own way looking at our own situation. In the same way, God does not 'make' culture but human beings make their own culture in their own ways. In doing and making so, we create and make according to our own convenience. Thus, it is universally known that, always the powerful and superior groups dominate. Every human being has his/her own weakness and strength, and when it comes to male and female, nowhere it is mentioned that all men are the same in every aspect and also women as vice versa. Credibility depends on individuals; therefore, the church's educational ministry should aim towards the goal in which everybody may experience a just society without any prejudices.

4. Reconstruction of Women's Issues and Gender Justice

It could be suggested that, the existing subject of 'women's studies' both in secular and theological education, needs to be re-examined and re-constructed in order to fulfill the goal of gender justice agendas. The main purpose of women's studies is no other than for seeking equality and partnership, fighting against all forms of violence on women. In other words, it is not simply about analyzing women's situation and status in the human society, but participating in the elimination of prejudices on women by critiquing their oppressive conditions. Thus, 'gender-justice' and 'issues on women human rights' needs to be placed properly in the existing content as a subject.

As mentioned earlier, analyzing women's status/conditions and conducting seminars on women's empowerment alone cannot bring radical changes in human society. From time immemorial, it is generally assumed that due to their weaknesses women need more instructions and awareness. Very interestingly, once in a seminar organized by the women's fellowship, one of the lay participants asked, 'why do only women need empowerment, and seminars all the time, what is wrong with us?' In one sense, all of us need to be educated. Because both men and women need to be aware of their responsibilities, privileges, rights and roles. Thus, gendered roles/stereotyped roles need to be examined thoroughly by critically analyzing all the root causes of discriminations and oppressions on women in the human society. The situation of gender-based violence needs to be challenged from the theological, psychological, anthropological, and sociological perspectives. We need to go beyond the efforts which we have achieved so far in order to bring gender justice. Education needs to be started from the very beginning of one's life. And to do that, the church's educational ministry needs to be re-evaluated and strengthened.

5. Need of Human Rights Education

Gender-based violence continues to be the most neglected human rights issue and it is of great concern for women today in the context of India and specifically in Nagaland context. Although, the Indian Constitution as well as the Universal Declaration of Human Rights guarantee to every person the right to life, liberty, security, dignity and the right to property or servitude, various forms of inequality, discrimination and oppression continue to affect women which again have been justified in the name of culture and religion. In addition to this, women are disproportionately affected by the unequal sharing of leadership and resources. In many places women are blocked from inheritance and property rights, and they are less able to gain skills and education.

The abuses suffered by women, go beyond the conventional notions of human rights violations. Thus, it was observed that, "For too long women have been denied a better quality of life, opportunities and privileges, for too long vast populations already living below the poverty line, have been pushed to the verge of destitution and hunger in the name of 'development' and 'modernization.' Needless to say, women have been the worst affected by this."[495] Thus, every community member should be educated, making them realize their roles where equality could be maintained without any differentiation between male and female. Since, from its inception, human race has developed and learnt different gender roles and moreover, women were regarded as inferior in everything, women silently endured much suffering. Even after the promotion of women's movement, women are still facing many hidden discriminations in the family and in the society. Those sufferings are not caused by strangers, or somebody unknown to them but their own husbands, sons, brothers and co-workers. Thus, the church needs to integrate Human Rights education in its educational ministry by critically evaluating the human values and its stewardship towards their fellow beings based on the biblical perspectives.

6. Women's Empowerment Education

Women's empowerment in its simplest form means the manifestation and redistribution of power that challenges patriarchal ideology and the male dominance. It is the transformation of the structures or institutions that reinforces and perpetuates gender discrimination. It is the process that enables women to gain access to and control of, material as well as information resources.[496] According to Pillai, "Empowerment is an active, multi-dimensional process which enables women to realize their full identity and power in all spheres of life." He also says, "Power is not a commodity to be transacted; nor can it be given away." He further says, "Power has to be acquired and once acquired, it needs to be exercised, sustained and preserved."[497] Empowerment is also a process

---

[495] Saroj Iyer, *The Struggle to be Human: Women's Human Rights* (Bangalore: Books for Change, 1999), p. 91.

[496] Sushama Sahay, *Women and Empowerment: Approaches and Strategies* (New Delhi: Discovery Publishing House, 1998), p. 201.

[497] *Ibid.*, p. 201.

of awareness and capacity-building leading to greater participation, to greater decision-making power and control, and to transformative action. The National Policy on Empowerment of women clearly identifies the challenge of gender-based violence. The policy has set certain clear cut goals and objectives to bring about the advancement, development and empowerment of women. Some of the main objectives of this policy include:

(a) Creating an environment through positive economic and social policies for full development of women to enable them to realize their full potential;
(b) The de-jure and de-facto enjoyment of all human rights and fundamental freedom by women on equal basis with men in all spheres – political, economic, social, cultural and civil;
(c) Equal access to participation and decision-making of women in social, political and economic life of the nation;
(d) Equal access to health care, equality in education at all levels, career and vocational guidance, employment, equal remuneration, occupational health and safety, social security and public office etc;
(e) Strengthening legal systems aimed at elimination of all forms of discrimination against women;
(f) Changing societal attitudes and community practices by active participation and involvement of both men and women;
(g) Mainstreaming a gender perspective in the development process;
(h) Elimination of discrimination and all forms of violence against women and the girl child; and
(i) Building and strengthening partnerships with civil society, particularly women's organizations.[498]

Thus, though the above mentioned policy aims to ensure equal access to every opportunity without gender discrimination, volumes of books on women's liberation have been produced, and so many memorandums have been presented in every consultation, but still a wide gap between men and women has existed in society. Gender inequality persists in various forms and at almost all levels. The underlying causes of gender-based violence are related to norms and practices deep-rooted in patriarchal socio-economic, political and religious structure of the society. On the other hand, there are also elements in the church activities that hinder the empowerment of women. In many churches there are certain rules and regulations which restrict women to use and apply God-given talents. If given a chance, they could do well with commitment and dedication, using what God has endowed them with–talents and gifts, care-giving, etc.

---

[498] Sheetal Sharma, "Women's Education: Key to Prosperity," in *Women's Link: Women and Education,* Vol. 13, No.1 January – March 2007, p. 3.

Even though, women are the live-wire workers of the church and backbones of the church activities, they are denied recognition and position in many ways just because they are women. The structure of the church administration continues to be patriarchal, hierarchal and top-down. This prevents women from full participation and when they participate they follow male-scripts for the positions they hold. Being within such structures, women find it difficult to develop their own potentiality for alternative forms of holding power and leadership. Even though, both in society and church there are structures which are tightly woven, there is always scope for modification, rectification, transformation, and education is the key for restructuring. Only education would empower women to achieve many social, psychological, economic and political dreams which are denied to them customarily.[499]

7. Men's Consciousness Towards Gender Justice

Women need to discuss with their male counterparts the issues of violence by the males both in the society and in the church. On the other hand, men need to re-evaluate their views of women and need to ask themselves some questions: Is there any part of my life where I am treating women with less respect than men? Are all my words about my wife or women in general, spoken as if I thought she was better than I? Does my wife have as much freedom as I do? Am I vulnerably sharing all of myself with my life partner? Am I sharing my thoughts, emotions, energy, time, experiences, money, and dreams? Do I respect her body when I am trying to get her attention to my desires?

In this connection, a male young church minister Raj Bharath says, "It is high time for us as men, to respect women, half of humankind, joint heirs, created in equal image of God, and dedicate ourselves to combat and resist violence in every form done to our women at homes, at office places etc. The just God is on their side and it is justice that will always be triumphant. If we treat women as commodities, we are indirectly involved in violence. Let us, as men, introspect and say no to violence and respect the dignity of women."[500] It could be argued that, these kinds of thoughts are often expressed in many occasions and many seminars that are conducted either by churches and community welfare organizations, yet it has appeared just for public documentations and have become academic debates for seminar deliberations.

Today, we can see just a few numbers of peace loving men who are coming forward to stand on the side of women in their struggles with much enthusiastic gesture and numerous writings regarding women's empowerment. They also participate in women's' liberation movement, women's seminars, consultations, funding towards women programmes, and making propagation against gender-

---

[499] *Ibid.*, p. 3.

[500] Raj Bharath Patta, "Ministry to Overcome Violence" in *Gurukul Daily Devotion* – 2006, p. 306.

based violence in the public places. On the other hand, the high level commissions (in every state government) which are headed by male bureaucrats, they try to implement many legal laws and begin to revise and restructure the existing regulations in order to show their concern and solidarity.

As acknowledged earlier, it is also encouraging to know the slogans of men's writings in support of women which are accepted and used in academic disciplines too. But unfortunately, when it comes to private spheres, men still hold on to the patriarchal role and maintain supremacy in almost all their activities. In the public field too, men dominate the over all leadership and ignore women's voice and opinions, by denying their suggestions, affinities, contributions. As mentioned in the preceding chapters, in the Naga society, there are numerous derogatory terms and vocabularies used for women, categorizing them in the level of commodities, irrespective of status and age. When it comes to property-sharing too, women are denied their rights.

When it comes to family life situation, a majority of the families are controled by male members knowing that they are the heir of the properties, and believing that they are stronger physically, abusing their economic, sexual, and moral power over women's lives. Therefore, as someone has said, 'a husband protects wives from outside violence, but wives are not protected from their husbands.' Of course, today some women are also trying to keep their husbands under their control, if they do not fulfill their wishes, yet, this is very rare compared to male dominations in general. As human beings are created equally in the image of God, what a woman needs is to have total protection, total education and total liberation not only for herself but for the good of her family and society. Therefore, as equal partner in the sight of God, men need to be conscious of their unruly attitudes towards women.

8. Solidarity among the Churches on Gender Justice

The Ecumenical Decade of the Churches in Solidarity with Women launched in 1988-1998 calls for churches to work together with women to achieve gender equality in all aspects. The decade is a "challenge to the churches to demonstrate visibly and vividly that the forty years of the WCC advocacy on behalf of women, and the many fine statements the Council has issued, are meant to change the actual life-styles and attitudes of churches and people towards women's potential for promoting the vision of a new age in Jesus Christ."[501] Ever since then, churches all over the world have joined together and conducted awareness programmes on different forms of violence on women.

Thus, lots of changes have taken place especially in the sister churches in the developing countries both in the state and church, and some are still working on women's emancipation by revising legal codes for women and child protection

[501] Mercy Oduyoye, *Who will Role the Stone Away?* The Ecumenical Decade of Churches in Solidarity with Women (Geneva: WCC, Publications, 1991, p. 50.

rules. In all these attempts, churches lend their support showing their solidarity with the oppressed. When we examine our own context, both the state and church have accepted the challenge and started working towards the eliminations of gender-based violence and overcoming violence in general. Laws have been made and added, related to violence on women and implemented in the state and national levels. Yet, sad to observe that law maker, they themselves are involved in violence against women. Also, empowerment of women for gender justice has been done mostly among the educated and a few elite. But women in general are yet to be educated. Therefore, churches need to show their solidarity by working together in giving awareness, analyzing traditional practices and critiquing cultural norms which devalue women.

9. Political Empowerment for Women

Women's empowerment is a global issue today, and discussions on women's political rights are at the forefront of many formal and informal campaigns worldwide. Although, the need of women's empowerment and women's liberation are always in discussion when it comes to political matters, power and authority matters a lot. Society always looks on the strength, status, economic positions and so on, since men are regarded as superior and inheritors in the family and in the society. Therefore, there is a great need for women to penetrate into all the spheres of public life, and that would be possible through appropriate awareness, provided they get recognition and opportunity.

10. Economic Empowerment for Women

It is undeniable that a majority of the women are suffering due to economic instability. Therefore, women need to be aware of their economic situation and be conscious of the value of their work, including their participation in economic activities. They need to look critically at as consumers, assessors to credit, bread-winners, and also for equality in wages and salary. Women as such are deprived of their economic life, denied their rights of getting equal share out of their labour. Even though they are not getting what they ought to have they are not aware of it. Rather they think that they are the weaker section and do not have the right to claim for equality. Even among women, the most unfortunate groups are the illiterate ones, because they were taught to be submissive and tolerant both from the religious and social teachings. Therefore, through the ministry of the church, women need to be empowered to realize their rights, especially their economic status, because every human being needs to survive and be nurtured in which economic empowerment is one of the sole concerns when we talk about the gender-based violence in the context. It can be also one of the concerns that affect the whole world.

11. Contextual Awareness on Gender-based Violence

In order to eradicate existing gender-based violence in the society, and to accomplish equality and partnership in every respect without gender bias, every person should have a sense of responsibility by sharing his/her responsibility and privilege. Thus, these few assumptions need to be kept in mind while educating the faith community in every society:

At Home:

Domestic work – It is the universal truth that home is the place where dominant meanings about gender get reproduced, challenged, and revised. Home is the place where both women and men are agents, but where the agency of women is often circumscribed by men. We need to recognize and value the domestic work on a societal level which is normally done by women. This was the result, as from the empirical research mentioned in chapter five, especially in the context of Naga society, where a majority of the respondents say domestic work is done by women. Thus, men should also need to learn to engage in domestic work because each and every person should know his/her place and especially, adults as they need to be responsible for his or her own personal maintenance.

Nurturing children – Women need to be released from carrying out the major responsibility for child care. If two people decide to have a child, then surely that child and its upbringing are the responsibility of both the parents and/or other adults.[502] In many a situation, the husband does not cooperate in nurturing children by commenting, 'women ought to do this.' It happens especially among the uneducated people too who stick to the traditional roles as norms. Therefore, men should provide nurture not only to children but to women and other men as well.

Therefore, both women and men need to take on their fair share of routinized and more occasional household tasks and other domestic responsibilities. Moreover, often parents socialize their children into culturally defined roles, even though those roles violate their own teachings. It is necessary therefore to develop educational ministries in the church which endeavour to overcome sexism and empower persons to develop new understandings of life for both men and women. In order to liberate persons from limited roles and statuses, and to open up new options for both men and women to exercise their full personhood in home, community, the church, and the world, Christian religious education can and ought to assume the major responsibility for that task.[503]

---

[502] Mary Stewart Van Leeuwen, *After Eden: Facing the Challenge of Gender Reconciliation* (Michigan: William B. Eerdmans Publishing Company Grand Rapids, 1993), p. 529.

[503] *Generation to Generation: Conversations on Religious Education and Culture* by John H. Westerhoff III and Gwen Kennedy Neville, New York-Philadelphia: The Pilgrim Press. 1979), p. 147.

In the Society:

Inheritance-Equal rights of inheritance should be given to all children regardless of sex.

Ownership-Equal ownership of poverty, both mobile and immobile, should be given to father and mother, sons and daughters.

Provision-Legal provision should be made to protect women in case of violence.

Recognition of household Work–Unpaid household work should be recognized as contributing to family economy.

Inclusiveness-All the development projects, social, government or church, should be made inclusive so as to take gender issues seriously and include them in all the plans.

Customary Laws and Rules-All the actions taken in regard to male bias need to be set right and made mandatory for both sexes. Laws and rules can be reaffirmed according to a specific community or peoples group.

Notions-The notion of inferiority and superiority about women and men should be removed and traditional views of women are weaker and men are stronger should be done away. Once the above mentioned concerns are taken into consideration in the society there would not be any bias treatment and no question about violence.

In the Church:

Equality-Need to challenge patriarchal interpretations of ecclesiology which advocates only male leadership and for equal participation of women and men in the ministry of the Church.

Reconstruction of Christian Traditions-Need to formulate new ways of reconstructing and re-interpreting all Christian traditions and church structures to bring them in line with the present ideas of justice and equality.

Re-interpretation of Christian Theology-Need to reshape and re-interpret traditional Christian theology which oppresses and de-humanizes women, thus, traditional God-language which legitimizes and reinforces the oppression of women should be reinterpreted.

Re-interpretation of Scriptures-Need to re-read and re-interpret the scriptures that have been distorted by male interpreters throughout the biblical history to suppress women, to recover a fuller and liberative meaning.[504]

If every faith community is willing to change its previous traditions and is willing to adopt the new way of working system and interpreting biblical messages with new eyes, there is hope for humanity, in which Christian education must take the risks to implement these steps.

---

[504] R. L. Hnuni, *Women in North East India* (2005), pp. 352-353.

Challenges to Overcome Gender-based Violence

The challenge is that of moving beyond the submissive passivity in the affairs of society without at the same time, indulging in angry rejection of the traditions of one's faith or in aggressively being competitive in self-promotion which moves against rather than with the redemption of the world. It is necessary to take initiative to exert right leadership, which is not based upon personal anger and hostility, and which does not seek to dominate or to seize exclusive privileges. In other words, it is necessary to avoid entering into competition for what have been seen as male prerogatives in a sinful history based upon bullying, and therefore it is necessary to discern new possibilities for quite different ways of social organization and community structures and cooperation. This calls for more than determination and aggressive energy; it also calls for contemplative sensitivity out of which new configurations can be imagined. It calls for a deeply rooted creativity.

1. Wholeness in Approach

With the above sense of openness and inclusiveness, the challenge seems to be much more in a community that boasts of rules, rituals and scriptures. Being structured thus, the religious activities under girding for wholeness need to be kept in mind. More than being a sudden radical departure, a gradual openness in furthering the cause of mitigating gender-based violence needs to be taken care of.

2. Biological Component

Another problem of challenge which faces us in our own days is that of disentangling what is biologically feminine from that which is culturally prescribed, and distinguishing both of these from what makes up the Christian vocation of women. The biological component of sexual determination is not static but responds to natural environment, nutritional factors which were extensively examined from different dimensions. For instance, in today's world, due to advancement in scientific technology, the biological component has been extensively modified by deliberate human intervention. Thus, this can be challenged if it destroys personhood, killing innocence, those who are yet to be born, that which has been done through abortion.

3. Scriptural Interpretation

One of the crucial challenges for Christian religious education practice is also to seek out difficult texts and difficult events in the tradition for re-interpretation. As a result, these texts and events will raise significant faith issues and will encourage persons to question and face their doubts. As a Christian religious educator Mary Elizabeth Moore comments in her article, 'Women and Men in the Social Order': "Sometimes texts seem to speak much more loudly to reinforce patriarchy than to point to a revolution in the social order. These texts are also part of the Jewish and

Christian heritage, and due to their formative power, interpretation and critique are vital to the revision of a sexist social order. These are the texts with which we must wrestle with, if we are bringing critique to them and to the world that they have helped to form."[505]

Challenge to Christianity-to Come of Age

Christianity has always been growing and changing, adapting to new situations, contexts and times, imposing alien cultural norms as it travelled and mingled with or retreating from cultural challenges. According to Nicola Slee, "There has never been and never will be only one form or expression of Christianity and belief: as a world faith, Christianity is as multiform, diverse, complex and fluid as any other historical tradition which has survived for millennia in vastly different contexts. Moreover, Christianity, along with every other world faith, faces contemporary challenges which are qualitatively new in comparison with anything these tradition's have previously faced."[506] Thus, the issues of gender-based violence arising throughout the world are part of Christianity, which is a qualitative challenge to churches in this present context. The challenge to the churches is not superficial, but fundamental and authentic, in which the over-all Christian faith education needs to intervene with the existing various social issues.

1. Beyond Superficial Change

The challenge posed by gender justice personalities and feminist theologians will not be fulfilled and met by superficial change, by mere tinkering with the surface of things. Simply naming God 'mother' as well as 'father' or 'parents, 'admitting women into the ministerial work by ordaining a few of them, imaging Christ as a woman, admitting more female students in theological institutions, stretching the boundaries of ecclesiastical practice, creating new subjects on women studies and allowing girls to get education without any restriction, none of this will do. The response of the tradition of gender-based violence must be far more serious and far more radical by challenging social norms and church's traditions which ignore women's rights. If we want to testify Christianity as the living faith which dispenses with all evils and gives salvation to everyone, it is high time, churches work towards tackling gender-based violence through its educational ministry.

2. Beyond Inequality

In order to bring equality, justice, aspiration and new vision in the church and in the society, both men and women must work together, to provide equal distribution of privileges and responsibilities and address the issues which subjugate women's emancipation in various ways. As men and women are equal

505 Mary Elizabeth Moore (1989), p. 86.

506 Nicola Slee, *Faith and Feminism: An Introduction to Christian Feminist Theology* (Wandsworth High Street, London: Darton Longman and Todd Ltd, 2003), p. 114.

members in the body of Christ, the church needs to extend her place where both sexes enjoy their God-given gifts. Today, people are no more in the old way of life in terms of education, living standard, world outlook, economic condition and taking leadership responsibilities. It is therefore, necessary that the church should also be able to adjust and adapt itself according to the changing needs of the time and situation as all other sectors of life do.

3. Beyond Iniquity

The church should enable its leadership to plot a cause where reality as it appears in terms of sin, evil and injustice be challenged as they impact gender-based violence.

4. Beyond Conservatism

The church needs to come to terms with cultural restructures and their interpretation in the light of biblical teachings. Cultural under-pinning needs to be re-interpreted, as it encounters globalization.

5. Beyond Insensitivity

The church should enable its members to exercise sensibility to the feelings, needs and demands of individuals, families and women as they feel oppression and discrimination. The church needs to be an inclusive community.

6. Beyond Structuralism

The church needs to get involved in society. That means the effects of the church's religious education and its ministry needs to go beyond the confines of the church, to reach out to people who need to be made aware of justice issues, incorporating leadership resources available in society by bringing awareness among people in general.

Considering all the above mentioned theories, Christian religious education should aim to challenge every individual and the society as a whole towards achieving that goal where the faith community goes beyond, learns to respect each other without any gender bias. Churches need to do a critical reflection on the opportunities for service that offers to both women and men the privileges and the responsibilities to bring about equality, justice and peace in the given society. And to begin with, those challenges need to be incorporated in the ongoing churches' educational ministry to bring about a holistic approach to the gender bias in church and in turn in society.

General Conclusion

Violence happens when the privileged section of a people uses power to influence, control, coerce, manipulate, or dominate especially the weak ones. Therefore, when it comes to gender issues, men assume a privileged section because of their superior attitude towards women. With those assumptions, the violence done to women by their male counterparts are beyond tolerable stage due to different forms of gender-based violence. The sufferings meted out to the female population through various means from conception till death cannot be denied in any given society. More specifically, churches as a called out community must challenge those crimes done to their fellow beings based on the biblical principles which manifest peace, justice and equality.

As examined elsewhere, gender-based violence has become endemic as a serious problem in our society today. A few evidences could be mentioned here to uncover the existing situation in which women experience oppression around the world. According to the national family health survey and national crimes records bureau of India reports of 2001, every 13 minutes a woman is burnt to death, every 34 minutes a rape takes place, every 42 minutes there is a sexual harassment, every 43 minutes a women is kidnapped and at least 20% of women aged between 15-45 have experienced domestic violence at some point in their lives, many of them on almost continuous basis.[507] No wonder, the crime situation faced by women have doubled everywhere as presented by the Media.

Thus, at any moment, women are experiencing untold discrimination, oppression, humiliation, and exploitation in different forms just because of their sex. But this rarely becomes a theological concern of the church, though she centers her belief in Jesus Christ who actually practiced His care for the value of persons as with much regard to women as to men. And the church is called to be a 'sign' of the Gospel. In the face of all cultural traditions, norms and oppositions

[507] Raj Bharath Patta, "Ministry to Overcome Violence" in *Gurukul Daily Devotion*-2006, p. 311.

which hinder the full participation of women in every area of life, the church is also called to demonstrate the good news of Christ, who exhibited through his life, deeds and actions in the right perspective. On this basis, the church has a vital role to play to uphold the dignity and status of women through her educational ministry by exhibiting a new way of Christian religious education.

The education which cultivates equality and mutual respect without any sex differences in every aspect need to be cultivated. The church should spell out and raise its voice against gender-based violence in different forms by presenting the right biblical message where there is no room for violence in any form. For so long churches have been just silent spectators without entering the gender-based violence issues. The urgent need for the churches is therefore to be sensitive towards those issues and critical in their theological stands on the gender-based violence issues in today's society of new inventions with new outlook.

Therefore, in order to bring about transformation in the traditionalized mindset where gender prejudices have no room but share equal responsibility and privilege irrespective of sex, one need to take certain risks. And to achieve peace and tranquility among all sections of the people everywhere, one needs to be educated in a way that makes realize the existing gender roles in which half of its own species are victimized.

Simply raising slogans on women's concerns, conducting women's empowerment programmes among a few fortunate/educated people who are in the top level positions, adding few topics on women's concerns in the educational syllabi and exploring outside world through women's initiatives alone cannot bring transformation in the society. Looking at the root causes in every culture by critically analyzing each custom and practice which demean and divide genders need to be critically examined. On the other hand, traditional biblical teachings which were over and over again emphasize women's subjectivity and men's objectivity need to be challenged by interpreting the right message by bringing out the real intention of God in creating human beings in His own image.

No doubt, the traditional understanding of Christian religious education seems to be biased in its mission. As we have already discussed in the preceding chapters, beginning from the early Church Fathers and some of the theologians, they have even categorized women's status differently. Thus, the faith community should take the leading role to challenge the existing gender-based violence and respond to the issue on hand. The church's educational ministry needs to be reviewed and modeled and as such their teaching aids, which teaches about personhood without prejudices.

Thus, in order to fulfill the mission of God, every one needs to awake from slumber to transform the old ways of understanding which contradict the present context and take courage to speak against all the prejudices existing in many societies. As Paulo Freire says, "The Christian Education in our situation demanded would enable human being to discuss courageously the problems of their context and to intervene in that context; it would warn men of the dangers of the time and offer them the confidence and the strength to confront those dangers instead of surrendering their sense of self through submission to the decisions of others."[508] Thus, Christian education needs to intervene in the context where women are exploited and oppressed due to their gender, based on the biblical principles which are the good news for the whole humanity.

The Bible expounds a variety of attitudes, feelings and needs of the people in terms of their position, status, dignity and identity. Written at a time when patriarchy ruled, it is not surprising to see men and males taking positions of authority/ leadership. However, it is also surprising to see how in many cases patriarchy was challenged, and even where women held positions of power, authority and status. All these strands have been the over all picture in the Bible although patriarchy mostly ruled. This was also the wholesome meaning of being made in the image of God. Men and women are equal partners in life. But it is much more, as we critically analyze the true message of the Bible. It clearly shows that it is a book which talks about liberation for the whole humanity or better, liberation for the whole universe. Therefore, the educational ministry of the church could be the best way to educate the faith community and go beyond, by interpreting its right message in the given context.

It would be worth concluding with the words of St. Paul- 'For in Christ Jesus you are all children of God through faith. As many of you as were baptized into Christ have clothed yourselves with Christ. There is no longer Jew or Greek, there is no longer slave or free, there is no longer male and female; for all of you are one in Christ Jesus' (Galatians 3:26-28). 'Nevertheless, in the Lord, a woman is not independent of man or man independent of woman. For just as women came from, so man comes through woman; but all things come from God' (1 Corinthians 11:11-12).

---

[508] Paulo Freire, *Education for Critical Consciousnes* (New York: Continuum, Publishing Company, 1994), p. 33.

Appendix-1

Gender Equality: Constitutional Provisions for Women in India

The principle of gender equality is enshrined in the Indian constitution in its preamble, Fundamental Rights, Fundamental Duties and Directive Principles of State Policy.

The constitution not only grants equality to women, but also empowers the State to adopt measures of positive discrimination in favour of women. Within the frame work of a democratic policy, our laws, development policies, Plans and programmes have aimed at women's advancement in different spheres. India has also ratified various international conventions and human rights instruments committing to secure equal rights of women. Key among them is the ratification of the Convention of Elimination of All forms of Discrimination against Women (CEDAW) IN 1993.

Constitutional Provisions

The Constitution of India not only grants equality to women but also empowers the State to adopt measures of positive discrimination in favour of women for neutralizing the cumulative Socio Economic, Education and political disadvantages faced by them. Fundamental Rights among others, ensure equality before the law and equal Protection of Law; prohibits discrimination against any citizen on grounds of religion, race, caste, sex or place of birth and guarantees equality of opportunity to all citizens in matters relating to employment. Articles 14,15,15 (3),16,39 (a), 39 (b)39 (c) and 42 of the Constitution are of specific importance in this regard.

1. Constitutional Privileges

(1) Equality before law for women (Article 14)
The State not to discriminate against any citizen on grounds only of religion, race, sex, caste, place of birth or any of them (Article 15 (i)) The State to make any special provision in favour of women and children (Article 15 (3)) Equality of opportunity for all citizens in matters relating to employment or appointment to any office under the State (Article 16)

(2) The State to direct its policy towards securing for men and women equally the right to an adequate means of livelihood (Article 39 (a)); and equal pay for equal work for both men and women (Article 39 (d))

(3) To promote justice, on a basis of equal opportunity and to provide free legal aid by suitable legislation or scheme or in any other way to ensure that opportunities for securing justice are not denied to any citizen by reason of economic or other disabilities (Article 39 A)

(4) The State to make provision for securing just and humane conditions of work and for maternity relief (Article 42)

(5) The State to promote with special care the educational and economic interests of the weaker sections of the people and to protect them from social injustice
And all forms of exploitation (Article 46)

(6) The State to raise the level of nutrition and the standard of living of its people (47)

(7) To promote harmony and the spirit of common brotherhood amongst all the people of India and to renounce practice derogatory to the dignity of Women (Article 51 (A) (e)

(8) Not less than one-third (including the number of seats reserved for Women belonging to the Scheduled Castes and the Scheduled Tribes) of the total number of seats to be filled by direct election in every Panchayat to be reserved for Wome and such seats to be allotted by rotation to different constituencies in a Panchayats (Article 243 D (3)

(9) Not less than one-third of the total number of offices of chairpersons in the Panchayats at each level to be reserved for Women (Article 243 D (4)

(10) Not less than one-third (including the number of seats reserved for Women belonging to the Scheduled caste and the Scheduled tribes) of the total number of seats to be filled direct election in every Municipality to be reserved for women and such seats to be allotted by rotation to different constituencies in a Municipality (Article 243 T (3))

(11) Reservation of offices of chairpersons in municipalities for the scheduled caste, the scheduled tribes and women in such manner as the legislature of a State may by law provide (Article243 T (4))

Special Enactments:

- Child marriage restraint Act-1929
- Devadasi Abolition Act-1934
- Suppression of Immoral Traffic in Women and Girls Act – 1956
- The Maternity Benefits Act – 1961 (amended in 1973)
- Anti-Dowry Act – 1961 (amended in1984 and 1986)
- The Medical Termination of Pregnancy Act – 1971
- The Child Marriage Restraint Act – 1974: Fixes the marriageable age for girls at 18 and for boys at 21.
- The Factories (Amendment) Act – 1976: Provides for establishment of crèches where 30 or more women are employed.
- The equal Remuneration Act – 1976
- The Contract Labour Acts, 1978: Provides for welfare facilities and crèches for the children of working women engaged in construction work.
- Family Courts Acts – 1984: facilitate speedy settlement of disputes relating to marriage and family affairs.
- The Immoral Traffic Prevention Act – 1986
- The Commission of Sati Prevention Act – 1987
- The Indecent Representation of Women (Prevention) Act – 1990
- The Pre-Natal Diagnostic Techniques Regulation and Prevention of misuse act – 1994
- Protection from domestic violence and right to matrimonial home -2005.

This source is adapted from the writings of Sr. Philomena D'Souza, FMA in *Woman Icon of Liberation: A Work-Book for Exploring and Achieving Total Liberation,* Mumbai: Better Yourself Books, 2005, pp. 217-219.

However, despite such progressive constitutional guarantees and special enactments, women are subjected to exploitation, alienation and dehumanization in most parts of India. They suffer from gender inequality, household inequality, educational inequality, economic inequality, and social brutality.

Appendix-2

National commission for women

For protection for rights of women and according to them equal status in the society, prior to the enactment of Human Rights Act, the National Commission for Women Act, 1990 was enacted by the Government of India. National Commission for women was constituted on 31st January, 1992 with an object of protecting rights of women. Cases of violation of provisions of the Constitution and the other laws relating to women can be taken up with appropriate authority set up under the Act. The Commission is also empowered to take suo motu notice of matters relating to deprivation of women's rights, non implementation of laws enacted for providing rights to women, for achieving the objective of equality and development; non compliance of policy decisions, guidelines or instructions aimed at mitigating hardships and ensuring welfare and providing relief to women.

Human Rights Acts, 1993

With the enactment of Human Rights Act, 1993 rights relating to life, liberty, equality and dignity of an individual, guaranteed by the Constitution, embodied in international conventions and enforceable by Courts in India stand acknowledged. Principles embodied in the convention for elimination of discrimination against women have now become an integral part of Indian Constitution and the Human Rights Act. Section 12 of the Protection of Human Rights Act obligates the Commission so established, with a duty for proper implementation as well as prevention of violation of human rights and fundamental freedoms.

The Pre-natal Diagnostic Techniques Act, 1994

The pre-natal Diagnostic Techniques (Regulation and prevention of misuse) Act, 1994, enacted to check female foeticide, regulating amongst others, use of pre-natal diagnostic technique for the purpose of detecting genetic or metabolic disorders or chromosomal abnormalities or certain congenital malformation or sex linked disorders and for prevention of misuse of such techniques for the purpose of prenatal sex determination leading to female foeticide.

Section 3 A prohibits sex selection. Section 3B prohibits sale of ultrasound machines etc. To persons, laboratories, clinics, etc. not registered under the Act. Section 4 regulates pre-natal diagnostic techniques. The Act prohibits determination and disclosure of foetus under Section 5 and 6. It also prohibits any advertisement relating to pre-natal determination of sex and prescribes punishment for its contravention. Ant person contravening provisions of this Act, under Section 22 and 26, is punishable with imprisonment and fine ranging from imprisonment of three months to five years and/or with fine up to fifty thousand rupees. Every offence under this Act shall be cognizable, non-bailable and non-compoundable.

The Protection of Women from Domestic Violence Act, 2005

The protection of Women from Domestic Violence Act, 2005 was enacted to provide for more effective protection of rights of women who are victims of violence of any kind occurring within the family and for matters connected therewith. It was intended to protect women from being victims of domestic violence and also to prevent occurrence of domestic violence in the society. The remedy under the Act is in addition to the statutory provisions of Indian Penal Code.

It covers women who are or have been in relationship with the abuser, where both parties have lived together in a shared household and are related by consanguinity marriage or through a relationship in the nature of marriage or adoption. In addition, relationships with family members living together as a join family are also included.

Even those women who are sister, widows, mothers, single woman, or living with the abuser are entitled to legal protection. However, the Act enables the wife or the female living in a relationship in the nature of marriage to file a complaint against any relative of the husband or the male partner; it does not enable any female relative of the husband or the male partner to file a complaint against the wife or the female partner.

It defines the expression "domestic violence" to include actual abuse or threat or abuse that is physical, sexual, verbal, emotional, or economic. Harassment by way of unlawful dowry demands to woman or her relatives is covered.

It provides for rights of women to secure housing. It also provides for the rights of a woman to reside in her matrimonial home or shared household, whether or not she has any rights or title therein. This rights is secured by an order of residence so passed by the magistrate. Also orders of protection can be passed in favour of the aggrieved person for preventing the respondent from aiding or committing an act of domestic violence entering a workplace or any other place frequented by the aggrieved person, attempting to communicate with her, isolating any assets used by both the parties and causing violence to the aggrieved person, her relatives or others who provide her assistance from the domestic violence.

It provides for appointment of protection Officers (Section 3) and registration of non-governmental organizations as service providers for providing assistance to the aggrieved person with respect to her medical examination, obtaining legal aid, safe shelter, etc. Aggrieved person, Protection Officers or any other person on behalf of the aggrieved person can file Complaint before the magistrate under Section 12 of the Act. On receivingsuch complain, magistrate after giving opportunity of hearing to the parties may pass:

- Protection Order under Section 18
- Order of Residence under Section 19
- Monetary Reliefs under Section 20
- Order of Custody under Section 21 and
- Order of Compensation under Section 22 of the Act.

The Sexual Harassment of Women at Workplace (Prevention Prohibition and Redressal) Act, 2013

Sexual harassment at workplace is considered violation of women's right to equality, life and liberty. It creates an insecure and hostile work environment, which discourages women's participation in work, thereby adversely affecting their social and economic empowerment and the goal of inclusive growth. Harassment results in violation of the fundamental rights of a woman to equality under Article 14 and 15 of the constitution of India and her right to life and to live with dignity under Article 21 of the Constitution of India, as also her right of freedom under Article 19 of the Constitution.

Section 3 of the act provides that no woman shall be subjected to sexual harassment at any workplace:

1. Implied or explicit promise of preferential treatment in her employment or
2. Implied or explicit threat of detrimental treatment in her employment or
3. Implied or explicit threat about her present or future employment status,
4. Interference with her work or creating an intimidating or offensive or hostile work environment for her or
5. Humiliating treatment to affect her health or safety.

Section 4 Provides for constitution of internal complains Committee by every employer of a workplace by an order in writing consisting of members amongst employees preferably committed to the cause of women or experience in social work or having legal knowledge with one member amongst Non-Governmental Organization or Associations committed to cause of women or familiar with issues relating to sexual harassment. (This source is extracted from the "Women and Law: Legal Literacy and Awareness," A project of department of Justice , Govt. of India, Implemented in Nagaland in the Districts of Tuensang and Mon by Nagaland State Legal Services Authority Old Secretariat Building, Kohima).

Appendix-3

Universal Declaration of Human Rights-Adopted and Proclaimed by General Assembly Resolution 217 A (111) 10 December 1948.

The General Assembly proclaims this Universal Declaration of Human Rights as a common standard of achievement for all peoples and all nations, to the end that every individual and every organ of society, keeping this Declaration constantly in mind, shall strive by teaching and education to promote respect for these rights and freedoms and by progressive measures, national and international, to secure their universal and effective recognition and observance, both among the peoples of Member States themselves and among the peoples of territories under their jurisdiction.

Article 1-All human beings are born free and equal in dignity and rights. They are endowed with reason and conscience and should act towards one another in a spirit of brotherhood.

Article 2-Everyone is entitled to all the rights and freedoms set forth in this Declaration, without distinction of any kind, such as race, colour, sex, language, religion, political or other opinion, national or social origin, property, birth or other status.

Article 3-Everyone has the right to life, liberty and security of person.

Article 4-No one shall be held in slavery or servitude, slavery and the slave trade shall be prohibited in all their forms.

Article 5-No one shall be subjected to torture or to cruelly, inhuman or degrading treatment or punishment.

Article 6 - Everyone has the right to recognition everywhere as a person before the law.

Article 7 - All are equal before the law and are entitled without any discrimination to equal protection against any discrimination in violation of this declaration and against any incitement to such discrimination.

Article 8 - Everyone has the right to an effective remedy by the competent national tribunals for acts violating the fundamental right granted to him by the constitution or by law.

Article 9 - No one shall be subjected to arbitrary arrest, detention or exile.

Article 10 - Everyone is entitled in fully equality to a fair and public hearing by an independent and impartial tribunal, in the determination of his rights and obligations and of any criminal charge against him.

Article 11 - (1) Everyone charged with a penal offence has the right to be presumed innocent until proved guilty according to law in a public trial at which he has had all the guarantees necessary for his defense.

(2) No one shall be held guilty of any penal offence on account of any act or omission which did not constitute a penal offence, under national or international law, at the time when it was committed. Nor shall a heavier penalty be imposed than the one that was applicable at the time the penal offence was committed.

Article 12 - No one shall be subjected to arbitrary interference with his privacy, family, home or correspondence, or to attacks upon his honour and reputation. Everyone has the right to the protection of the law against such interference or attacks.

Article 13 - (1) Everyone has the right to freedom of movement and residence within the borders of each state.

(2) Everyone has the right to leave any country, including his own, and to return to his country.

Article 14 - (1) Everyone has the right to seek and to enjoy in other countries asylum from persecution.

(2) This right may not be invoked in the case of prosecutions genuinely arising from non-political crimes or from acts contrary to the purposes and principles of the United Nations.

Articles 15 - (1) Everyone has the right to a nationality.

(2) No one shall be arbitrarily deprived of his nationality nor denied the right to change his nationality.

Article 16 - (1) Men and women of full age, without any limitation due to race, nationality or religion, have the right to marry and to found a family. They are entitled to equal rights as to marriage, during marriage and at its dissolution.

Marriage shall be entered into only with the free and full consent of the intending spouses.

The family is the natural and fundamental group unit of society and is entitled to protection by society and the state.

Article 17 - (1) Everyone has the right to own property alone as well as in association with others.

(2) No one shall be arbitrarily deprived of his property.

Article 18 - Everyone has the right to freedom of thought, conscience and religion; this right includes freedom to change his religion or belief, and freedom, either alone or in community with others and in public or private, to manifest his religion or belief in teaching, practice, worship and observance.

Article 19 - Everyone has the right to freedom of opinion and expression; this right includes freedom to hold opinions without interference and to seek, receive and impart information and ideas through any media and regardless of frontiers.

Article 20 - (1) Everyone has the right to freedom of peaceful assembly and association.

(2) No one may be compelled to belong to an association.

Article 21 - (1) Everyone has the right to take part in the government of his country, directly or through freely chosen representatives.

(2) Everyone has the right to equal access to public service in his country.

(3) The will of the people shall be the basis of the authority of government; this will, shall be expressed in periodic and genuine election which shall be by universal and equal suffrage and shall be held by secret vote or by equivalent free voting procedures.

Article 22 - Everyone, as a member of society, has the right to social security and is entitled to realization, through national effort and international co-operation and in accordance with the organization and resources of each State, of the economic, social and cultural rights indispensable for his dignity and the free development of his personality.

Article 23 - (1) Everyone has the right to work, to free choice of employment, to just and favourable conditions of work and to protection against unemployment.

(2) Everyone, without any discrimination, has the right to equal pay for equal work.

(3) Everyone who works has the right to just and favourable remuneration ensuring for himself and his family an existence worthy of human dignity, and supplemented, if necessary, by other means of social protection.

(4) Everyone has the right to form and to join trade unions for the protection of his interests.

Article 24 - Everyone has the right to rest and leisure, including reasonable limitation of working hours and periodic holidays with pay.

Article 25 - (1) Everyone has the right to a standard of living adequate for the health and well-being of himself and of his family, including food, clothing, housing and medical care and necessary social services, and the right to security in the event of unemployment, sickness, disability, widowhood, old age or other lack of livelihood in circumstances beyond his control.

(2) Motherhood and childhood are entitled to special care and assistance. All children, whether born in or out of wedlock, shall enjoy the same social protection.

Article 26 - (1) Everyone has the right to education. Education shall be free, at least in the elementary and fundamental stages. Elementary education shall be compulsory. Technical and professional education shall be made generally available and higher education shall be equally accessible to all on the basis of merit.

(2) Education shall be directed to the full development of the human personality and to the strengthening of respect for human rights and fundamental freedoms. It shall promote understanding, tolerance and friendship among all nations, racial or religious groups, and shall further the activities of the United Nations for the maintenance of peace.

(3) Parents have a prior right to choose the kind of education that shall be given to their children.

Article 27 - (1) Everyone has the right freely to participate in the cultural life of the community, to enjoy the arts and to share in scientific advancement and its benefits.

(2) Everyone has the right to the protection of the moral and material interest resulting from any scientific, literary or artistic production of which he is the author.

Article 28 - Everyone is entitled to a social and international order in which the rights and freedoms set forth in this Declaration can be fully realized.

Article 29 - (1) Everyone has duties to the community in which alone the free and full development of his personality is possible.

(2) In the exercise of his rights and freedoms, everyone shall be subject only to such limitations as are determined by law solely for the purpose of securing due recognition and respect for the rights and freedoms of others and of meeting the just requirements of morality, public order and the general welfare in a democratic society.

(3) These rights and freedoms may in no case be exercised contrary to the purposes and principles of the United Nations.

Article 30 - Nothing in this Declaration may be interpreted as implying for any State, group of person any right to engage in any activity or to perform any act aimed at the destruction of any of the rights and freedoms set forth herein.

Appendix-4

A Chronology of Support for Women's Human Rights (Adopted from United Nations, World's Women 1970-1990: Trends and Statistics (New York, 1991), p. 7.

UN Commission on the Status of Women calls for global monitoring of activities related to women and promotion of the rights of women.

UN Convention on the Political Rights of women; mandates political equality for women throughout the world through granting the right to vote and hold office.

1957, 1962 Conventions guaranteeing equal rights to women in marriage and divorce.

Declaration on the Elimination of Discrimination against women.

Decade of Women. The World Conference on Women initiates the collection of statistics on women.

Convention on the Elimination of All forms of Discrimination against Women.

World Conference on Women, Copenhagen: further collection of statistics on the status of women.

World Conference on Women, Nairobi: reviews the collected statistics about women's condition and adopts "Forward-Looking Strategies for the Advancement of Women."

Convention on the Rights of the Child.

Second Conference on Human Rights: identified gender-based violence as an abuse of women's health rights.

World Conference on Women, Beijing: established specific goals and timetables which could serve as benchmarks to evaluate the progress of governments on issues such as the elimination of laws that discriminate against women and increasing the number of women in public service.

Appendix-5

A brief summary of key points to guide all Gender-based violence programming and programming implementation check list which was implemented by a range of international NGOs in Guinea and Sierra Leone for refugees and internally displaced persons. The programme was initially designed to respond to the needs of the many women and girls who had been captured by the RUF rebel group in Sierra Leone whose stories of sexual abuse, exploitation and torture were among the worst imaginable. Gender-based violence in emergency situations is widespread and presents a programming challenge for all sectors. The international community should accept this challenge and work to promote an environment where the physical and emotional integrity of every individual is protected and respected.

Key summary points:

1. Belief in the full and equal rights of all human beings is central to Save the children's mission and policies.
2. Gender-based violence is an egregious violation of human rights and it must not be tolerated under any circumstance.
3. Gender-based violence can be substantially eliminated through appropriate prevention-oriented programming and the enforcement and recognition of international law.
4. One should remain sensitive to cultural norms and practices in programme design and implementation, but programme staff should not be reluctant to intervene when necessary to save the children.
5. Gender-based violence concerns should be considered in design and integrated into all Save the Children emergency field programming.
6. Save the Children staff and volunteers should use the best interest principle to guide all programming efforts for children in emergencies, particularly those affected by gender-based violence.

7. Save the Children staff and volunteers should receive training on how to handle sensitive matters related to gender-based violence, including interview procedures and the importance of client confidentiality. (This is adopted from the book-*Women's Commission for Refugee Women and Children, (2002), UNHCR policy on Refugee Women and guidelines on their Protection; An Assessment of ten Years of Implementation.* New York: Women's Commission for Refugee Women and Children).

References

Amaladoss, S.J. Michael, *The Asian Jesus*, Chennai: IDCR/ISPCK, 2005.

Amer, Jonatsungba, *Biblical Principles of Christian Education Applied to Christian Schools in Nagaland,* Mokokchung: Merangkong Baptist Church, 1993.

Ariarajah, S. Wesley, *Axis of Peace: Christian faith in times of Violence and War,* Geneva: World Council of Churches, 2004.

Aier, Imti, L., *Naga Social and Customary Genealogy,* Mokokchung: Pioneer Book Stall, Second edition, 1969.

Atsongchanger, Mar, *Christian Education and Social Change,* Guwahati: Christian Literature Center, 1995.

Askew, Sue and Carol Ross, *Boys' Don't Cry: Boys and Sexism in Education,* Milton Keynes: Open University Press, 1988.

Alemchiba, M., *A brief historical account of Nagaland*, Kohima: Naga Institute of Culture, 1970.

Ao, Tajen, *Ao Naga Customary Laws,* Mokokchung: Aowati Imchen, 1980.

Aier, Alongla P., *From Darkness To Light: A publication of the Nagaland Baptist Church Coun cil on the occasion of the celebration of 125 years of Christianity in Nagaland,* 1997.

Ahuja, Ram, *Violence Against Women,* Jaipur and New Delhi: Rawat Publications, 2003.

Ahuja, Ram, *Society in India: Concepts, Theories and Recent Trends,* Jaipur and New Delhi, Rawat Publications, Reprinted, 2004.

Ahuja, Ram, *Rights of Women: A Feminist Perspective,* Jaipur and New Delhi: Rawat Publications, 1992.

Agnes, Flavia, *Law and Gender Inequality: The Politics of Women's Rights in India,* New Delhi: Oxford University Press, 2001.

Agnes, Flavia, *Feminist Jurisprudence: Contemporary Concerns,* Mumbai: Majlis, 2003.

Arthur, Chris, *Biting the Bullet: Some Personal Reflections on Religious Education,* Edinburgh: The Saint Andrew Press, 1990.

Barash, D and Webel, C.P., *Peace and Complex Studies,* Thousand Oaks, CA. Sage Publications, 2002.

Bhasin, Kamla, *Understanding Gender,* New Delhi: Kali for Women, 2000.

Bhasin, Kamla and Nighat Said Khan, *Some questions on Feminism and its Relevance in South Asia,* New Delhi: Kali for Women, Reprint 2000.

Brown, R.M., *Religion and Violence,* Philadelphia: West-Minster, 1987.

Berge, Lars and Gunnel Cederlof, *Political Visions and Social Realities in Contemporary South India*: Dalarna University International Studies Series 1, 2003.

Byrne, H.W., *Christian Education for the Local Church: An Evangelical and Functional Approach,* Michigan: Zondervan Publishing House, Grand Rapids, 1963.

Bendangangshi, *Glimpses of Naga History,* Mokokchung: Supongwati Ao, 2000.

Ballard, Paul H., *A Christian Perspective on Violence*, London: British Council of Churches, 1979.

Bhuimali, Anil, *Education, Employment and Empowering Women*, New Delhi: Serials Publications, 2004.

Brown, Kristine and Susan Hood, *Academic Encounters: Life in Society,* New Delhi: Cambridge University Press, Reprinted 2006.

Chatrath, K.J.S. , *Education for Human Rights and Democracy,* Shimla: Indian institute of advance study Rashtrapati Nivas and United Nations Educational, Scientific and Cultural Organization (UNESCO), 1998.

Cooper-White, Pamela, *The Cry of Tamar: Violence Against Women and the Churches Response,* Minneapolis: Fortress Press, 1995.

Chunakara, Mathew George, (ed), *Globalization and its Impact on Human Rights,* Hongkong: Christian Conference of Asia, 1998.

Clapsis, Emmanuel, *Violence and Christian Spirituality: An Ecumenical Conversation*, Geneva 2, Switzerland: WCC Publication, World Council of Churches, 2007.

Chandhoke, Neera, *The Conceits of Civil Society,* New Delhi: Oxford University Press, 2003.

Chauhan, O.P., Lalit Dadwal, *Human Rights Promotion and Protection,* New Delhi: Anmol Publications PVT. LTD., 2004.

Chatterji, Saral K., *Society and Culture in North-East India: A Christian Perspective,* ISPCK, Delhi: The Christian Institute for the Study of Religion and Society, Bangalore, 1996.

Cahill, Lisa Sowle, *Sex, Gender and Christian Ethics,* New York: Cambridge University Press 1996.

Datar, Chhaya, *The Struggle Against Violence,* Calcutta: Mandira Sen for Stree, Reprint, 1995.

Dietrich, Gabriele, *A New Thing on Earth: Hopes and Fears facing Feminist Theology,* Delhi: ISPCK, 2001.

D'Silva, Allwyn, *Responding to India's Social Challenges: The Promotion of Human Rights* (A NBCLC Series on Current Issues). (Year unknown).

Das, Somen, *Women in India: Problems and Prospects,* ISPCK, 1997.

D'sa, Fr. Thomas, *The Church in India in the Emerging Third Millennium,* Bangalore: N.B.C.L.C, 2005.

Darling, Barbara-Smith, *Can Virtue Be Taught?,* Notre Dame, Indiana: University of Notre Dame Press, 1993.

Desjardins, Michel, *Peace, Violence and the New Testament,* Sheffield, England: Sheffield Academic Press, 1997.

Das, Somen, *Bible Study Series: Towards a transformed and transforming Community,* Delhi: ISPCK, 2005.

Elwin, Verrier, *The Nagas and the Nineteenth Century,* London: Oxford University Press, 1969.

Edgar, Andrew and Peter Sedgwick, *Key Concepts in Cultural Theory,* New York and London: Routledge, 2004.

Freire, Paulo, *Education for Critical Consciousness,* New York: Continuum, Publishing Company, 1994.

Freire, Paulo, *Pedagogy of the Oppressed, 30th Anniversary Edition, translated by Myra Ramos with an Introduction by Donaldo Macedo,* New York: The Continuum Publishing Group Inc, 2000.

Freire, Paulo, *Cultural Action for Freedom,* Cambridge, Massachusetts: Penguin Books, 1972.

Evenson, C. Richard, *Foundations for Educational ministry: Yearbooks in Christian Education Volume III,* USA: Fortress Press, 1971.

Foster, Charles R., *The Future of Christian Education: Educating Congregations,* Nashville: Abingdon Press, 1994.

Fortune, Marie M., *Sexual Violence: The Unmentionable Sin,* Cleveland, Ohio: The Pilgrim press, 1983.

Freeman, Jo, *Women: A Feminist Perspective,* California: Mayfield Publishing Company, Second edition 1979.

Gnanadason, Aruna, *No longer a Secret: The Church and Violence against Women,* Geneva: World Council of Churches Publications, 1993.

Girard, Rene, *Violence and the Sacred,* Baltimore: Johns Hopkins U.P., 1977.

Guimaraes, Marcelo Rozende, *A New World is Possible: Ten good reasons to educate for Peace*. Translated by Philip Lee, 357 Kennington Lane, London: World Association for Christian Communication, 2005.

Ghosh, B. B., *Nagaland District Gazetters: Mokokchung District,* Kohima: Government of Nagaland, 1979.

Gore, M. S., *Education for Women's Equality,* New Delhi: Center for Women's Development Studies, 1988.

Garrett, Stephanie, *GENDER,* London. New York: Tavistock Publications, 1987.

Hooks, Bell, *FEMINISM IS FOR EVERYBODY: Passionate politics,* Cambridge, MA: South End Press, 2000.

Hooks, Bell, *Teaching to Transgress: Education as the Practice of Freedom,* New York London: Routledge, 1994.

Horam, M., *Nagas Old ways and New trends,* New Delhi: Cosmo Publication, 1988.

Hunter, Rodney J. *The Dictionary of Pastoral Care and Counseling,* Nashville: Abingdon Press, 1999.

Harris, James H., *Pastoral Theology: A Black-Church Perspective,* Minneapolis: Fortress Press, 1991.

Harris, Maria and Gabriel Moran, *Reshaping Religious Education: Conversation on Contemporary Practice,* Louisville, Kentucky: Westminster John Knox Press, 1998.

Hutton, J.P., *The Angami Nagas,* London: Oxford University Press.

Huizer, Gerrit and Bruce Mannheim, *The Politices of Anthropology: From Colonialism and Sexism Towards a View From Below,* The Hague. Paris: Mouton Publishers, 1979.

Haker, Hille, Susan Ross and Marie-Theres Wacker, *Women's Voices in World Religions: Concilium,* London: SCM Press, 2006/3.

Imchen, Narola, *Women In Church and Society: The Story of Ao Naga Women,* Jorhat: Eastern Theological College, 2001.

Imchen, Narola, *Women's Issues in the 21st Century,* Jorhat: Women's Study Centre, November, 2001.

Iyer, Saroj, *The Struggle to be Human: Women's Human Rights,* Bangalore: Books for Change, 1999.

Imchen Panger, *Ancient Ao Naga Religion and Culture,* New Delhi: Har-Anand Publications, 1993.

Isherwood, Lisa and Dorothea McEwen, *An A to Z of Feminist Theology,* Sheffield S119AS, England: Sheffield Academic Press Ltd, 1996.

Jagessar, Michael N and Anthony G Reddie, *Black Theology in Britain A Reader: Cross cultural Theologies*, London, UK: Equinox Publishing Ltd., 2007.

Jesudasan, Usha and Gert Ruppell, *Healing as Empowerment: Discovering Grace in Community,* 2005.

Jeanrond, Werner G. and Lisa Sowle Cahill, *Religious Education of Boys and Girls*, London: SCM Press, Concilium, 2002/4.

Joseph, Ammu and Kalpana Sharma, *Terror Counter-Terror: Women Speak out,* New Delhi: Kali for Women, 2003.

Jamir, N. Talitemjen & A. Lanunungsang, *Naga Culture: A Case Study of the Ao Naga Society and Culture,* Mokokchung: Nagaland University Tribal Research Centre, 2005.

Joy, Elizabeth, *Lived Realities: Faith Reflections on Gender Justice,* Bangalore: CISRS Publications Trust, 1999.

Jeyaraj, Nirmala, *Women and Society: A Reader in Women's Studies*, Madurai: ISPCK, Delhi and Lady Doak College, 2005.

Kirkup, Gill and Laurie Smith Keller, *Inventing Women: Science, Technology and Gender,* UK: Polity Press in association with the Open University, 1992.

Kassmann, Margot, *Overcoming Violence: The Challenge to the Churches in All Places,* Geneva: World Council of Churches, 1998.

Koshy, Ninan, *The War on Terror: Recording the World*, Hong Kong: DADA Press, 2002.

Keran, Desai, *The Inheritance of Loss,* New Delhi: Penguin Books, 2006.

Kroeger, Catherine Clark & Nancy Nason-Clark, *No Place for Abuse: Biblical & Practical Resources to Counteract Domestic Violen*ce, Illinois: InterVarsity Press, 2001.

Kerber, K. L., *Psycho-Feminism: Conceptualization and Criticism*, Delhi: Global Vision Publishing House, 2002.

Longchar, A. Wati, *The Traditional Tribal World view and Modernity*, Jorhat: N. Limala Lkr, 1995.

Longchar, Purtongzuk, *Historical Development of the Ao Nagas in Nagaland,* Dimapur: Print Home, Near Indian Bank, 2002.

Luithui, Luingam and Nandita Haksar, *Nagaland File: A Question of Human Rights,* New Delhi: Lancer International, 1984.

Longkumer, Limatula & Talijungla Longkumer, *Side by Side: Naga Women Doing Theology in Search of Justice and Partnership* CCA-EGY & NWYF, 2004.

Longkumer, Limatula, *No More Sorrow in God's Garden of Justice: Tribal Women Doing Theology,* Jorhat: Women's Study Department, 2007.

Loades, Ann, *Feminist Theology: A Reader*, London: SPCK/WIJKP, 1990.

Lip. M. and Nina Lee Colwill, *The Psychology of Sex Differences*, New Jersey: Prentice-Hall, Inc., 1978.

Maggay, Melba Padilla, *Women, Culture and revelation*, New Delhi: Regnum-Asia Books, 1994.

Moore, Allen J., *Religious Education as Social Transformation,* Birmingham, Alabama: Religious Press, 1998.

Mayr, Marlene, *Does the Church Really Want Religious Education?,* Birmingham, Alabama: Religious Education Press, 1988.

Miller-McLemore, Bonnie J. & Brita L. Gill-Austern, *Feminist & Womanist: Pastoral Theology,* Nashville: Abingdon Press, 1999.

Marie, *Fortune, Sexual Violence,* New York: Pilgrim Press, 1983.

Mills, J.P., *The Ao Nagas,* Oxford University Press.

Mabry, Hunter P., *A Manual for Researchers and Writers of Course Assignments, Theses, Dissertations and other Research Reports:* Second Edition, Bangalore: The Board of Theological Education Senate of Serampore College, 2003.

Moses.Y., *Discerning Mission Today: Essays in Honour of Ipe Joseph,* New Delhi: ISPCK, 2004.

Moltmann, Jurgen, *God for a Secular Society: The Public Relevance of Theology,* London: SCM Press, 1999.

Miller, Randolph Crump, *Education for Christian Living,* New Jersey: Prentice-Hall, INC. 1956.

Manderson, Lenore and Linda Rae Bennett, *Violence Against Women in Asian Societies,* London and New York: Routledge Curzon, Taylor & Francis Group, 2003.

Mananzan, Mary John, *Women in Asia: Status and Image,* Singapore: Christian Conference of Asia, 1979.

Misra, Rabi N., *Women Education and Development*, Laxmi Nagar, Delhi: Discovery Publishing House, 2006.

Manchala, Deenabandhu, *Nurturing Peace: Theological Reflections on Overcoming Violence*, Geneva: WCC Publications, World Council of Churches, 2005.

McGinnis, Kathleen and James, *Parenting for Peace and Justice,* New York: Orbis Books, 1982.

Messer, Donald E., *Breaking the Conspiracy of Silence: Christian Churches and the Global Aids Crisis,* Minneapolis: Fortress Press, 2004.

Madhurima, *Violence Against Women: Dynamic of Conjugal Relations*, New Delhi: Gyan Publishing House, 1996.

Meroff, Deborah, *Save our Sisters: An Action Guide for Helping Girls and Women at Risk Worldwide*, Secunderabad: GS Books, Reprint 2017

Nurser, John, *For All Peoples and All Nations: Christian Churches and Human Right,* Geneva: World Council of churches Publications, 2005.

Nuh, V. K., *In Search of Praxis Theology for the Nagas,* New Delhi: Regency Publications, 2003.

Nason-Clark, Nancy & Gatherine Clark Kroeger, *Refuge from Abuse: Healing and Hope for Abused Christian Women,* Illinois: InterVarsity Press, 2004.

Narasaiah, M. L., *Women and Development*, New Delhi: Discovering Publishing House, 2006.

Oduyoye, Mercy Amba, *Daughters of Anowa: African Women & Patriarchy,* New york: Orbis Books, 2002.

Paechter, Carrie, *Educating the Other: Gender, Power and Schooling,* London. Washington, D.C: The Falmer Press, 1998.

Poonacha, Veena and Divya Pandey, *Responses to Domestic Violence in the States of Karnataka and Gujarat,* Mumbai: Research Centre for Women's Studies, 1999.

Poonacha, Veena, *Understanding Women's Studies: Contribution to Women's Studies Series* 11, Mumbai: The Research Centre for Women Studies, 1999.

Prabhakar, Samson, *Peace Initiatives for A Just Society* (A Consultation held on Dec. 6-8, 2001).

Prabhakar, Samson, *Essays on Christian Education and Liturgy*, Bangalore: South Asia Theological Research Institute, 2003.

Prabhakar, Samson, *Towards a Culture of Peace in South Asia,* Bangalore: South Asia Theological Research Institute, 2004.

Prabhakar, Samson, *Inter-play of Religion, Politics and Communalism*, Bangalore: BTESSC/SATHRI, 2004.

Prabhakar, Samson, *Overcoming Violence,* Bangalore: South Asia Theological Research Institute, 2004.

Prabhakar, Samson, *Dalit and Minjung Theologies: A Dialogue,* Bangalore: BTESSC/SATHRI, 2006.

Paulus, Vimala, *Introducing Christian Education,* Madras: The Christian Literature Society, 1986.

Poonacha, Veena, *Understanding Women,s Studies*, Mumbai: Research Centre for Women's Studies, 1999.

Parsons, Talcott, Edward Shils, Kaspar D. Naegele and Jesse R. Pitts, *Theories of Society: Foundations f Modern Sociological Theory, Volume II.* New York: The Free Press of Glencoe, INC. Second Printing March 1962.

Polling, James Newton, *Deliver Us From EVIL: Resisting Racial and Oppression,* Minneapolis: Fortress Press, 1996.

Pazmino, Robert W., *Foundational Issues in Christian Education: An Introduction in Evangelical Perspective*, Michigan: A Division of Baker Book House Co, Grand Rapids, Second Printing, November, 1999 *Gender.*

Pazmino, Robert w., *The Abuse of Power: A Theological Problem,* Nashville: Abingdon Press, 1991.

Pandey, Janak, *Psychology in India the State-of-the-Art: Personality and Mental Processes,* New Delhi: Sage Publication, 1988.

Pillai, Jaya Kothai, *Women and Empowerment,* New Delhi: Gyan Publishing House, 1995.

Qureshi, Muniruddin, *Social Status of Indian Women,* New Delhi: Anmol Publications Pvt. Ltd., 2003.

Rood, Wayne R., *Understanding Christian Education*, New York: Abingdon Press, 1970.

Russell, Letty M., *Household of Freedom: Authority in Feminist Theology,* Philadelphia: The Westminster Press, 1987.

Raiser, Konrad, *For a Culture of life: Transforming Globalization and Violence,* Geneva: WCC Publications, 2002.

Reddie, Anthony G., *Dramatizing Theologies: A Participative Approach to Black God-Talk*, London: Equinox Publishing Ltd, 2006.

Renzetti, Claire M, Lynne Goodstein, *Women, Crime, and Criminal Justice: Original Feminist Readings,* California: Roxbury Publishing Company, 2001.

Robevans and Toshharai, *The Church and Education in Asia*, Singapore: Christian Conference of Asia, 1980.

Ruth W.,Beulah, *Protect Yourself: 15 Sets of Coping Clues for Girl and Women,* Secunderabad: OM Headlinez, 2014.

Sanday, Peggy Reeves, *Female Power and Male Dominance On the Origins of Sexual Inequality,* Melbourne Sydney: Cambridge University Press, Reprinted 1990.

Seymour, J.L., *Mapping Christian Education: Approaches to Congregational Learning,* Abingdon Press, Nashville, 1997.

Seymour, Jack L. and Donald E. Miller, *Theological Approaches to Christian Education,* Nashville, Abingdon Press, 1990.

Siddons, Philip, *Speaking Out for Women: A Biblical View,* Valley Forge: Judson Press, 1980.

Shamsi, Nayyar, *Human Rights in New World Order,* New Delhi: Anmol Publications PVT. LTD., 2004.

SVD, L. Stanislaus, *Education As Mission,* New Delhi: Ishvani Kendra/ISPCK, 2004.

Strasburger, Victor C., *Adolescents and the Media: Medical and Psychological Impact,* New Delhi: SAGE Publications, 1995.

Sahay, Sushama, *Women and Empowerment: Approaches and Strategies*, New Delhi: Discovery Publishing House, 1998.

Swerdloff, Peter, *Men and Women: Human Behaviour,* Nederland: Time-Life International, 1977.

Slee, Nicola, *Praying Like a Woman*, London: Society for Promoting Christian Knowledge, 2004.

Slee, Nicola, *Women's Faith Development, Patterns and Processes: Explorations in Practical, Pastoral and Empirical Theology*, England: Ashgate Publishing Limited, 2004.

Sumi, Akheto, *Understanding the Nature and Purpose of Christian Religious Education*, Jorhat: Barkataki and Company Private Limited, First Edition 2005.

Sexism in the 1970s: Discrimination Against Women, A Report of a World Council of Churches Consultation West Berlin 1974.

Tamez, Elsa, *Through Her Eyes, Women's Theology from Latin America*, Maryknoll, NY, 1989.

Thomas D'Sa, *The Church in India in the Emerging Third Millennium,* Bangalore: NBCLC., 2005.

Thanzauva, K., *Transforming Theology: A Theological Basis for Social Transformation*, Bangalore: Asian Trading Corporation, 2002.

Thiagaraj, Henry, *Human Rights from the Dalit Perspective,* Chennai: Dalid Liberatrion Education Trust, Second Revised print: December, 1998.

Talesra, Hemlata, Nalini Pancholy, Mangi Lal Nagda, *Human Rights Education: A Global Perspective,* New Delhi: Regency Publications, 2000.

Tournier, Paul, *The Violence Within,* San Francisco: Harper & Row Publishers, 1977.

Taylor, Ann, Wladyslaw Sluckin, D.R. Davies, J.T. Reason, R. Thomson and A.M. Colman, *Introducing Psychology,* New York: Penguin Books, Second Edition, revised and enlarge, 1982.

Trew, Karen and John Kremer, *Gender and Psychology*, London, New York, Sydney, Auckland: Arnold, 1998.

Thompson, Norma H., *Religious Education and Theology,* Birmingham, Alabama: Christian Education Press, 1982.

Treston, Kevin, *A New Vision of Religious Education: Theory, History, Practice, and Spirituality for DREs, Catechists, and Teachers*, Mystic, Connecticut: Twenty-Third Publications, 1993.

Trible, Philic, 'Feminist Hermeneutics and Biblical Studies,' in *A Loads* (ed), *Feminist Theology: A Reader*, London: SPCK, 1990.

Vander Ben, Ans J., *Christian Response in a World of Crisis: A Brief History of the WCC's Commission of the Churches on International Affairs,* Geneva: World Council of Churches, 1986.

Vindhya, U., *Psychology in India: Intersecting Crossroads*, New Delhi: Concept Publishing Company, 2003.

Woods, Edith, *Education That Transforms: Perspectives on Christian Education for Asia,* Bangalore: Theological Book Trust Bangalore, 1995.

Wynn, J.C., *Christian Education for Liberation: and Other Upsetting Ideas,* Nashville: Abingdon, 1977.

Wilhoit, Jim, *Christian Education and the Search for Meaning,* Michigan: Baker Book House, Second printing, September 1993.

Wielenga, Bastiaan, *Reflections on the Biblical Call to Choose Life,* Bangalore: Students Christian Movement of India, Reprinted April, 1998.

Wimberly, Anne Streaty, *Soul Stories: African American Christian Education,* Nashville: Abingdon Press, 1994.

Yong-Bock, Kim, "*Education for the 21st Century in Asia" in Religious Education in Asia: Challenges, Perspectives, and Visions for the 21st Century,* ed. Edna Ordeza, Hongkong: CCA, 2003.

Westerhoff III, John H. and Gwen Kennedy Neville, *Generation to Generation: Conversations on Religious Education and Culture,* New York. Philadelphia: The Pilgrim Press, 1979.

Webster, Ellen Low and John C.B., *The Church and Women in the Third World,* Philadelphia: The Westminster Press, 1985.

Westerhoff, John, *Will Our Children Have Faith,* New York: Seabury Press, 1976.

Women of Courage: Asian Women Reading the Bible, Asian Women's Resource Centre for Culture and Theology, ed. by Editorial Team of AWRC: Lee Oo Chung, et, al, Seoul, Korea: Asian Women's Resource Centre for Culture and Theology, 1992.

Zachariah, Mathew, *Christian Education and Cultural Transformation in India,* Madras: The Christian Literature Society, 1981.

Dictionaries

Alastair V., *A Dictionary of Pastoral Care*, London: SPCK, 1987.

Oxford Advanced Learner's Dictionary of Current English, New York: Oxford University Press, Sixth edition 2000 (14th impression, 2003).

Tan Sutclipfe, John M., *A Dictionary of Religious Education* (Year and Publisher unknown).

Hastings, James, D.D., *Dictionary of the Bible,* Edinburgh: T&T Clark, Second Edition, 1963.

Brown, Lesley, *The New Shorter Oxford English Dictionary,* Oxford: Clarendon Press, 1993.

Winick, Charles, *Dictionary of Anthropology, Totowa,* New Jersey: Littlefield, Adams & Co., 1977.

Encyclopedias

Bareh, H.M., *Encyclopedia of North East India, Nagaland,* Vol. VI, New Delhi: Mittal Publications, 2001.

Kalia, H.L. and N.K. Singh, Rita Singh, *Encyclopedia of the World Psychologists,* Delhi: Global Vision Publishing House, 2002.

Mohan, Poornima, *Encyclopedia of Women*, Delhi: Indian Publisher's Distributors, 2000.

Kazdin, Alan E., *Encyclopedia of Psychology,* Vol. 8, New York: Oxford University Press, 2000.

International Encyclopedia of Sociology, London: Fitzroy Dearborn Publishers, Vol. 1, 1995.

Encyclopedia of Women and Gender: Sex Similarities and Differences and the Impact of Society on Gender, L-Z Volume Two, San Diego, San Francisco, New York, Boston, London, Sydney, Tokyo: Academic Press, 2001.

Journals, Magazines

Asia Journal of Theology, Vol. 11, No. 1, April 1997.

"Theologies and Cultures: Rethinking Globalization, creating theological space for integral research and dialogue to promote cultures of justice and peace Christianity and culture," Research Center of Chang Jung Christian University and Tainan Theological College and Seminary, Vol. 1, No. 1, November 2004.

Christian Education Journal, Autumn 1992, Vol. XIII, No. 1.

Women's Link: Women and Media, Vol.12, No.2, April-June 2006.

Social Action: A Quarterly Review of Social Trends, January – March 2007, Vol. 57, No. 1.

Quilt Asian Women Weave: A Journal on Human Rights, Bangalore: Asian Women's Human Rights Council, No. 5, March 2000.

Waking for Justice, Making Peace, Report of the 12th Asia YMCA Leaders' Conference, Tozanso, October 1987.

In God's Image: Asian Women Overcoming Violence, Journal of Asian Women's Resource Center for Culture and Theology, Vol. 24, No.1, March 2005.

In God's Image: Women and Peacemaking, Journal of Asian Women's Resource Centre for Culture and Theology, Vol. 25, No. 2, June 2006.

Communalism Compact, Temple of Justice: Hurts, Harmony Work, Proud Moment for a Secular Democracy, April-May 2004, Year 10 No. 97.

In God's Image: Women Searching for a New Humanity, Journal of Asian Womens' Resource Centre for Culture and Theology. Vol. 25, No. 4, December 2006.

Luiz Carlos Susin and Maria Pilar Aquino, *Reconciliation in a World of Conflicts,* London: SCM Press, Concilium, 2003/5.

Kristu Jyoti: Promoting Dialogue at the Grassroots, Vol. 18 No. 4, December 2002.

Kristu Jyoti: Three-Dimensional Christian Value Education, Education-The Crisis of values, Thomas Stephens: A Pioneer in Adaptation; Suffering in the Book of Job, Internet-Merits and Demerits. Vol. 18, No. 1, March 2002.

Kristu Jyoti: Psychological Dynamics of a Pluralistic Society-11, Vol. 21, No. 1, March 2005.

Understanding Human Rights, Metro Manila: A SALAG Publication, (year of publication not mentioned).

The Church in India: Status, Trends and Challenges, Ethne, a fresh perspective, Jan-March, 2004.

Journal of Dharma: Religion and Education, Dharmaram College Golden Jubilee Commemorative Volume, April-June 2006, Vol. 31, No. 2.

Cross Currents: Current Issues in Interfaith Work, Spring 2005, S10/S12 Canada.

Theology of our times: Eco Sensitivity, Ecumenical Christian Center Indian School of Ecumenical Theology, No. 9, July 2003.

Christian Education Belongs to the Whole Church, Newsletter for Education and Ecumenical Formation, world Council of Churches, EEF-NET 16-April 2005.

Reformed World, Vol. 54, Nos. 3-4, September-December 2004.

Asia Sunday 2005: *Building Communities of Peace for All,* Christian Conference of Asia.

Vidya Jyoti: Journal of Theological Reflection, Hope and Easter.., Vol. 69, No.3 March 2005.

Vidya Jyoti: Journal of Theological Reflection, "The Field is the World" (Mt.13:38), Vol. 69, No. 7, July 2005.

Vidya Jyoti: Journal of Theological Reflection, "Facing Conflict," Vol. 69, No. 9, September 2005.

Indian Theological Studies, Vol. XV, No.1, March 2003.

Journal of Ecumenical Studies, Vol. 39, Nos. 1-2, Winter-Spring, 2002.

Jnanadeepa: Pune Journal of Religious Studies: Religion, Violence and New World-Order, Vol. 8, No.1, January 2005.

Jnanadeepa: Pune Journal of Religious Studies: The Eucharist and Life, Vol. 8, No. 2, July 2005.

Bangalore Theological Forum, United Theological College, Bangalore, India. Vol. XXXV, No. 2, December 2003.

Journals of Communication Studies, Makhanlal Chaturvedi Rashtriya Palratarita Vishwavidyalaya, Vol. 4, No. 2 Grishm (Summer) April-June 2005.

Reformed World: The Crisis in World Christianity and the Challenges to Mission in the 21st century, Vol. 54, Nos. 3-4 September-December 2004.

Building Communities of Peace for All: Themes and Stories, Christian Conference of Asia.

Voices from the Third World, The Struggle of the Marginalized: Challenges to Theology and Ecumenical Movement, Vol. XXIII, No.1, June 2000.

Voices from the Third World, Globalization, Gender and Inter-faith, Inter-religious Dialogue, Vol. XXII, No.1, June 1999.

International Review of Mission: Come Holy Spirit - Health and Reconcile, Vol. 94, No. 372, January 2005.

Ministerial formation: Education and Ecumenical Formation, World Council of Churches, January 2005, No .104.

Journal of Constructive Theology Vol. 10. No. 2, December 2004.

Social Action: A Quarterly Review of Social Trends, A Social Action Trust Publication, Vol. 55, No. 1, January-March 2005.

Fullness of Life for All (CCA Joint Program Area Committees Meeting, Bangkok, 21-24 February 2001).

Mizoram Theological Journal, Aizwal Theological College, Durtlang, Mizoram, Vol. X, No. 2, April-June, 2005.

Mizoram Theological Journal, Aizwal Theological College, Durtlang, Mizoram, Vol. X, January-March, 2005.

CTC Bulletin: Bulletin of the Program Area on Faith, Mission and Unity (Theological Concerns) Christian Conference of Asia, Vol. XXI, No. 3, December 2005.

Realities: Faith Reflections on Gender Justice, Bangalore: CISRS Publication Trust, 1999.

Kumkumshidi (Revitalize), Watsu Mungdang Silver Jubilee (1982-2007) *Nungo kaket*, Mokokchung, 2007. (Women's Convention Souvenir).

Women's Link: Women and Education, Vol. 13, No.1 January – March 2007.

"It's Time to talk about it!" Study of Culture: Violence Against Women in Culture, Society and the Church, Published by the United Evangelical Mission (UEM).

An Introduction to Law: Legal Literacy and Awareness. Published by Nagaland State Legal service Authority District Court Building, Kohima (n.p).

Women and Law: Legal Literacy and Awareness. A project of department of Justice, Govt. of India Implemented in Nagaland in the Districts of Tuensang and Mon by Nagaland State Legal Services Authority, Old Secretariat Building, Kohima. (n.p).

Newspapers

Vijay times, Bangalore, June–October, 2005.

The Times of India, Bangalore, January, 2006 - July, 2007.

The Times of India, Bangalore, Tuesday, 22nd March, 2008.

The Hindu, Bangalore, Friday, February 10, 2006, p. 5.

The Hindu, Bangalore, Thursday, 3rd March, 2008.

Nagaland Post, Dimapur, Sunday, March 8, 2015.

Raj Bharath Patta, "Ministry to Overcome Violence" in *Gurukul Daily Devotion-2006,* p. 311.

Paulo Freire, *Education for Critical Consciousnes* (New York: Continuum, Publishing Company, 1994), p. 33.